BALTASAR GRACIÁN

THE ART OF WORLDLY WISDOM or
THE ORACLE
TRANS. BY JOSEPH JACOBS, [1892]

THE CRITICK
TRANS. BY SIR PAUL RYCAUT

®2018 Neo Books (Neoeditorialbooks@gmail.com). This book is a product of its time, and it does not necessarily reflect the same views on race, gender, sexuality, ethnicity, and interpersonal relations as it would if it was written today.

CONTENTS

- BOOK ONE THE ART OF WORLDLY WISDOM 1
  - PREFACE 2
- **TESTIMONIA** 3
  - INTRODUCTION 6
  - TO THE READER 19
  - ABOUT THE NOTES 94
- BOOK TWO THE CRITICK 95
  - THE EPISTLE DEDICATORY 96
  - THE TRANSLATOR TO THE READER. 97
  - THE SPRING OF CHILDHOOD, AND THE SUMMER OF YOUTH. 100
  - THE FIRST CRISIS 100
  - THE SECOND CRISIS 106
  - THE THIRD CRISIS 113
  - THE FOURTH CRISIS 122
  - THE FIFTH CRISIS 134
  - THE SIXTH CRISIS 144
  - THE SEVENTH CRISIS 159
  - THE EIGHTH CRISIS 174
  - THE NINTH CRISIS 186
  - THE TENTH CRISIS 199
  - THE ELEVENTH CRISIS 211
  - **THE TWELFTH CRISIS** 226
  - THE THIRTEENTH CRISIS 239
  - THE CONCLUSION 253
  - *FINIS.* 255

BOOK ONE
THE ART OF WORLDLY WISDOM

or
THE ORACLE

Auf des Glückes großer Waage
Steht die Zunge selten ein;
Du mußt steigen oder sinken,
Du mußt herrschen und gewinnen,
Oder dienen und verlieren,
Leiden oder triumphieren,
Amboß oder Hammer sein.

On the great scales of fortune,
The balance rarely keeps still;
You must rise or sink,
You must rule and win
Or serve and lose,
Suffer or triumph,
Be the anvil or the hammer.

GOETHE, ***Ein Kophtisches Lied***.

When you are an anvil, hold you still,
When you are a hammer, strike your fill.
G. HERBERT, ***Jacula Prudentum***.

PREFACE

My attention was first drawn to the Oráculo Manual by Mr. (now Sir Mountstuart) Grant Duff's admirable article on Balthasar Gracian in the Fortnightly Review of March 1877. I soon after obtained a copy of Schopenhauer's excellent version, and during a journey in Spain I procured with some difficulty a villainously printed edition of Gracian's works (Barcelona, 1734, "Por Joseph Giralt"), which contains the Oráculo Manual towards the end of the first volume (pp. 431-494).

I have translated from this last, referring in the many doubtful places of its text to the first Madrid edition of 1653, the earliest in the British Museum. I have throughout had Schopenhauer's version by my side, and have found it, as Sir Mountstuart Grant Duff says, "a most finished piece of work," though I have pointed out in the Notes a few cases where he has failed, in my opinion, to give Gracian's meaning completely or correctly. I have little doubt that I am a fellow-sinner in this regard: I know no prose style that offers such difficulty to a translator as Gracian's laconic and artificial epigrams. It is not without reason that he has been called the Intraducible. The two earlier English versions miss his points time after time, and I found it useless to refer to them. On the other hand, I have ventured to adopt some of Sir Mountstuart Grant Duff's often very happy renderings in the extracts contained in his *Fortnightly* article.

I have endeavoured to reproduce Gracian's Laconism and *Cultismo* in my version, and have even tried to retain his many paronomasias and jingles of similar sound. I may have here and there introduced others of my own to redress the balance for cases where I found it impossible to produce the same effect in English. In such cases I generally give the original in the Notes. Wherever possible I have replaced Spanish proverbs and proverbial phrases by English ones, and have throughout tried to preserve the characteristic rhythm and brevity of the Proverb. In short, if I may venture to say so, I have approached my task rather in the spirit of Fitzgerald than of Bohn.

The gem on the title, representing a votive offering to Hermes, the god of Worldly Wisdom, is from a fine paste in the British Museum of the best period of Greek glyptic art. I have to thank Mr. Cecil Smith of that Institution for kind advice in the selection.

Let me conclude these prefatory words with a piece of advice as oracular as my original: When reading this little book for the first time, read only fifty maxims and then stop for the day.

JOSEPH JACOBS.

TESTIMONIA

IL est si concis si rompu et si estrangement coupé qu'il semble qu'il ait pris l'obscurité à tasche: aussi le Lecteur a besoin d'en deuiner le sens & souvent quand il l'a compris il trouve qu'il s'est estudié à faire une énigme d'une chose fort commune.

F. VAN AERSSENS, *Voyage d'Espagne*, 1667, p. 294.

Il a beaucoup d'élévation, de subtilité, de force et même de bon sens: mais on ne sait le plus souvent ce qu'il veut dire, et il ne le sait pas peut-être lui-même. Quelques-uns de ses Ouvrages ne semblent être fait, que pour n'être point entendus.

BOUHOUR'S *Entretiens d'Ariste et d'Eugène*, 1671, p. 203.

Luisa de Padilla, a Lady of great Learning, and Countess of *Aranda*, was in like manner angry with the famous Gratian upon his publishing his Treatise of the *Discreto*, wherein she fancied that he had laid open those Maxims to common Readers, which ought only to be reserved for the knowledge of the Great. These Objections are thought by many of so much weight that they often defend

the above-mention'd Authors by affirming they have affected such an Obscurity in their Style and Manner of Writing, that tho' every one may read their Works there will be but very few who can comprehend their Meaning.

The Spectator, No. 379 (1712).

En cherchant toujours l'énergie et le sublime il devient outré et se perd dans les mots. Gracian est aux bons moralistes ce que Don Quichotte est aux vrais héros. Its ont l'un et l'autre un faux air de grandeur qui en impose aux sots et qui fait rire les sages.

ABBÉ DESFONTAINES, 1745.

Qué de elogios no se deben al autor del *Criticon*! En medio de las antitesis, paronomasias y toda la metralla culta es una de las obras más recomendables de nuestra literatura por la felicidad de la invention, la inagotable riqueza de imagination y de sales, por la viveza de sus pinturas y por la gracia, soltura y naturalidad del estilo.

DON MANUEL SIEVELA, *Biblioteca selecta de literatura española* (1819).

Si hubiese Gracian procedido con más sobriedad en el uso de estos juegos y conceptos ¿qual es el escritor de su tiempo de tantos dotes y caudal nativo para ser el más fecondo y elezante, sabiendo, como lo manifesto, en dónde estaban las delicadezas y los donaires, esto es, lo amargo, lo dulce, lo picante, lo salado de la lengua castellana?

DON ANTONIO CAPMANY, *Teatro de la elocuencia española*, tomo v.

The *Oráculo Manual* has been more used than any other of the author's works. It is intended to be a collection of maxims of general utility, but it exhibits good and bad precepts, sound judgments, and refined sophisms, all confounded together. In this work Gracian has not forgotten to inculcate his practical principles of Jesuitism to be all things to all men ("hacerse a todos"), nor to recommend his favourite maxim, "to be common in nothing" ("en nada vulgar"), which, in order to be valid, would require a totally different interpretation from that which he has given it.

BOUTERWEK.

The person, however, who settled the character of *cultismo* and in some respects gave it an air of philosophical pretension, was Baltazar Gracian, a Jesuit of Aragon, who lived between 1601 and 1658, exactly the period when the cultivated style took possession of Spanish prose and rose to its greatest consideration.

G. TICKNOR, *History of Span. Lit.* iii. 222.

Dabei ist es das Einzige seiner Art und nie ein anderes über denselben Gegenstand geschrieben worden; denn nur ein Individuum aus der feinsten aller Nationen, der spanischen, konnte es versuchen. . . . Dasselbe lehrt die Kunst derer Allesich befliessigen und ist daher für Jedermann. Besonders aber ist es geeignet das Handbuch aller derer zu werden, die in der grossen Welt leben, ganz vorzüglich aber junger Leute, die ihr Glück darin zu machen bemüht sind und denen es mit Einem Mal und zum Voraus die Belehrung giebt die sie sonst erst durch lange Erfahrung erhalten.

A. SCHOPENHAUER, *Litterarische Notiz we seiner Uebersetzung* (1831, published 1861).

Avec beaucoup d'esprit, d'instruction & de facilité il n'a rien produit qui puisse aujourd'hui soutenir l'examen de la critique la plus impartiale.

PUIBUSQUE, *Histoire comparée des littératures espagnole et française*, 1843, i. p. 559.

Gracian aurait pu être un excellent écrivain s'il n'avait pas voulu devenir un écrivain extraordinaire. Doué d'une vaste érudition, d'un esprit fin, d'un talent profond d'observation, il était né pour éclairer son siècle; mais la vanité de devenir novateur corrompit son gout, en le portant à introduire dans la prose ce langage précieux, ces expressions alambiquées que Gongora avait introduit dans les vers.

A. DE BACKER, *Bibliothèque des écrivains de la Compagnie de Jésus*, 1869, *s.v.* Gracian.

Asi como las máximas de Antonio Perez fueron muy populares entre cortesanos ó doctos ó ilustrados, así españoles como extranjeros, por aquella delicadeza especial de estilo, las del Padre Baltasar Gracian alcanzaron la misma estima por ese atildamiento en el decir: atildamiento que tenia en si un inexplicable atractivo, y que aunque algo participaba del general culteranismo de la literatura española en aquel siglo, encerraba cierto buen gusto deslumbrador y lisonjero para el lector que Con profundisimos conceptos preciaba con la fuerza de su ingenio aquellos.

DON ADOLFO DE CASTRO, *Obras escogidas de Filósofia*, 1873, p. cviii.

Taking the book as a guide, especially for those who intend to enter public life, I have never chanced to meet with anything which seemed to me even distantly to approach it . . . It would possibly be rather difficult to disprove the thesis that the Spanish nation has produced the best maxims of practical wisdom, the best proverb, the best epitaph, and the best motto in the world, If I had to sustain it, I would point with reference to the first head to the *Oráculo Manual*.

Sir M. E. GRANT DUFF on "Balthasar Gracian" in *Fortnightly Review*, March 1877.

Some have found light in the sayings of Balthasar Gracian, a Spaniard who flourished at the end of the seventeenth century. . . . I do not myself find Gracian much of a companion, though some of his aphorisms give a neat turn to a commonplace.

J. MORLEY on "Aphorisms," *Studies*, 1891, p. 86.

INTRODUCTION

I. Of Balthasar Gracian and his Works

WE may certainly say of Gracian what Heine by an amiable fiction said of himself: he was one of the first men of his century. For he was born 8th January 1601 N.S. [1] at Belmonte, a suburb of Calatayud, in the kingdom of Aragon. Calatayud, properly Kalat Ayoub, "Job's Town," is nearly on the site of the ancient Bilbilis, Martial's birthplace. As its name indicates, it was one of the Moorish settlements, and nearly one of the most northern. By Gracian's time it had again been Christian and Spanish for many generations, and Gracian himself was of noble birth. For a Spaniard of noble birth only two careers were open, arms and the Church. In the seventeenth century arms had yielded to the cassock, and Balthasar and his three brothers all took orders. Felipe, his eldest, joined the order of St. Francis; the next brother, Pedro, became a Trinitarian during his short life; and the third, Raymundo, became a Carmelite[2]. Balthasar himself tells us (*Agudeza*, c. xxv.) that he was brought up in the house of his uncle, the licentiate Antonio Gracian, at Toledo, from which we may gather that both his father and his mother, a Morales, died in his early youth. He joined the Company of Jesus in 1619, when in its most flourishing state, after the organising genius of Acquaviva had given solid form to the bold counter-stroke of Loyola to the Protestant Revolution. The *Ratio Studiorum* was just coming into full force, and Gracian was one of the earliest men in Europe to be educated on the system which has dominated the secondary education of Europe almost down to our own days. This point is of some importance, we shall see, in considering Gracian's chief work.

Once enrolled among the ranks of the Jesuits, the individual disappears, the Jesuit alone remains. There is scarcely anything to record of Gracian's life except that he was a Jesuit, and engaged in teaching what passes with the Order for philosophy and sacred literature, and became ultimately Rector of the Jesuit College at Tarragona. His great friend was Don Vincencio Juan de Lastanosa, a dilettante of the period, who lived at Huesca, and collected coins, medals, and other archæological bric-a-brac. Gracian appears to have shared his tastes, for Lastanosa mentions him in his description, of his own cabinet. A long correspondence with him was once extant and seen by Latassa, who gives the dates and places where the letters were written. From these it would seem that Gracian moved about

---

[1] The ordinary authorities vary between 1594 and 1604. I follow Latassa y Ortin, *Biblioteca nueva de los escritores Aragoneses*, Pamplona, 1799, iii. 267 *seq.*, practically the only original source for Gracian's life and works.
[2] Gracian mentions his brothers in his *Agudeza*.

considerably from Madrid to Zarogoza, and thence to Tarragona. From another source we learn that Philip III. often had him to dinner to provide Attic salt to the royal table. He preached, and his sermons were popular. In short, a life of prudent prosperity came to an end when Balthasar Gracian, Rector of the Jesuit College at Tarragona, died there 6th December 1658, at the age of nearly fifty-eight years.

Of Gracian's works there is perhaps more to say even while leaving for separate consideration that one which is here presented to the English reader and forms his chief claim to attention. Spanish literature was passing into its period of swagger, a period that came to all literatures of modern Europe after the training in classics had given afresh the sense of style. The characteristic of this period in a literature is suitably enough the appearance of "conceits" or elaborate and far-fetched figures of speech. The process began with Antonia Guevara, author of *El Libro Aureo*, from which, according to some, the English form of the disease known as Euphuism was derived. But it received a further impetus from the success of the *stilo culto* of Gongora in poetry. [3] Gongorism drove "conceit" to its farthest point: artificiality of diction could go no farther in verse: it was only left for Gracian to apply it to prose.

He did this for the first time in 1630 in his first work, *El Heroe*. This was published, like most of his other works, by his lifelong friend Lastanosa, and under the name of Lorenzo Gracian, a supposititious brother of Gracian's, who, so far as can be ascertained, never existed. The whole of *El Heroe* exists, in shortened form, in the *Oráculo Manual*.[4] The form, however, is so shortened that it would be difficult to recognise the original *primores*, as they are called, of *El Heroe*. Yet it is precisely in the curtness of the sentences that the peculiarity of the stilo culto consists. Generally elaborate metaphor and far-fetched allusions go with long and involved sentences of the periodic type. But with Gracian the aim is as much towards shortness as towards elaboration. The embroidery is rich but the jacket is short, as he himself might have said. As for the subject-matter, the extracts in the *Oráculo* will suffice to give some notion of the lofty ideal or character presented in*El Heroe*, the ideal indeed associated in the popular mind with the term hidalgo. [5]

---

[3] On Gongora and his relation to *Cultismo* see Ticknor, *Hist. Span. Lit.* iii. 18 *seq.*; also Appendix G, "On the origin of Cultismo." Ticknor is, however, somewhat prejudiced against any form of Cultismo.
[4] See Notes to Maxims xxvi, xxxviii, xl, xlii, xliv, xl, lxiii, lxv, lxvii, xciv, xcviii, cvi, cxxvii.
[5] See Notes to Maxims ii, xx, xxii, xxv, xlix, li, liii, lv, lvi, lix, lxix, lxxi, lxxvi, lxxxvii, cxxii, cxxvii, cclxxvii, ccxcv.

A later book, *El Discreto*, first published in 1647, gives the counterpoise to *El Heroe* by drawing an ideal of the prudent courtier as contrasted with the proud and spotless hidalgo. This too is fully represented in the book before us, but the curtailment is still more marked than in the case of *El Heroe*. There is evidence that Gracian wrote a similar pair of contrasts, termed respectively *El Galante* and *El Varon Atento*, which were not published but were incorporated in the Oráculo Manual by Lastanosa. The consequences of this utilisation of contrasts will concern us later.

Reverting to Gracian's works somewhat more in their order, his *éloge* of Ferdinand, the Magus of Columbus' epoch, need not much detain us. It is stilted and conventional and does not betray much historical insight. Gracian's *Agudeza y Arte de Ingenio* is of more importance and interest as the formal exposition of the critical principles of *Cultismo*. It is concerned more with verse than prose and represents the *Poetics* of Gongorism. A curious collection of flowers of rhetoric in Spanish verse could be made from it. Of still more restricted interest is the *Comulgador* or sacred meditations for holy communion. I do not profess to be a judge of this class of literature, if literature it can be called, but the fact that the book was deemed worthy of an English translation as lately as 1876 seems to show that it still answers the devotional needs of Catholics. It has a personal interest for Gracian, as it was the only book of his that appeared under his own name.

There remains only to be considered, besides the Oráculo Manual, Gracian's *El Criticon*, a work of considerable value and at least historic interest which appeared in the three parts dealing with Youth, Maturity, and Old Age respectively during the years 1650-53. This is a kind of philosophic romance or allegory depicting the education of the human soul. A Spaniard named Critilo is wrecked on St: Helena, and there finds a sort of Man Friday, [6] whom he calls Andrenio. Andrenio, after learning to communicate with Critilo, gives him a highly elaborate autobiography of his soul from the age of three days or so. They then travel to Spain, where they meet Truth, Valour, Falsehood, and other allegorical females and males, who are labelled by Critilo for Andrenio's benefit in the approved and frigid style of the allegorical teacher. Incidentally, however, the ideals and aspirations of the Spaniard of the seventeenth century are brought out, and from this point of view the book derives the parallel with the *Pilgrim's Progress* which Ticknor had made for it[7]. It is certainly one of the most characteristic products of Spanish literature, both for style and subject-matter.

---

[6] It is not impossible that the English translation of *The Critick* by Rycaut, 1681, may have suggested the Friday incidents of *Robinson Crusoe*, which was intended to be a more didactic book than it looks.

[7] Ticknor also suggests that the *Criticon* was derived from the *Euphormion* of Barclay, the author of *Argenis*.

Nearly all these works of Gracian were translated into most of the cultured languages of Europe, English not excepted. [8] Part of this ecumenical fame was doubtless due to the fact that Gracian was a Jesuit, and brethren of his Order translated the works of one of whom the Order was justly proud. But this explanation cannot altogether account for the wide spread of Gracian's works, and there remains a deposit of genuine ability and literary skill involved in most of the works I have briefly referred to—ability and skill of an entirely obsolete kind nowadays, but holding a rank of their own in the seventeenth and eighteenth centuries, when didacticism was all the rage. It is noteworthy that the *Testimonia* I have collected for the most part pass over the *Oráculo*, the only work at which a modern would care to cast a second glance, and go into raptures over *El Criticon* and its fellows, or the reverse of raptures on Gracian's style, which after all was the most striking thing about his works.

That style reaches its greatest perfection in the *Oráculo Manual*, to which we might at once turn but for a preliminary inquiry which it seems worth while to make. It is a book of maxims as distinguished from a book of aphorisms, and it is worth while for several reasons inquiring into maxims in general and maxim literature in particular before dealing with what is probably the most remarkable specimen of its class.

Before, however, doing this we may close this section of our introductory remarks by "putting in," as the lawyers say, the Latin inscription given by Latassa from the foot of the portrait of Gracian, which once stood in the Jesuit College at Calatayud, a portrait of which, alas! no trace can now be found. The lines sum up in sufficiently forcible Latin all that need be known of Balthasar Gracian and his works.

P. BALTHASAR GRACIAN VT IAM AB ORTV EMINERET IN BELLOMONTE NATVS EST PROPE BILBILIM CONFINIS MARTIALIS PATRIA PROXIMVS INGENIO, VT PROFVNDERET ADHVC CHRISTIANAS ARGVTIAS BILBILIS QVÆ PŒNE EXHAVSTA VIDEBATVR IN ETHNICIS. ERGO AVGENS NATALE INGENIVM INNATO ACVMINE SCRIPSIT ARTEM INGENII ET ARTE FACIT SCIBILE QVOD SCIBILES FACIT ARTES.
SCRIPSIT ITEM ARTEM PRVDENTIAE ET A SE IPSO ARTEM DIDICIT. SCRIPSIT ORACVLVM ET VOCES SVAS PROTVLIT. SCRIPSIT DISERTVM VT SE IPSVM DESCRIBERET ET VT SCRIBERET HEROEM HEROICA PATRAVIT. HÆC ET ALIA EIVS SCRIPTA MOECENATES REGES HABVERVNT

---

[8] See the details in the Bibliographical Appendix to this Introduction.

IVDICES ADMIRATIONEM LECTOREM MVNDVM TYPOGRAPHVM ÆTERNITATEM. PHILIPPVS III. SÆPE ILLIVS ARGVTIAS
INTER PRANDIVM VERSABAT NE DEFICERENT SALES REGIIS DAPIBVS. SED QVI PLAVSVS EXCITAVERAT CALAMO DEDITVS MISSIONIBVS EXCITAVIT PLANCTVS VERBO EXCITATVRVS DESIDERIVM IN MORTE QVA RAPTVS FVIT VI. DECEMBRIS AN. MDCLVIII SED ALIQVANDO EXTINCTV3 ÆTERNVM LVCEBIT.

II. Of Maxims

Many men have sought to give their views about man and about life in a pithy way; a few have tried to advise men in short sentences what to do in the various emergencies of life. The former have written aphorisms, the latter maxims. Where the aphorism states a fact of human nature, a maxim advises a certain course of action. The aphorism is written in the indicative, the maxim in an imperative mood.[9] "Life is interesting if not happy," is an aphorism, of Professor Seely's, I believe. "Ascend a step to choose a friend, descend a step to choose a wife," is a maxim of Rabbi Meir, one of the Doctors of the Talmud.

Now it is indeed curious how few maxims have ever been written. Wisdom has been extolled on the house-tops, but her practical advice seems to have been kept secret. Taking our own literature, there are extremely few books of practical maxims, and not a single one of any great merit. Sir Walter Raleigh's *Cabinet Council*, Penn's *Maxims*, and Chesterfield's *Letters* almost exhaust the list, and the last generally contains much more than mere maxims. Nor are they scattered with any profusion through books teeming with knowledge of life, the galaxy of English novels. During recent years extracts of their "beauties" have been published in some profusion— *Wit and Wisdom of Beaconsfield*; *Wise, Witty, and Tender Sayings of George Eliot*; *Extracts from Thackeray*, and the rest—but the crop of practical maxims to be found among them is extremely scanty. Aphorisms there are in plenty, especially in George Eliot, but he that is doubtful what course to pursue in any weighty crisis would wofully waste his time if he sought for advice from the novelists.

Nor are the moralists more instructive in this regard. Bacon's *Essays* leave with one the impression of fulness of practical wisdom. Yet, closely examined, there is very little residue of practical advice left in his pregnant sayings. Even the source of most of this kind of writing, the Biblical book of

---

[9] Not to be misleading, I may mention that Gracian's are generally in the infinitive.

Proverbs, fails to answer the particular kind of test I am at present applying. However shrewd some of them are, startling us with the consciousness how little human nature has changed, it is knowledge of human nature that they mainly supply. When we ask for instruction how to apply that knowledge we only get variations of the theme "Fear the Lord." Two thousand years of experience have indeed shown that the Fear or Love of the Lord forms a very good foundation for practical wisdom. But it has to be supplemented by some such corollary as "Keep your powder dry" before it becomes of direct service in the conduct of life.

It is indeed because of the unpractical nature of practical maxims that they have been so much neglected. You must act in the concrete, you can only maximise in general terms. Then, again, maxims can only appeal to the mind, to the intellect: the motive force of action is the will, the temperament. As Disraeli put it: "The conduct of men depends on the temperament, not upon a bunch of musty maxims" (*Henrietta Temple*). It is only very distantly that a maxim can stir the vague desire that spurs an imitative will. True, at times we read of men whose whole life has been coloured by a single saying. But these have generally been more appeals to the imagination, like Newman's "Securus judicat orbis terrarum," or the "Heu! fuge crudeles terras, fuge litus avarum," which had so decisive an effort on Savonarola's life. It is rare indeed that a man's whole life is tinged by a single practical maxim like Sir Daniel Gooch, who was influenced by his father's advice, "Stick to one thing."

Perhaps one of the reasons that have led literary persons to neglect the Maxim as a literary form has been their own ignorance of Action and, still more, their exaggerated notions of its difficulties and complexities. Affairs are not conducted by aphorisms: war is waged by a different kind of Maxims from those we are considering. Yet after all there must be some general principles on which actions should be conducted, and one would think they could be determined. Probably the successful men of action are not sufficiently self-observant to know exactly on what their success depends, and, if they did, they would in most cases try to "keep it in the family," like their wealth or their trade secrets.

And perhaps after all they are right who declare that action has little to do with intellect, and much with character. To say the truth, one is not impressed with the intellectual powers of the millionaires one meets. The shadiest of journalists could often explain their own doings with more point than they. Yet there are surely intellectual qualifications required for affairs: the Suez Canal must have required as great an amount of research, emendation, sense of order, and organisation as, say, the *Corpus Inscriptionum Latinarum*. But there is no such punishment for slovenly scholarship in action as there is in letters. The Suez Canal can be dug only once: Lucretius or Latin inscriptions can be edited over and over again. Altogether we need not be surprised if the men of action cannot put the principles of action into pointed sentences or maxims.

And if men of action cannot, it is not surprising that men of letters do not. For they cannot have the interest in action and its rewards which is required for worldly success, or else they would not be able to concentrate their thoughts on things which they consider of higher import. To a man of letters the world is the devil, or ought to be if he is to have the touch of idealism which gives colour and weight to his words. How then is he to devote his attention to worldly wisdom and the maxims that are to teach it? It is characteristic in this connection that the weightiest writer of maxims in our language is Bacon, who attempted to combine a career of affairs and of thought, and spoilt both by so doing.

It is perhaps due to the subtle and all-embracing influence of Christianity on modern civilisation that this divorce between idealism and the world has come about. The strenuous opposition to the world among earnest Christians has led to their practical withdrawal from it. Just as the celibacy of the clergy meant that the next generation was to be deprived of the hereditary influence of some of the purest spirits of the time, so the opposition of Christianity to the world has brought it about that the world has been un-Christian. Only one serious attempt has been made to bridge the chasm. The *idée mère* of Jesuitism was to make the world Christian by Christians becoming worldly. It was doubtless due to the reaction against the over -spiritualisation of Christianity pressed by the Protestant Reformation, but its practical result has been to make the Jesuit a worldly Christian. The control of the higher education of Europe by the Jesuits has tended, on the other hand, to make society more Christian. If then we were to look for an adequate presentation of worldly wisdom touched with sufficient idealism to make it worthy of a man of letters, we should look for it from a Jesuit, or from one trained among the Jesuits.

After all this elaborate explanation why so few maxims have been composed it may seem contradictory to give as a further and final reason because so many exist—under another form. For what are the majority of proverbs but maxims under another name, or rather maxims without the name of their author? We say of proverbs, indeed, that they arise among the people, but it is one definite individual among the people that gives them the piquant form that makes them proverbial. It was, we may be sure, a definite English gaffer who first said, "Penny wise, pound foolish." If we knew his name, we should call it maxim; as his name is unknown it ranks as a proverb. In this connection the Talmudic proverbs and maxims are of great interest. Owing to the worthy Rabbinic principle, "Say a thing in the name of the man who said it," we can in almost all cases trace Talmudic proverbs to their authors; or, in other words, Talmudic proverbs remain maxims. There is only one analogous case in English; a few of Benjamin Franklin's maxims, *e.g.* "Three removes are as good as a fire," [10] have become proverbs.

The abundance of proverbs is extraordinary. There is a whole bibliography devoted to the literature of proverbs (Duplessis,*Bibliographie Parémiologique*, Paris, 1847), and this needs nowadays a supplement as large again as the original (partly supplied by the bibliographical Appendix of Haller, *Altspanische Sprichwörter*, 1883). Indeed in the multitude of proverbs consists the greatest proof of their uselessness as guides to action, for by this means we get proverbs at cross purposes. Thus take the one I have just referred to, "Penny wise, pound foolish," which has a variant in the proverb, "Do not spoil the ship for a ha'porth of tar."

A man who was hesitating as to the amount or expense he would incur in any undertaking would be prompted by these sayings to be lavish. But then how about the proverb, "Take care of the pence and the pounds will take care of themselves"? Between the two proverbs he would come to the ground, and if he has the νοῦς to decide between them, he does not need the proverbs at all.

Hence it is perhaps that the nation that is richest in proverbs is the one that has proved itself among European peoples the least wise in action. To the Spaniards has been well applied the witticism about Charles II.: "They never said a foolish thing and never did a wise one." Certainly if proverbs be a proof of wisdom the Spaniards have given proofs in abundance. Don Quixote is full of them and the Spanish collections are extraordinarily rich. Now the nation that can produce good proverbs should be able to produce good maxims; hence we should expect the best book of maxims to emanate from a Spaniard.

One characteristic of both these forms of practical wisdom is their artificiality. One has to think twice before the point of a proverb or a maxim is perfectly clear. "The early bird catches the worm" seems at first sight as meaningless a proposition as "There are milestones on the Dover Road." Hence it is when a literature is passing through its artificial stage that maxims would naturally appear. So that it was clearly preordained that when the book of maxims should appear it would be by a Jesuit, so as to be worldly yet not too worldly; by a Spaniard, so that it should have the

---

[10] Most persons have heard the cynical continuation of a modern: "Three fires are as good as a failure and three failures are as good as a fortune."

proverbial ring; and during the prevalence of cultismo, so that it should have the quaintness to attract attention.

III Of the "Oráculo Manual"

Having thus proved *à priori* that the ideal book of maxims was destined to be the *Oráculo Manual* of Balthasar Gracian, let us proceed to prove our proof, as schoolboys do with their sums. That it is the best book of maxims is a foregone conclusion, because there is none other. Schopenhauer, who translated the book, observes that there is nothing like it in German, and there is certainly none approaching it in English, and if France or Italy can produce its superior, it is strange that its fame has remained so confined to its native country.

Not that there are not books teaching the art of self-advancement in almost all languages. The success of Dr. Smiles's volume on Self-Help is a sufficient instance of this.[11] Curiously enough, Dr. Smiles's book has had its greatest success in Italy, where it has given rise to quite a *letteratura selfelpista*, as the Italians themselves call it. Or rather not curiously, for if you wish to find the most unromantic set of ideals nowadays you must go search among the Romance nations.

Gracian does not, however, compete with Dr. Smiles. He does not deal with *Brodweisheit*; he assumes that the vulgar question of bread and butter has been settled in favour of his reader. He may be worldly, but he is thinking of the great world. He writes for men with a position and how to make the most of it. Nor is the aim he puts before such persons an entirely selfish one. "The sole advantage of power is that you can do more good" is the only rational defence of ambition, and Gracian employs it (Max. cclxxxvi).

Indeed the tone of the book is exceptionally high. It is impossible to accuse a man of any meanness who is the author of such maxims as—

"One cannot praise a man too much who speaks well of them who speak ill of him" (clxii).

"Friends are a second existence" (cxi).

"When to change the conversation? When they talk scandal" (ccl).

"In great crises there is no better companion than a bold heart" (clxvii).

"The secret of long life: lead a good life" (xc).

---

[11] One of our public men, I have been told, is known among his friends by the sobriquet of "Self-help by smiles."

"Be able to boast that if gallantry, generosity, and fidelity were lost in the world men would be able to find them again in your own breast" (clxv).

"A man of honour should never forget what he is because he sees what others are" (cclxxx).

And there are whole sections dealing with such topics as Rectitude (xxix), Sympathy with great Minds (xliv), a genial Disposition (lxxix), and the like.

Not that he is without the more subtle devices of the worldly wise. One could not wish to have anything more cynical or stinging than the following:—

"Find out each man's thumbscrew" (xxvi).

"A shrewd man knows that others when they seek him do not seek *him*, but their advantage in him and by him" (cclii).

"The truth, but not the whole truth" (clxxxi).

"Keep to yourself the final touches of your art" (ccxii).

"Do not take payment in politeness" (cxci).

"Have a touch of the trader" (ccxxxii).

"Think with the few and speak with the many" (xliii).

"Never have a companion who casts you in the shade" (clii).

"Never become paradoxical in order to avoid the trite" (cxliii).[12]

"Do not show your wounded finger" (cxlv).

The characteristic of the book is this combination or rather contrast of high tone and shrewdness. Gracian is both wisely worldly and worldly wise. After all, there does not seem to be any inherent impossibility in the combination. There does not seem any radical necessity why a good man should be a fool. One always has a certain grudge against Thackeray for making his Colonel Newcome so silly at times, though perhaps the irony, the pathos, the tragedy of the book required it. As a matter of fact the holiest of men have been some of the shrewdest, for their friends at least, if not for themselves.

The explanation of the combination in Gracian is simple enough. He was a Jesuit, and the Jesuits have just that combination of high tone and worldly wisdom as their *raison d'être*. And in the case of the *Oráculo* the mixture was easily effected by Gracian or his friend Lastanosa. For Gracian had written at least two series of works in which this contrast was represented by separate books. Two of these describing the qualities of the Hero and the Prudent Man (*El Heroe* and *El Discreto*) were published and

---

[12] Mr. Oscar Wilde's attention may be respectfully called to this maxim.

are represented in the *Oráculo*.[13] Two others dealing with the Gallant and the Cautious Man (*El Galante* and *El Varon Atento*) are referred to by Lastanosa in the preface to *El Discreto*, and are also doubtless represented in the book before us. One may guess that the section on Highmindedness (cxxviii) or on Nobility of Feeling (cxxxi) comes from *El Galante*, while "Better mad with the rest of the world than wise alone" (cxxxiii) smacks of *El Varon Atento*. At times we get the two tones curiously intermingled: "Choose an heroic ideal" (lxxv) seems at first sight a noble sentiment, but Gracian goes on to qualify it by adding, "but rather to emulate than to imitate."

The modernness of the tone is the thing that will strike most readers apart from these contrasts. Here and there one may be struck by an archaic note. "Never compete" would scarcely be the advice of a worldly teacher nowadays. But on the whole there is a tone of modern good society about the maxims which one would scarcely find in contemporary English works like Peacham's, or even in contemporary French authors like Charron. The reason is that modern society is permeated by influences which Gracian himself represented. The higher education of Europe for the last two and a half centuries has been in the hands of Jesuits or in schools formed on the *Ratio Studiorum*. And Society in the stricter sense traces from the Hôtel Rambouillet, where one-half the influence was Spanish. Gracian thus directly represents the tone of the two Societies which have set the tone of our society of to-day, and it is no wonder therefore if he is modern.

Even in his style there is something of a modern epigrammatic ring. At times there is the euphuistic quaintness, *e.g.* "One must pass through the circumference of time before arriving at the centre of opportunity." But as a rule the terseness and point of the maxim approximate to the modern epigram. "El escusarse antes de ocasion es culparse "might be both the source and the model of *Qui s'excuse s'accuse*. The terseness is indeed excessive and carried to Tacitean extremes. "A poco saber camino real," "Ultima felicidad el filosofar," "Harto presto, si bien." Gracian jerks out four or five words where a popular preacher would preach a sermon. Yet I cannot agree with the writers who call him obscure. He is one of the writers that make you think before you grasp his meaning, but the meaning is there, and put plainly enough, only tersely and very often indirectly, after the manner of proverbs. There is indeed no doubt that he and his predecessors were influenced by the form of the Spanish proverb in drawing up aphorisms and maxims. I say predecessors, for aphorismic literature at any rate was no novelty in Spain. Among the long list of books on aphorisms possessed by the late Sir William Stirling-Maxwell, and still at Keir, there are fully a dozen

---

[13] See *supra*, p. xxi. and notes.

Spanish ones who precede Gracian(Hernando Diaz, Lopez de Corelas, and Melchior de Santa Cruz are the most important, though the latter is more full of anecdotage). Among them is a book of *Aforismos* by Antonio Perez, whose *Relaciones* has been the chief means of blackening Philip II.'s character. [14] The former are undoubtedly of the same style as Gracian, and probably influenced him, though, as they are aphorisms and not maxims, I have not been able to quote parallels in the Notes. Thus "Una obra vale millares de graçias" (Perez, *Afor*. i. 198) has the same proverbial ring. It is curious to see Lytton's "The pen is mightier than the sword" anticipated by Perez' "La pluma corta mas que espadas afiladas" (*ibid*. 199), or Voltaire's "Speech was given us to conceal our thoughts" in Perez' "Las palabras, vestido de los conçeptos" (ii. 130). This last example has all Gracian's terseness, while Perez' "Amigos deste Siglo, rostros humanos, coraçones de fieras" [15] (ii. 71) has both terseness and cynicism. Certainly the only other work in Spanish or any other literature preceding Gracian on anything like the same lines is this book of *Aforismos* by Antonio Perez.

It is somewhat of a question, to my mind, how far Gracian was the author of the final form of the maxims as we have them in the *Oráculo*. Those taken from *El Heroe* and *El Discreto* differ from their originals with great advantage. They are terser, more to the point and less euphuistic. Now the Address to the Reader has all these qualities, and we may assume was written by its signatory, Don Vincencio de Lastanosa. It is just possible that we owe to him the extreme terseness and point of the majority of the maxims of the *Oráculo Manual*. It must not, however, be assumed that they are all as pointed and epigrammatic as those I have quoted. Gracian seems advisedly to have imbedded his jewels in a duller setting. At times he vies with the leaders of the great sect of the Platitudinarians, and he can be as banal as he is brilliant. Even as it is, his very brilliancy wearies, and after fifty maxims or so one longs for a more fruity wisdom, a more digressive discussion of life like those learned, wise, and witty essays of Mr. Stevenson, which may some day take higher rank as literature than even his novels.

Perhaps, after all, the weariness to which I refer may be due to the cautious tone of the book. To succeed one must be prudent; [16] that is the great moral of the book, and if so, does it seem worth while to succeed? If life is to be denuded of the aleatory element, is it worth living? Well, Gracian meets you when in that temper too. It is indeed remarkable how frequently he refers to luck; how you are to trust your luck, weigh your luck, follow your

---

[14] On Perez see Mr. Froude's paper in his *Spanish Story of the Armada*. Perez was over in England and was of the Sidney set.
[15] "Friends nowadays, human faces, hearts of brutes."
[16] The second title of the book is *Arte de Prudencia*, which I have adopted as the main title of my version.

luck, know your unlucky days, and so forth. Is all this a confession that after all life is too complex a game for any rules to be of much use? Granted, but there is one thing certain about life, and that is put by Goethe in the lines which I, following Schopenhauer,[17] have placed at the head of my translation. One must be either hammer or anvil in this world, and too great an excess of idealism only means that the unideal people shall rule the world. To guard against both extremes we have the paradoxical advice I have heard attributed to Mr. Ruskin, "Fit yourself for the best society, and then—never enter it."

Whether any ideal person will learn to rule the world by studying Gracian's or any one else's maxims is somewhat more doubtful, for reasons I have given above in discussing proverbs. The man who can act on maxims can act without them, and so does not need them. And there is the same amount of contradiction in maxims as in proverbs. Thus, to quote an example from the book before us, from Max. cxxxii it would seem best to keep back an intended gift: "long expected is highest prized"; whereas from Max. ccxxxvi we learn that "the promptness of the gift obliges the more strongly." Which maxim are we to act upon? That depends on circumstances, and the judgment that can decide on the circumstances can do without the maxims. I cannot therefore promise success in the world to whomsoever may read this book; otherwise I should perhaps not have published it.

But whether Gracian's maxims are true or useful scarcely affects their value. To the student of literature as such, the flimsiest sentiment or the merest paradox aptly put is worth the sublimest truth ill expressed. And there can be little doubt that Gracian puts his points well and vigorously. I cannot hope to have reproduced adequately all the vigour and force of his style, the subtlety of his distinctions, or the shrewdness of his mother-wit. But enough, I hope, has emerged during the process of translation to convince the reader that Gracian's *Oráculo Manual* has much wisdom in small compass and well put.

---

[17] Gracian was his favourite author; "Mein Gracian" he called him on one occasion (*Memorabilien*, p. 505).

To the Reader

No laws for the just, no counsels for the wise. Yet no one ever knew as much as he had need. One thing you must forgive, another, thank me for. I have called this manual of worldly wisdom an Oracle, for it is one in curtness and sententiousness. On the other hand, I offer you in one all the twelve works of Gracian. Each of these is so highly thought of that his Prudent Man had scarcely appeared in Spain than it was enjoyed among the French, in whose language it was translated and at whose court it was printed. May this be Wisdom's bill of fare at the banquet of her sages, in which she inscribes the items of the feast of reason to be found in Gracian's other works.

DON VINCENCIO JUAN DE LASTANOSA.

i *Everything is at its Acme*; especially the art of making one's way in the world. There is more required nowadays to make a single wise man than formerly to make Seven Sages, and more is needed nowadays to deal with a single person than was required with a whole people in former times.

ii[18] *Character and Intellect:* the two poles of our capacity; one without the other is but halfway to happiness. Intellect sufficeth not, character is also needed. On the other hand, it is the fool's misfortune, to fail in obtaining the position, the employment, the neighbourhood, and the circle of friends that suit him.

iii[19] *Keep Matters for a Time in Suspense*. Admiration at their novelty heightens the value of your achievements, it is both useless and insipid to play with the cards on the table. If you do not declare yourself immediately, you arouse expectation, especially when the importance of your position makes you the object of general attention. Mix a little mystery with everything, and the very mystery arouses veneration. And when you explain, be not too explicit, just as you do not expose your inmost thoughts in ordinary intercourse. Cautious silence is the holy of holies of worldly wisdom. A resolution declared is never highly thought of; it only leaves room for criticism. And if it happens to fail, you are doubly unfortunate. Besides you imitate the Divine way when you cause men to wonder and watch.

iv *Knowledge and Courage* are the elements of Greatness. They give immortality, because they are immortal. Each is as much as he knows, and the wise can do anything. A man without knowledge, a world without light. Wisdom and strength, eyes and hands. Knowledge without courage is sterile.

v[20] *Create a Feeling of Dependence*. Not he that adorns but he that adores makes a divinity. The wise man would rather see men needing him than thanking him. To keep them on the threshold of hope is diplomatic, to trust to their gratitude boorish; hope has a good memory, gratitude a bad one. More is to be got from dependence than from courtesy. He that has satisfied his thirst turns his back on the well, and the orange once sucked falls from the golden platter into the waste-basket. When dependence disappears, good behaviour goes with it as well as respect. Let it be one of

---

[18] *character and intellect*—Orig. "Genio y ingenio"; Schop. "Herz und Kopf"; Eng. I. "Wit and a Genius." The first section of El Discreto has the same title.
two poles—Orig. "los dos exes del lucimiento de prendas"; M.G.D. "The two axes of the brilliance of our accomplishments."
[19] cf. ccliii.
the Divine way; cf. "It is the glory of God to conceal a thing," Prov. xxv. 2
[20] *Not he that adorns*—Orig. "No hace el númen el que lo dora sino el que lo adora"; Schop. "Den Götzen macht nicht der Vergolder sondern der Anbeter."
golden platter—Orig. "del oro al lodo"; lit. from the gold to the mire.

the chief lessons of experience to keep hope alive without entirely satisfying it, by preserving it to make oneself always needed even by a patron on the throne. But let not silence be carried to excess lest you go wrong, nor let another's failing grow incurable for the sake of your own advantage.

vi[21] ***A Man at his Highest Point.*** We are not born perfect: every day we develop in our personality and in our calling till we reach the highest point of our completed being, to the full round of our accomplishments, of our excellences. This is known by the purity of our taste, the clearness of our thought, the maturity of our judgment, and the firmness of our will. Some never arrive at being complete; somewhat is always awanting: others ripen late. The complete man, wise in speech, prudent in act, is admitted to the familiar intimacy of discreet persons, is even sought for by them.

vii ***Avoid Victories over Superiors.*** All victories breed hate, and that over your superior is foolish or fatal. Superiority is always detested, *à fortiori* superiority over superiority. Caution can gloss over common advantages; for example, good looks may be cloaked by careless attire. There be some that will grant you precedence in good luck or good temper, but none in good sense, least of all a prince; for good sense is a royal prerogative, any claim to that is a case of *lèse majesté*. They are princes, and wish to be so in that most princely of qualities. They will allow a man to help them but not to surpass them, and will have any advice tendered them appear like a recollection of something they have forgotten rather than as a guide to something they cannot find. The stars teach us this finesse with happy tact; though they are his children and brilliant like him, they never rival the brilliancy of the sun.

viii ***To be without Passions.*** 'Tis a privilege of the highest order of mind. Their very eminence redeems them from being affected by transient and low impulses. There is no higher rule than that over oneself, over one's impulses: there is the triumph of free will. While passion rules the character, no aiming at high office; the less the higher. It is the only refined way of avoiding scandals; nay, 'tis the shortest way back to good repute.

ix ***Avoid the Faults of your Nation.*** Water shares the good or bad qualities of the strata[22] through which it flows, and man those of the climate in which he is born. Some owe more than others to their native land, because there is a more favourable sky in the zenith. There is not a nation even among the most civilised that has not some fault peculiar to itself which other nations blame by way of boast or as a warning. 'Tis a triumph of cleverness to correct in oneself such national failings, or even to hide them:

---

[21] From *El Discreto*.
[22] *strata*—so Schop. "Schichten"; Orig. "venas donde pasa." TWC. It could be simply translated as in the original, literally "water veins".

you get great credit for being unique among your fellows, and as it is less expected of you it is esteemed the more. There are also family failings as well as faults of position, of office or of age. If these all meet in one person and are not carefully guarded against, they make an intolerable monster.

x *Fortune and Fame*. Where the one is fickle the other is enduring. The first for life, the second afterwards; the one against envy, the other against oblivion. Fortune is desired, at times assisted: fame is earned. The desire for fame springs from man's best part. It was and is the sister of the giants; it always goes to extremes—horrible monsters or brilliant prodigies.

xi *Cultivate those who can teach you*. Let friendly intercourse be a school of knowledge, and culture be taught through conversation: thus you make your friends your teachers and mingle the pleasures of conversation with the advantages of instruction. Sensible persons thus enjoy alternating pleasures: they reap applause for what they say, and gain instruction from what they hear. We are always attracted to others by our own interest, but in this case it is of a higher kind. Wise men frequent the houses of great noblemen not because they are temples of vanity, but as theatres of good breeding. There be gentlemen who have the credit of worldly wisdom, because they are not only themselves oracles of all nobleness by their example and their behaviour, but those who surround them form a well-bred academy of worldly wisdom of the best and noblest kind.

xii *Nature and Art*: material and workmanship. There is no beauty unadorned and no excellence that would not become barbaric if it were not supported by artifice: this remedies the evil and improves the good. Nature scarcely ever gives us the very best; for that we must have recourse to art. Without this the best of natural dispositions is uncultured, and half is lacking to any excellence if training is absent. Every one has something unpolished without artificial training, and every kind of excellence needs some polish.

xiii *Act sometimes on Second Thoughts[23], sometimes on First Impulse*. Man's life is a warfare against the malice[24] of men. Sagacity fights with strategic changes of intention: it never does what it threatens, it aims only at escaping notice. It aims in the air with dexterity and strikes home in an unexpected direction, always seeking to conceal its game. It lets a purpose appear in order to attract the opponent's attention, but then turns round and conquers by the unexpected. But a penetrating intelligence anticipates this by watchfulness and lurks in ambush. It always understands

---

[23] Orig. "intencion segunda." The expression and idea is derived from scholastic logic. Terms of second intention, *i.e.* logical technical terms, are doubly abstract, being abstractions of terms of first intention.
[24] Orig. "milicia . . . contra la malicia."

the opposite of what the opponent wishes it to understand, and recognises every feint of guile. It lets the first impulse pass by and waits for the second, or even the third. Sagacity now rises to higher flights on seeing its artifice foreseen, and tries to deceive by truth itself, changes its game in order to change its deceit, and cheats by not cheating, and founds deception on the greatest candour. But the opposing intelligence is on guard with increased watchfulness, and discovers the darkness concealed by the light and deciphers every move, the more subtle because more simple. In this way the guile of the Python combats the far darting rays of Apollo.

xiv **The Thing Itself and the Way it is done**. "Substance" is not enough: "accident"[25] is also required, as the scholastics say. A bad manner spoils everything, even reason and justice; a good one supplies everything, gilds a No, sweetens truth, and adds a touch of beauty to old age itself. The *how* plays a large part in affairs, a good manner steals into the affections. Fine behaviour is a joy in life[26], and a pleasant expression helps out of a difficulty in a remarkable way.

xv **Keep Ministering Spirit**s. It is a privilege of the mighty to surround themselves with the champions of intellect; these extricate them from every fear of ignorance, these worry out for them the moot points of every difficulty. 'Tis a rare greatness to make use of the wise[27], and far exceeds the barbarous taste of Tigranes, who had a fancy for captive monarchs as his servants. It is a novel kind of supremacy, the best that life can offer, to have as servants by skill those who by nature are our masters. 'Tis a great thing to know[28], little to live: no real life without knowledge. There is remarkable cleverness in studying without study, in getting much by means of many, and through them all to become wise. Afterwards you speak in the council chamber on behalf of many, and as many sages speak through your mouth as were consulted beforehand: you thus obtain the fame of an oracle by others' toil. Such ministering spirits distil the best books and serve up the quintessence of wisdom. But he that cannot have sages in service should have them for his friends.

xvi **Knowledge and Good Intentions** together ensure continuance of success. A fine intellect wedded to a wicked will was always an unnatural monster. A wicked will envenoms all excellences: helped by knowledge it

---

[25] Orig. "circumstancia"; again a scholastic term referring to the modes of real being.
[26] cf. Emerson: "Beautiful behaviour is the finest of the fine arts."
[27] Make friends of the wise," said the Seven Sages, *ap.* Stobaeus, *Flor.* iii. 80.
[28] Orig. "Ay mucho que saber y es poco el vivir"; Schop. takes it as a variant of Hippocrates' maxim, "Art is long," etc., and renders "Das Wissen ist lang, das Leben kurz." See, however, ccxlvii.

only ruins with greater subtlety. 'Tis a miserable superiority that only results in ruin. Knowledge without sense[29] is double folly.

xvii ***Vary the Mode of Action***; not always the same way, so as to distract attention, especially if there be a rival. Not always from first impulse[30]; they will soon recognise the uniformity, and by anticipating, frustrate your designs. It is easy to kill a bird on the wing that flies straight: not so one that twists. Nor always act on second thoughts: they can discern the plan the second time. The enemy is on the watch, great skill is required to circumvent him. The gamester never plays the card the opponent expects, still less that which he wants.

xviii ***Application and Ability***[31]. There is no attaining eminence without both, and where they unite there is the greatest eminence. Mediocrity obtains more with application than superiority without it. Work is the price which is paid for reputation. What costs little is little worth. Even for the highest posts it is only in some cases application that is wanting, rarely the talent. To prefer moderate success in great things than eminence in a humble post has the excuse of a generous mind, but not so to be content with humble mediocrity when you could shine among the highest. Thus nature and art are both needed, and application sets on them the seal.

xix ***Arouse*** [32]***no Exaggerated Expectations on entering***. It is the usual ill-luck of all celebrities not to fulfil afterwards the expectations beforehand formed of them. The real can never equal the imagined, for it is easy to form ideals but very difficult to realise them. Imagination weds Hope and gives birth to much more than things are in themselves. However great the excellences, they never suffice to fulfil expectations, and as men find themselves disappointed with their exorbitant expectations they are more ready to be disillusionised than to admire. Hope is a great falsifier of truth; let skill guard against this by ensuring that fruition exceeds desire. A few creditable attempts at the beginning are sufficient to arouse curiosity without pledging one to the final object. It is better that reality should surpass the design and is better than was thought. This rule does not apply to the wicked, for the same exaggeration is a great aid to them; they are defeated amid general applause, and what seemed at first extreme ruin comes to be thought quite bearable.

xx ***A Man of the Age***. The rarest individuals depend on their age. It is not every one that finds the age he deserves, and even when he finds it he does not always know how to utilise it. Some men have been worthy of a

---

[29] "Ciencia sin seso locura doble"; cf. Span. prov. "Ciencia es Locura si buen seso no la cura." TWC. The original literally says: Science, without brains, is double folly.
[30] Orig. "intencion," a reference to xiii, where see Note
[31] Galton, *Hereditary Genius*, p. 38, adds zeal or energy.
[32] *El Heroe*, § 16

better century, for every species of good does not always triumph. Things have their period; even excellences are subject to fashion. The sage has one advantage[33]: he is immortal. If *this* is not his century many others will be.

xxi **The Art of being Lucky**. There are rules of luck: it is not all chance with the wise: it can be assisted by care. Some content themselves with placing them-selves confidently at the gate of Fortune, waiting till she opens it. Others do better, and press forward and profit by their clever boldness, reaching the goddess and winning her favour on the wings of their virtue and valour. But on a true philosophy there is no other umpire than virtue and insight; for there is no luck or ill-luck except wisdom and the reverse.

xxii **A Man of Knowledge to the Point**. Wise men arm themselves with tasteful and elegant erudition; a practical knowledge of what is going on not of a common kind but more like an expert. They possess a copious store of wise and witty sayings, and of noble deeds, and know how to employ them on fitting occasions. More is often taught by a jest than by the most serious teaching. Pat knowledge helps some more than the seven arts, be they ever so liberal.

xxiii **Be Spotless**: the indispensable condition of perfection. Few live without some weak point, either physical or moral, which they pamper because they could easily cure it. The keenness of others often regrets to see a slight defect attaching itself to a whole assembly of elevated qualities, and yet a single cloud can hide the whole of the sun. There are likewise patches on our reputation which ill-will soon finds out[34] and is continually noticing. The highest skill is to transform them into ornament. So Cæsar hid his natural defects with the laurel.

xxiv **Keep the Imagination under Control**; sometimes correcting, sometimes assisting it. For it is all-important for our happiness, and even sets the reason right. It can tyrannise, and is not content with looking on, but influences and even often dominates life, causing it to be happy or burdensome according to the folly to which it leads. For it makes us either contented or discontented with ourselves. Before some it continually holds up the penalties of action, and becomes the mortifying lash of these fools. To others it promises happiness and adventure with blissful delusion. It can do all this unless the most prudent self-control keeps it in subjection.

xxv **Know how to take a Hint**.[35] 'Twas once the art of arts to be able to discourse; now 'tis no longer sufficient. We must know how to take a hint,

---

[33] A favourite maxim of Schopenhauer, quoted by him in his *Wille in d. Natur*, 1836, p. 34, and written on his own copy of *Die Welt als Wille*, obviously applying it to himself. (See Grisebach, *Edita and Inedita*, p. 104.)
[34] Orig. "para luego y aun repara."
[35] Orig. "Buen entendedor"; from *El Discreto*. Eng. I. "A good Pryer"; Eng. II. "A good Understanding." The reference is to the Span. prov. "A buen entendedor pocas palabras," *Don*

especially in disabusing ourselves. He cannot make himself understood who does not himself easily understand. But on the other hand there are pretended diviners of the heart and lynxes of the intentions. The very truths which concern us most can only be half spoken, but with attention we can grasp the whole meaning. When you hear anything favourable keep a tight rein on your credulity; if unfavourable, give it the spur.

xxvi **Find out each Man's Thumbscrew.** 'Tis the art of setting their wills in action. It needs more skill than resolution. You must know where to get at any one. Every volition has a special motive which varies according to taste. All men are idolaters, some of fame, others of self-interest, most of pleasure. Skill consists in knowing these idols in order to bring them into play. Knowing any man's mainspring of motive you have as it were the key to his will. Have resort to primary motors, which are not always the highest but more often the lowest part of his nature: there are more dispositions badly organised than well. First guess a man's ruling passion, appeal to it by a word, set it in motion by temptation, and you will infallibly give checkmate to his freedom of will.

xxvii **Prize Intensity more than Extent.** Excellence resides in quality not in quantity. The best is always few and rare: much lowers value. Even among men giants are commonly the real dwarfs[36]. Some reckon books by the thickness, as if they were written to try the brawn[37] more than the brain. Extent alone never rises above mediocrity: it is the misfortune of universal geniuses that in attempting to be at home everywhere, are so nowhere. Intensity gives eminence, and rises to the heroic in matters sublime.

xxviii **Common in Nothing.** First, not in taste. O great and wise[38], to be ill at ease when your deeds please the mob! The excesses of popular applause never satisfy the sensible. Some there are such chameleons of popularity[39] that they find enjoyment not in the sweet savours of Apollo but in the breath of the mob. Secondly, not in intelligence. Take no pleasure in the wonder of the mob, for ignorance never gets beyond wonder. While vulgar folly wonders wisdom watches for the trick.

xxix **A Man of Rectitude** clings to the sect of right with such tenacity of purpose that neither the passions of the mob nor the violence of the tyrant can ever cause him to transgress the bounds of right. But who shall be such

---

Quixote, ii. cc. 37, 60. Sly uses the later half in *Taming of Shrew* Induction, "Therefore *pocas palabras*, let the world slide, sessa!"
[36] cf. Bacon's apophthegm, "Nature did never put her jewels in garrets."
[37] A slight embellishment. Orig. "para exercitar antes los braços que los ingenios."
[38] Phocion; ap. Plutarch, *Reg. et Imp. Apophthegm.* Phocion, 4.
[39] cf. ccxcv

a Phœnix of equity? What a scanty following has rectitude! Many praise it[40] indeed, but—for others. Others follow it till danger threatens; then the false deny it, the politic conceal it. For it cares not if it fights with friendship, power, or even self-interest: then comes the danger of desertion. Then astute men make plausible distinctions so as not to stand in the way of their superiors or of reasons of state. But the straightforward and constant regard dissimulation as a kind of treason, and set more store on tenacity than on sagacity. Such are always to be found on the side of truth, and if they desert a party, they do not change from fickleness, but because the others have first deserted truth.

xxx **Have naught to do with Occupations of Ill-repute**, still less with fads that bring more notoriety than repute. There are many fanciful sects, and from all the prudent man has to flee. There are bizarre tastes that always take to their heart all that wise men repudiate; they live in love with singularity. This may make them well known indeed, but more as objects of ridicule than of repute. A cautious man does not even make profession of his wisdom, still less of those matters that make their followers ridiculous. These need not be specified, for common contempt has sufficiently singled them out.

xxxi **Select the Lucky and avoid the Unlucky**[41]. Ill-luck is generally the penalty of folly, and there is no disease so contagious to those who share in it. Never open[42] the door to a lesser evil, for other and greater ones invariably slink in after it. The greatest skill at cards is to know when to discard; the smallest of current trumps is worth more than the ace of trumps of the last game. When in doubt, follow the suit of the wise and prudent; sooner or later they will win the odd trick[43].

xxxii **Have the Reputation of being Gracious**. 'Tis the chief glory of the high and mighty to be gracious, a prerogative of kings to conquer universal goodwill. That is the great advantage of a commanding position—to be able to do more good than others. Those make friends[44] who do friendly acts. On the other hand, there are some who lay themselves out for not being gracious, not on account of the difficulty, but from a bad disposition. In all things they are the opposite of Divine grace.

xxxiii **Know how to Withdraw**. If it is a great lesson in life to know how to deny, it is a still greater to know how to deny oneself as regards both affairs and persons. There are extraneous occupations which eat away

---

[40] cf. "Probitas laudatur et alget," Juv. *Sat.* i. 74.
[41] Quoted by Addison in Spectator, No. 293. The Rothschilds are said to act on this principle in their business relations.
[42] cf. ccliv
[43] Orig. merely "hallan con la ventura."
[44] cf. xl, cxi.

precious time. To be occupied in what does not concern you is worse than doing nothing. It is not enough for a careful man not to interfere with others, he must see that they do not interfere with him. One is not obliged[45] to belong so much to all as not to belong at all to oneself. So with friends, their help should not be abused or more demanded from them than they themselves will grant. All excess is a failing, but above all in personal intercourse. A wise moderation in this best preserves the goodwill and esteem of all, for by this means that precious boon of courtesy is not gradually worn away. Thus you preserve your genius free to select the elect, and never sin against the unwritten laws of good taste.

xxxiv **Know your strongest Point**— your pre-eminent gift; cultivate that and you will assist the rest. Every one would have excelled in something if he had known his strong point. Notice in what quality you surpass, and take charge of that. In some judgment excels, in others valour. Most do violence to their natural aptitude, and thus attain superiority in nothing. Time disillusionises us too late of what first flattered the passions.

xxv *Think over Things, most over the most Important*. All fools[46] come to grief from want of thought. They never see even the half of things, and as they do not observe their own loss or gain, still less do they apply any diligence to them. Some make much of what imports little and little of much, always weighing in the wrong scale. Many never lose their common sense, because they have none to lose. There are matters which should be observed with the closest attention of the mind, and thenceforth kept in its lowest depths. The wise man thinks over everything, but with a difference, most profoundly where there is some profound difficulty, and thinks that perhaps there is more in it than he thinks. Thus his comprehension extends as far as his apprehension.

xxxvi *In Acting or Refraining, weigh your Luck*. More depends on that than on noticing your temperament. If he is a fool who at forty applies to Hippocrates for health, still more is he one who then first applies to Seneca for wisdom. It is a great piece of skill to know how to guide your luck even while waiting for it. For something is to be done with it by waiting so as to use it at the proper moment, since it has periods and offers opportunities, though one cannot calculate its path, its steps are so irregular. When you find Fortune favourable, stride boldly forward, for she favours the bold[47] and, being a woman, the young. But if you have bad luck, keep retired so as not to redouble the influence of your unlucky star.

---

[45] cf. cclx
[46] cf. Stevenson, Kidnapped, c. xiv. as: "I have seen wicked men and fools, a great many of them; and I believe they both got paid in the end; but the fools first."
[47] cf. Span. prov. "Al hombre osado la Fortuna le da la mano", TWC: lit, Fortune lends a hand to the bold.

xxxvii **Keep a Store of Sarcasms, and know how to use them.** This is the point of greatest tact in human intercourse. Such sarcasms are often thrown out to test men's moods, and by their means one often obtains the most subtle and penetrating touchstone of the heart. Other sarcasms are malicious, insolent, poisoned by envy or envenomed by passion, unexpected flashes which destroy at once all favour and esteem. Struck by the slightest word of this kind, many fall away from the closest intimacy with superiors or inferiors which could not be the slightest shaken by a whole conspiracy of popular insinuation or private malevolence. Other sarcasms, on the other hand, work favourably, confirming and assisting one's reputation. But the greater the skill with which they are launched, the greater the caution with which they should be received and the foresight with which they should he foreseen. For here a knowledge of the evil is in itself a means of defence, and a shot foreseen always misses its mark.

xxxviii **Leave your Luck while Winning.** All the best players do it. A fine retreat is as good as a gallant attack. Bring your exploits under cover when there are enough, or even when there are many of them. Luck long lasting was ever suspicious; interrupted seems safer, and is even sweeter to the taste for a little infusion of bitter-sweet. The higher the heap of luck, the greater the risk of a slip, and down comes all. Fortune pays you sometimes for the intensity of her favours by the shortness of their duration. She soon tires of carrying any one long on her shoulders.

xxxix **Recognise when Things are ripe, and then enjoy them.** The works of nature all reach a certain point of maturity; up to that they improve, after that they degenerate. Few works of art reach such a point that they cannot be improved. It is an especial privilege of good taste to enjoy everything at its ripest. Not all can do this, nor do all who can know this. There is a ripening point too for fruits of intellect; it is well to know this both for their value in use and for their value in exchange.

xl[48] **The Goodwill of People.** 'Tis much to gain universal admiration; more, universal love. Something depends on natural disposition, more on practice: the first founds, the second then builds on that foundation. Brilliant parts suffice not, though they are presupposed; win good opinion and 'tis easy to win goodwill. Kindly acts besides are required to produce kindly feelings, doing good with both hands, good words and better deeds, loving so as to be loved. Courtesy is the politic witchery of great personages. First lay hand on deeds and then on pens; words follow swords; for there is goodwill to be won among writers, and it is eternal.

---

[48] *El Heroe*, § 12

xli ***Never Exaggerate***. It is an important object of attention not to talk in superlatives, so as neither to offend against truth nor to give a mean idea of one's understanding. Exaggeration is a prodigality of the judgment which shows the narrowness of one's knowledge or one's taste. Praise arouses lively curiosity, begets desire, and if afterwards the value does not correspond to the price, as generally happens, expectation revolts against the deception, and revenges itself by under-estimating the thing recommended and the person recommending. A prudent man goes more cautiously to work, and prefers to err by omission than by commission. Extraordinary things are rare, therefore moderate ordinary valuation. Exaggeration is a branch of lying, and you lose by it the credit of good taste, which is much, and of good sense, which is more.

xlii ***Born to Command***. It is a secret force of superiority not to have to get on by artful trickery but by an inborn power of rule. All submit to it without knowing why, recognising the secret vigour of connatural authority. Such magisterial spirits are kings by merit and lions by innate privilege. By the esteem which they inspire, they hold the hearts and minds of the rest. If their other qualities permit, such men are born to be the prime motors of the state. They per-form more by a gesture than others by a long harangue.

xliii[49] ***Think with the Few and speak with the Many***. By swimming against the stream it is impossible to remove error, easy to fall into danger; only a Socrates can undertake it. To dissent from others' views is regarded as an insult, because it is their condemnation. Disgust is doubled on account of the thing blamed and of the person who praised it. Truth is for the few, error is both common and vulgar. The wise man is not known by what he says on the house-tops, for there he speaks not with his own voice but with that of common folly, however much his inmost thoughts may gainsay it. The prudent avoid being contradicted as much as contradicting: though they have their censure ready they are not ready to publish it. Thought is free, force cannot and should not be used to it. The wise man therefore retires into silence, and if he allows himself to come out of it, he does so in the shade and before few and fit persons.

xliv ***Sympathy with great Minds***. It is an heroic quality to agree with heroes. 'Tis like a miracle of nature for mystery and for use[50]. There is a natural kinship of hearts and minds: its effects are such that vulgar ignorance scents witchcraft. Esteem established, goodwill follows, which at times reaches affection. It persuades without words and obtains without earning. This sympathy is sometimes active, sometimes passive, both alike felicific; the more so, the more sublime. 'Tis a great art to recognise, to

---

[49] *El Discreto*, "Hombre juizio."
[50] Orig. "por lo oculto y por lo ventajoso."

distinguish and to utilise this gift. No amount of energy suffices without that favour of nature.

xlv **Use, but do not abuse, Cunning**. One ought not to delight in it, still less to boast of it. Everything artificial should be concealed, most of all cunning, which is hated. Deceit is much in use; therefore our caution has to be redoubled, but not so as to show itself, for it arouses distrust, causes much annoy, awakens revenge, and gives rise to more ills than you would imagine. To go to work with caution is of great advantage in action, and there is no greater proof of wisdom. The greatest skill in any deed consists in the sure mastery with which it is executed.

xlvi **Master your Antipathies**. We often allow ourselves to take dislikes, and that before we know anything of a person. At times this innate yet vulgar aversion attaches Itself to eminent personalities. Good sense masters this feeling, for there is nothing more discreditable than to dislike those better than ourselves. As sympathy with great men en-nobles us, so dislike to them degrades us.

xlvii **Avoid "Affairs of Honour"** —one of the chiefest aims of prudence. In men of great ability the extremes are kept far asunder, so that there is a long distance between them, and they always keep in the middle of their caution, so that they take time to break through it. It is easier to avoid such affairs than to come well out of them. They test our judgment; it is better to avoid them than to conquer in them. One affair[51] of honour leads to another, and may lead to an affair of dishonour. There are men so constituted by nature or by nation that they easily enter upon such obligations. But for him that walks by the light of reason, such a matter requires long thinking over. There is more valour needed not to take up the affair than to conquer in it. When there is one fool ready for the occasion, one may excuse oneself from being the second.

xlviii **Be Thorough**. How much depends on the person. The interior must be at least as much as the exterior. There are natures all frontage, like houses that for want of means have the portico of a palace leading to the rooms of a cottage. It is no use boring[52] into such persons, although they bore you, for conversation flags after the first salutation. They prance through the first compliments like Sicilian barbs, but silence soon succeeds, for the flow of words soon ceases where there is no spring of thoughts. Others may be taken in by them because they themselves have but a view of the surface, but not the prudent, who look within them and find nothing there except material for scorn.

---

[51] Orig. has a play upon "empeño" and "despeño," which I have tried to reproduce.
[52] Orig. "No ay en estos donde parar ó todo para."

xlix[53] **Observation and Judgment**. A man with these rules things, not they him. He sounds at once the profoundest depths; he is a phrenologist by means of physiognomy. On seeing a person he understands him and judges of his inmost nature. From a few observations he deciphers the most hidden recesses of his nature. Keen observation, subtile insight, judicious inference: with these he discovers, notices, grasps, and comprehends everything.

l **Never lose Self-respect**, or be too familiar with oneself. Let your own right feeling be the true standard of your rectitude, and owe more to the strictness of your own self-judgment than to all external sanctions. Leave off anything unseemly more from regard for your own self-respect than from fear of external authority. Pay regard to that and there is no need of Seneca's imaginary tutor.

li[54] **Know how to Choose well**. Most of life depends thereon. It needs good taste and correct judgment, for which neither intellect nor study suffices. To be choice, you must choose, and for this two things are needed: to be able to choose at all, and then to choose the best. There are many men of fecund and subtle mind, of keen judgment, of much learning, and of great observation who yet are at a loss when they come to choose. They always take the worst as if they had tried to go wrong. Thus this is one of the greatest gifts from above.

lii **Never be put out**. 'Tis a great aim of prudence never to be embarrassed. It is the sign of a real man. of a noble heart, for magnanimity is not easily put out. The passions are the humours of the soul, and every excess in them weakens prudence; if they overflow through the mouth, the reputation will be in danger. Let a man therefore be so much and so great a master over himself that neither in the most fortunate nor in the most adverse circumstances can anything cause his reputation injury by disturbing his self-possession, but rather enhance it by showing his superiority.

liii[55] **Diligent and Intelligent**. Diligence promptly executes what intelligence slowly excogitates. Hurry is the failing of fools; they know not the crucial point and set to work without preparation. On the other hand, the wise more often fail from procrastination; foresight begets deliberation, and remiss action often nullifies prompt judgment. Celerity is the mother of

---

[53] *El Discreto*, c. xviii
[54] *El Discreto*, c. ix.
[55] *El Discreto*, c. xx

good fortune. He has done much who leaves nothing over till to-morrow. *Festina lente*[56] is a royal motto.

liv *Know how to show your Teeth*. Even hares can pull the mane of a dead lion. There is no joke about courage. Give way to the first and you must yield to the second, and so on till the last, and to gain your point at last costs as much trouble as would have gained much more at first. Moral courage exceeds physical; it should be like a sword kept ready for use in the scabbard of caution. It is the shield of great place; moral cowardice lowers one more than physical. Many have had eminent qualities, yet, for want of a stout heart, they passed inanimate lives and found a tomb in their own sloth. Wise Nature has thoughtfully combined in the bee the sweetness of its honey with the sharpness of its sting.

lv[57] *Wait*. It's a sign of a noble heart dowered with patience, never to be in a hurry, never to be in a passion. First be master over yourself if you would be master over others. You must pass through the circumference of time before arriving at the centre of opportunity. A wise reserve seasons the aims and matures the means. Time's crutch effects more than the iron club of Hercules. God Himself chasteneth not with a rod but with time. He (Charles V) spake[58] a great word who said, "Time and I against any two." Fortune herself rewards waiting with the first prize.

lvi[59] *Have Presence of Mind*. The child of a happy promptitude of spirit. Owing to this vivacity and wideawakeness there is no fear of danger or mischance. Many reflect much only to go wrong in the end: others attain their aim without thinking of it beforehand. There are natures of Antiperistasis[60] who work best in an emergency[61]. They are like monsters who succeed in all they do offhand, but fail in aught they think over. A thing occurs to them at once or never: for them there is no court of appeal. Celerity wins applause because it proves remarkable capacity; subtlety of judgment, prudence in action.

lvii *Slow and Sure*. Early enough if well. Quickly done[62] can be quickly undone. To last an eternity requires an eternity of preparation. Only excellence counts; only achievement endures. Profound intelligence is the

---

[56] Orig. "Correr á espacio." This is not given in Dielitz' elaborate work on *Wahl-und Denksprüche*, Gorlitz, 1884, so I suspect it was Gracian's version of Augustus' motto, σπεῦδε βραχέως, generally translated *Festina lente*.
[57] *El Discreto*, c. iii, mainly from the end. It is called an *Allegoria*.
[58] Charles V. according to *El Discreto*, I.e. Schop. attributes the saying to Philip II.
[59] *El Discreto*, c. xiv.
[60] *natures of Antiperistasis*. The energy aroused by opposition. Johnson gives example from Cowley (M.G.D.) It occurs also in Bacon (*Colours*, vii.) and Browne (*Rel. Med.* II. x.) Macaulay also uses it in his essay on Bacon (Oxford Diet.).
[61] So Galton, *Hereditary Genius*, p. 48, who speaks of men "formed to shine under exceptional circumstances," as in the Indian Mutiny.
[62] cf. Herbert, *Jacula Prudentum*, "Good and quickly seldom meet."

only foundation for immortality. Worth much costs much. The precious metals are the heaviest.

lviii **Adapt Yourself to your Company**. There is no need to show your ability before every one. Employ no more force than is necessary. Let there be no unnecessary expenditure either of knowledge or of power. The skilful falconer only flies enough birds to serve for the chase. If there is too much display to-day there will be nothing to show to-morrow. Always have some novelty wherewith to dazzle. To show something fresh each day keeps expectation alive and conceals the limits of capacity.

lix **Finish off well**[63]. In the house of Fortune, if you enter by the gate of pleasure you must leave by that of sorrow and *vice versâ*. You ought therefore to think of the finish, and attach more importance to a graceful exit than to applause on entrance. 'Tis the common lot of the unlucky to have a very fortunate outset and a very tragic end. The important point is not the vulgar applause on entrance—that comes to nearly all—but the general feeling at exit. Few in life are felt to deserve an encore. Fortune rarely accompanies any one to the door: warmly as[64] she may welcome the coming, she speeds but coldly the parting guest.

lx **A Sound Judgment**. Some are born wise, and with this natural advantage enter upon their studies, with a moiety already mastered. With age and experience their reason ripens, and thus they attain a sound judgment. They abhor everything whimsical as leading prudence astray, especially in matters of state, where certainty is so necessary, owing to the importance of the affairs involved., Such men deserve to stand by the helm of state[65] either as pilots or as men at the wheel.

lxi [66]**To Excel in what is Excellent**. A great rarity among excellences. You cannot have a great man without something pre-eminent. Mediocrities never win applause. Eminence in some distinguished post distinguishes one from the vulgar mob and ranks us with the elect. To be distinguished in a Small post is to be great in little: the more comfort, the less glory. The highest eminence in great affairs has the royal characteristic of exciting admiration and winning goodwill.

lxii **Use good Instruments**[67]. Some would have the subtlety of their wits proven by the meanness of their instruments. 'Tis a dangerous

---

[63] *El Discreto*, c. xi. cf. lxvi. *Few in life*—Orig. "Que son raros los deseados."
[64] Orig. "lo que se muesta de cumplida con los que vienen de descortes con los que van." M.G.D. "Seldom does fortune conduct a parting guest to the threshold."
[65] So Schop. "Solche Leute verdienen am Staatsruder zu stehen, sei es zur Lenkung oder zum Rath"; Orig. "Merecen estos la asistencia al gobernarle ó para exercicio ó para consejo."
[66] *El Heroe*, p. vi.
[67] Chap. iii. of Sir H. Taylor's *The Statesman* is entitled "A Statesman's most pregnant Function lies in the Choice and Use of Instruments."

satisfaction, and deserves a fatal punishment. The excellence of a minister never diminished the greatness of his lord. All the glory of exploits reverts to the principal actor; also all the blame[68]. Fame only does business with principals. She does not say, "This had good, that had bad servants," but, "This was a good artist, that a bad one." Let your assistants be selected and tested therefore, for you have to trust to them for an immortality of fame.

lxiii [69]**To he the First of the Kind is an Excellence**, and to be eminent in it as well, a double one. To have the first move is a great advantage when the players are equal. Many a man would have been a veritable Phœnix if he had been the first of the sort. Those who come first are the heirs of Fame; the others get only a younger brother's allowance: whatever they do, they cannot persuade the world they are anything more than parrots. The skill of prodigies may find a new path to eminence, but prudence accompanies them all the way. By the novelty of their enterprises sages write their names in the golden book of heroes. Some prefer to be first in things of minor import than second in greater exploits.

lxiv **Avoid Worry**. Such prudence brings its own reward. It escapes much, and is thus the midwife of comfort and so of happiness. Neither give nor take bad news unless it can help. Some men's ears are stuffed with the sweets of flattery; others with the bitters of scandal, while some cannot live without a daily annoyance no more than Mithridates could without poison. It is no rule of life to prepare for yourself lifelong trouble in order to give a temporary enjoyment to another, however near and dear. You never ought to spoil your own chances to please another who advises and keeps out of the affair, and in all cases where to oblige another involves disobliging yourself, 'tis a standing rule that it is better he should suffer now than you afterwards and in vain.

lxv[70] **Elevated Taste**. You can train it like the intellect. Full knowledge whets desire and increases enjoyment. You may know a noble spirit by the elevation of his taste: it must be a great thing that can satisfy a great mind. Big bites for big mouths, lofty things for lofty spirits. Before their judgment the bravest tremble, the most perfect lose confidence. Things of the first importance are few; let appreciation be rare. Taste can be imparted by intercourse: great good luck to associate with the highest taste. But do not affect to be dissatisfied with everything: 'tis the extreme of folly, and more odious if from affectation than if from Quixotry. Some would have God create another world and other ideals to satisfy their fantastic imagination.

---

[68] cf. Sir A. Helps's *Essays in Intervals of Business* (Macmillan, 1890), p. 44: "You have to choose persons for whose faults you are to be punished, to whom you are to be the whipping boy."
[69] from *El Heroe*, primor vii
[70] *El Heroe*, primor v. Eng. II. "The Fine Taste," and so quoted by Addison, Spectator, No. 40n.

lxvi **See that Things end well**[71]. Some regard more the rigour of the game than the winning of it, but to the world the discredit of the final failure does away with any recognition of the previous care. The victor need not explain. The world does not notice the details of the measures employed; but only the good or ill result. You lose nothing if you gain your end. A good end gilds everything, however unsatisfactory the means. Thus at times it is part of the art of life to transgress the rules of the art, if you cannot end well otherwise.

lxvii[72] **Prefer Callings "en Evidence."** Most things depend on the satisfaction of others. Esteem is to excellence what the zephyr is to flowers, the breath of life. There are some callings which gain universal esteem, while others more important are without credit. The former, pursued before the eyes of all, obtain the universal favour; the others, though they are rarer and more valuable, remain obscure and unperceived, honoured but not applauded. Among princes conquerors are the most celebrated, and therefore the kings of Aragon[73] earned such applause as warriors, conquerors, and great men. An able man will prefer callings *en evidence* which all men know of and utilise, and he thus becomes immortalised by universal suffrage.

lxviii **It is better to help with Intelligence than with Memory**. The more as the latter needs only recollection, the former νοῦς. Many persons omit the *à propos* because it does not occur to them; a friend's advice on such occasions may enable them to see the advantages. 'Tis one of the greatest gifts of mind to be able to offer what is needed at the moment: for want of that many things fail to be performed. Share the light of your intelligence, when you have any, and ask for it when you have it not, the first cautiously, the last anxiously. Give no more than a hint: this *finesse* is especially needful when it touches the interest of him whose attention you awaken. You should give but a taste at first, and then pass on to more when that is not sufficient. If he thinks of No, go in search of Yes. Therein lies the cleverness, for most things are not obtained simply because they are not attempted.

lxix[74] **Do not give way to every common Impulse**. He is a great man who never allows himself to be influenced by the impressions of others. Self-reflection is the school of wisdom. To know one's disposition and to allow for it, even going to the other extreme so as to find the *juste milieu* between nature and art. Self-knowledge is the beginning of self-

---

[71] cf. lix. *A good end gilds*. Here the Jesuit speaks.
[72] *El Heroe*, primor viii.
[73] Gracian was himself an Aragonese.
[74] *El Discreto*, c. xiii.

improvement. There be some whose humours are so monstrous that they are always under the influence of one or other of them, and put them in place of their real inclinations. They are torn asunder by such disharmony and get involved in contradictory obligations. Such excesses not only destroy firmness of will; all power of judgment gets lost, desire and knowledge pulling in opposite directions.

lxx **Know how to Refuse**. One ought not to give way in everything nor to everybody. To know how to refuse is therefore as important as to know how to consent. This is especially the case with men of position. All depends on the *how*. Some men's No is thought more of than the Yes of others: for a gilded No is more satisfactory than a dry Yes. There are some who always have No on their lips, whereby they make everything distasteful. No always comes first with them, and when sometimes they give way after all, it does them no good on account of the unpleasing herald. Your refusal need not be point-blank: let the disappointment come by degrees. Nor let the refusal be final; that would be to destroy dependence; let some spice of hope remain to soften the rejection. Let politeness compensate and fine words supply the place of deeds. Yes and No are soon said, but give much to think over.

lxxi[75] **Do not Vacillate**. Let not your actions be abnormal either from disposition or affectation. An able man is always the same in his best qualities; he gets the credit of trustworthiness. If he changes, he does so for good reason or good consideration. In matters of conduct change is hateful. There are some who are different every day; their intelligence varies, still more their will, and with this their fortune. Yesterday's white is to-day's black: to-day's No was yesterday's Yes. They always give the lie to their own credit and destroy their credit with others.

lxxii **Be Resolute**. Bad execution of your designs does less harm than irresolution in forming them. Streams do less harm flowing than when dammed up. There are some men so infirm of purpose that they always require direction from others, and this not on account of any perplexity, for they judge clearly, but from sheer incapacity for action. It needs some skill to find out difficulties, but more to find a way out of them. There are others who are never in straits . their clear judgment and determined character it them for the highest callings: their intelligence tells them where to insert the thin end of the wedge, their resolution how to drive it home. They soon get through anything: as soon as they have done with one sphere of action, they are ready for another. Affianced to Fortune, they make themselves sure of success.

---

[75] *El Discreto*, c. vi

lxxiii **Utilise Slips**. That is how smart people get out of difficulties. They extricate themselves from the most intricate labyrinth by some witty application of a bright remark. They get out of a serious contention by an airy nothing or by raising a smile. Most of the great leaders are well grounded in this art. When you have to refuse, it is often the polite way to talk of something else. Sometimes it proves the highest understanding not to understand.

lxxiv **Do not be Unsociable**. The truest wild beasts live in the most populous places. To be inaccessible is the fault of those who distrust themselves, whose honours change their manners. It is no way of earning people's goodwill by being ill-tempered with them. It is a sight to see one of those unsociable monsters who make a point of being proudly impertinent. Their dependants who have the misfortune to be obliged to speak with them, enter as if prepared for a fight with a tiger armed with patience and with fear. To obtain their post these persons must have ingratiated themselves with every one, but having once obtained it they seek to indemnify themselves by disobliging all. It is a condition of their position that they should be accessible to all, yet, from pride or spleen, they are so to none. 'Tis a civil way to punish such men by letting them alone, and depriving them of opportunities of improvement by granting them no opportunity of intercourse.

lxxv **Choose an Heroic Ideal**; but rather to emulate than to imitate. There are exemplars of greatness, living texts of honour. Let every one have before his mind the chief of his calling not so much to follow him as to spur himself on. Alexander wept not on account of Achilles dead and buried, but over himself, because his fame had not yet spread throughout the world. Nothing arouses ambition so much in the heart as the trumpet-clang of another's fame. The same thing that sharpens envy, nourishes a generous spirit.

lxxvi[76] **Do not always be Jesting**. Wisdom is shown in serious matters, and is more appreciated than mere wit. He that is always ready for jests is never ready for serious things. They resemble liars in that men never believe either, always expecting a lie in one, a joke in the other. One never knows when you speak with judgment, which is the same as if you had none. A continual jest[77] soon loses all zest. Many get the repute of being witty, but thereby lose the credit of being sensible. Jest has its little hour, seriousness should have all the rest.

---

[76] *El Discreto*, c. ix.
[77] Orig. "No ay mayor desayre que el continuo donayre."

lxxvii **Be all Things to all Men**[78] —a discreet Proteus, learned with the learned, saintly with the sainted. It is the great art to gain every one's suffrages; their goodwill gains general agreement. Notice men's moods and adapt yourself to each, genial or serious as the case may be. Follow their lead, glossing over the changes as cunningly as possible. This is an indispensable art for dependent persons. But this *savoir faire* calls for great cleverness. He only will find no difficulty who has a universal genius[79] in his knowledge and universal ingenuity in his wit.

lxxviii **The Art of undertaking Things**. Fools rush in through the door; for folly is always bold. The same simplicity which robs them of all attention to precautions deprives them of all sense of shame at failure. But prudence enters with more deliberation. Its forerunners are caution and care; they advance and discover whether you can also advance without danger. Every rush forward is freed from danger by caution, while fortune some-times helps in such cases. Step cautiously where you suspect depth. Sagacity goes cautiously forward while precaution covers the ground. Nowadays there are unsuspected depths in human. intercourse, you must therefore cast the lead at every step.

lxxix **A Genial Disposition**. If with moderation 'tis an accomplishment, not a defect. A grain of gaiety seasons all. The greatest men join in the fun[80] at times, and it makes them liked by all. But they should always on such occasions preserve their dignity, nor go beyond the bounds of decorum. Others, again, get themselves out of difficulty quickest by a joke. For there are things you must take in fun, though others perhaps mean them in earnest. You show a sense of placability, which acts as a magnet on all hearts.

lxxx **Take care to get Information**. We live by information, not by sight. We exist by faith in others. The ear is the area-gate of truth but the front-door of lies. The truth is generally seen, rarely heard; seldom she comes in elemental purity, especially from afar; there is always some admixture of the moods of those through whom she has passed. The passions tinge her with their colours wherever they touch her, sometimes favourably, sometimes the reverse. She always brings out the disposition, therefore receive her with caution from him that praises, with more caution from him that blames. Pay attention to the intention of the speaker; you should know beforehand on what footing he comes. Let reflection assay falsity and exaggeration.

---

[78] A touch of Gracian's training as Jesuit
[79] Orig. "varon universal de ingenio en noticias y de genio en gustos" cf. ii.
[80] cf. cclxxv.

lxxxi **Renew your Brilliance**. 'Tis the privilege of the Phœnix. Ability is wont to grow old, and with it fame. The staleness of custom weakens admiration, and a mediocrity that's new[81] often eclipses the highest excellence grown old. Try therefore to be born again in valour, in genius, in fortune, in all. Display startling novelties, rise afresh like the sun every day. Change too the scene[82] on which you shine, so that your loss may be felt in the old scenes of your triumph, while the novelty of your powers wins you applause in the new.

lxxxii **Drain Nothing to the Dregs, neither Good nor Ill**. A sage[83] once reduced all virtue to the golden mean. Push right to the extreme and it becomes wrong: press all the juice from an orange and it becomes bitter. Even in enjoyment never go to extremes. Thought too subtle is dull. If you milk a cow too much you draw blood, not milk.

lxxxiii **Allow Yourself some venial Fault**. Some such carelessness is often the greatest recommendation of talent. For envy exercises ostracism, most envenomed when most polite, It counts it to perfection as a failing that it has no faults; for being perfect in all it condemns it in all. It becomes an Argus, all eyes for imperfection: 'tis its only consolation. Blame is like the lightning; it hits the highest. Let Homer nod now and then and affect some negligence in valour or in intellect—not in prudence—so as to disarm malevolence, or at least to prevent its bursting with its own venom. You thus leave your cloak[84] on the horns of Envy in order to save your immortal parts.

lxxxiv **Make use of your Enemies**. You should learn to seize things not by the blade, which cuts[85], but by the handle, which saves you from harm: especially is this the rule with the doings of your enemies. A wise man gets more use from his enemies than a fool from his friends. Their ill-will often levels mountains of difficulties which one would otherwise not face. Many have had their greatness made for them by their enemies. Flattery is more dangerous than hatred, because it covers the stains which the other causes to be wiped out. The wise will turn ill-will into a mirror more faithful than that of kindness. and remove or improve the faults referred to. Caution thrives well when rivalry and ill-will are next-door neighbours.

lxxxv **Do not play Manille**[86]. It is a fault of excellence that being so much in use it is liable to abuse. Because all covet it, all are vexed by it. It is

---

[81] cf. cclxix.
[82] cf. cxcviii
[83] Aristotle
[84] an image taken from the bull-fight, when the matador allows the bull to rush at his cloak held sideways. Gracian uses the same image in El Criticon, i. 3.
[85] cf. ccxxiv
[86] *Manille*. Schop. suggests that this is the Manillio of Hombre, the second best trump (cf. Pope, *Rape of Lock*, iii. 51). But there is a game mentioned by Littré s.v., which is obviously the one

a great misfortune to be of use to nobody; scarcely less to be of use to everybody. People who reach this stage lose by gaining, and at last bore those who desired them before. These Manilles wear away all kinds of excellence: losing the earlier esteem of the few, they obtain discredit among the vulgar. The remedy against this extreme is to moderate your brilliance. Be extraordinary in your excellence, if you like, but be ordinary in your display of it. The more light a torch gives, the more it burns away and the nearer 'tis to going out. Show yourself less and you will be rewarded by being esteemed more.

lxxxvi **Prevent Scandal.** Many heads go to make the mob, and in each of them are eyes for malice to use and a tongue for detraction to wag. If a single ill report spread, it casts a blemish on your fair fame, and if it clings to you with a nickname, your reputation is in danger. Generally it is some salient defect or ridiculous trait that gives rise to the rumours. At times these are malicious additions of private envy to general distrust. For there are wicked tongues that ruin a great reputation more easily by a witty sneer than by a direct accusation. It is easy to get into bad repute, because it is easy to believe evil of any one: it is not easy to clear yourself. The wise accordingly avoid these mischances, guarding against vulgar scandal with sedulous vigilance. It is far easier to prevent than to rectify.

lxxxvii[87] **Culture and Elegance.** Man is born a barbarian, and only raises himself above the beast by culture. Culture therefore makes the man; the more a man, the higher. Thanks to it, Greece could call the rest of the world barbarians. Ignorance is very raw; nothing contributes so much to culture as knowledge. But even knowledge is coarse If without elegance. Not alone must our intelligence be elegant, but our desires, and above all our conversation. Some men are naturally elegant in internal and external qualities, in their thoughts, in their address, in their dress, which is the rind of the soul, and in their talents, which is its fruit. There are others, on the other hand, so *gauche* that everything about them, even their very excellences, is tarnished by an intolerable and barbaric want of neatness.

lxxxviii **Let your Behaviour be Fine and Noble.** A great man ought not to be little in his behaviour. He ought never to pry too minutely into things, least of all in unpleasant matters. For though it is important to know all, it is not necessary to know all about all. One ought to act in such cases with the generosity of a gentleman, conduct worthy of a gallant man. To overlook forms a large part of the work of ruling. Most things must be left unnoticed among relatives and friends, and even among enemies. All

---

referred to by Gracian. In this the nine of diamonds, called Manille, can be made any value the player wishes. Manille thus means a combination of a jack of all Trades and a universal drudge.
[87] *El Discreto*, c. xvii.

superfluity is annoying, especially in things that annoy. To keep hovering around the object or your annoyance is a kind of mania. Generally speaking, every man behaves according to his heart and his understanding.

lxxxix **Know Yourself** —in talents and capacity, in judgment and inclination. You cannot master yourself unless you know yourself. There are mirrors for the face but none for the mind. Let careful thought about yourself serve as a substitute. When the outer image is forgotten, keep the inner one to improve and perfect. Learn the force of your intellect and capacity for affairs, test the force of your courage in order to apply it, and keep your foundations secure and your head clear for everything.

xc **The Secret[88] of Long Life** Lead a good life. Two things bring life speedily to an end: folly and immorality. Some lose their life because they have not the intelligence to keep it, others because they have not the will[89]. Just as virtue is its own reward, so is vice its own punishment. He who lives a fast life runs through life in a double sense. A virtuous life never dies. The firmness of the soul is communicated to the body, and a good life is long not only in intention but also in extension.

xci **Never set to work at anything if you have any doubts of its Prudence**. A suspicion of failure in the mind of the doer is proof positive of it in that of the onlooker, especially if he is a rival. If in the heat of action your judgment feels scruples, it will afterwards in cool reflection condemn it as a piece of folly. Action is dangerous where prudence is in doubt: better leave such things alone. Wisdom does not trust to probabilities; it always marches in the mid-day light of reason. How can an enterprise succeed which the judgment condemns as soon as conceived? And if resolutions passed *nem. con.* by inner court often turn out unfortunately, what can we expect of those undertaken by a doubting reason and a vacillating judgment?

xcii **Transcendant Wisdom**. I mean in everything. The first and highest rule of all deed and speech, the more necessary to be followed the higher and more numerous our posts, is: an ounce of wisdom[90] is worth more than tons of cleverness. It is the only sure way, though it may not gain so much applause. The reputation of wisdom is the last triumph of fame. It is enough if you satisfy the wise, for their judgment is the touchstone of true success.

---

[88] cf. Fuller, "He lives long who lives well."
[89] So, it is said, negroes and savages die in circumstances where Europeans keep alive simply because they have "the will to live, the competence to be."
[90] Orig. "Mas vale un grano de cordura que arrobas de sutileza." TWC: It lit. says "A grain of sanity is worth more than buckets of sutility."

xciii **Versatility**. A man of many excellences equals many men. By imparting his own enjoyment of life to his circle he enriches their life. Variety in excellences is the delight of life. It is a great art to profit by all that is good, and since Nature has made man in his highest development an abstract of herself, so let Art create in him a true microcosm by training his taste and intellect.

xciv[91] **Keep the extent of your Abilities unknown**. The wise man does not allow his knowledge and abilities to be sounded to the bottom, if he desires to be honoured by all. He allows you to know them but not to comprehend them. No one must know the extent of his abilities, lest he be disappointed. No one ever has an opportunity of fathoming him entirely. For guesses and doubts about the extent of his talents arouse more veneration than accurate knowledge of them, be they ever so great.

xcv **Keep Expectation alive**. Keep stirring it up. Let much promise more, and great deeds herald greater. Do not rest your whole fortune on a single cast[92] of the die. It requires great skill to moderate your forces so as to keep expectation from being dissipated.

xcvi **The highest Discretion**.[93] It is the throne of reason, the foundation of prudence: by its means success is gained at little cost. It is a gift from above, and should be prayed for as the first and best quality. 'Tis the main piece of the panoply, and so important that its absence makes a man imperfect, whereas with other qualities it is merely a question of more or less. All the actions of life depend on its application; all require its assistance, for everything needs intelligence. Discretion consists in a natural tendency to the most rational course, combined with a liking for the surest.

xcvii **Obtain and preserve a Reputation**. It is the usufruct of fame. It is expensive to obtain a reputation, for it only attaches to distinguished abilities, which are as rare as mediocrities are common. Once obtained, it is easily preserved. It confers many an obligation, but it does more. When it is owing to elevated powers or lofty spheres of action, it rises to a kind of veneration and yields a sort of majesty. But it is only a well-founded reputation that lasts permanently.

xcviii [94]**Write your Intentions in Cypher**. The passions are the gates of the soul. The most practical knowledge consists in disguising them. He that plays with cards exposed runs a risk of losing the stakes. The reserve

---

[91] *El Heroe*, i
[92] cf. clxxxv.
[93] Orig. "la gran sinderesis." TWC: The Spanish annotated versions say that sinderesis means "to reflect, to use good judgement
[94] *El Heroe*, ii

of caution should combat the curiosity of inquirers: adopt the policy[95] of the cuttlefish. Do not even let your tastes be known, lest others utilise them either by running counter to them or by flattering them.

xcix **Reality and Appearance**. Things pass[96] for what they seem, not for what they are. Few see inside; many take to the outside. It is not enough to be right, if right seem false and ill.

c **A Man without Illusions, a wise Christian, a philosophic Courtier**. Be all these, not merely seem to be them, still less affect to be them. Philosophy is nowadays discredited, but yet it was always the chiefest concern of the wise. The art of thinking has lost all its former repute. Seneca introduced it at Rome: it went to court for some time, but now it is considered out of place there. And yet the discovery of deceit was always thought the true nourishment of a thoughtful mind, the true delight of a virtuous soul.

ci **One half of the World laughs at the other, and Fools are they all**. Everything is good or everything is bad according to the votes they gain. What one pursues another persecutes[97]. He is an in-sufferable ass that would regulate everything according to his ideas. Excellences do not depend on a single man's pleasure. So many men, so many tastes, all different. There is no defect which is not affected by some, nor need we lose heart if things please not some, for others will appreciate them. Nor need their applause turn our head, for there will surely be others to condemn. The real test of praise is the approbation of famous men and of experts in the matter. You should aim to be independent of any one vote, of any one fashion, of any one century.

cii **Be able to stomach big slices of Luck**. In the body of wisdom not the least important organ is a big stomach, for great capacity implies great parts. Big bits of luck do not embarrass one who can digest still bigger ones. What is a surfeit for one may be hunger for another. Many are troubled as it were with weak digestion, owing to their small capacity being neither born nor trained for great employment. Their actions turn sour, and the humours that arise from their undeserved honours turn their head and they incur great risks in high place: they do not find their proper place[98], for luck finds no proper place in them. A man of talent therefore should show that he has more room for even greater enterprises, and above all avoid showing signs of a little heart.

---

[95] Orig. "A linces de discurso gibias de interioridad," I have omitted the lynxes, who have little to do with cuttle-fish (pl. of Sp. *jibia*).
[96] A favourite expression of Gracian's; cf. cxxx, cxlvi; cf. also the German proverb, "Was scheint, das gilt."
[97] Orig. "Lo que este sigue, el otro persigue."
[98] Orig. "No caben en si porque no cabe en ellos la suerte."

ciii **Let each keep up his Dignity**. Let each deed of a man in its degree, though he be not a king, be worthy of a prince, and let his action be princely within due limits. Sublime in action, lofty in thought, in all things like a king, at least in merit if not in might. For true kingship lies in spotless rectitude, and he need not envy greatness who can serve as a model of it. Especially should those near the throne aim at true superiority, and prefer to share the true qualities of royalty rather than take parts in its mere ceremonies, yet without affecting its imperfections but sharing in its true dignity.

civ **Try your hand at Office**. It requires varied qualities, and to know which is needed taxes attention and calls for masterly discernment. Some demand courage, others tact. Those that merely require rectitude are the easiest, the most difficult those requiring cleverness. For the former all that is necessary is character; for the latter all one's attention and zeal may not suffice. 'Tis a troublesome business to rule men, still more fools or blockheads: double sense is needed with those who have none. It is intolerable when an office engrosses a man with fixed hours and a settled routine. Those are better that leave a man free to follow his own devices, combining variety with importance, for the change refreshes the mind. The most in repute are those that have least or most distant dependence on others; the worst is that which worries us both here and hereafter.

cv **Don't be a Bore**. The man of one business or of one topic is apt to be heavy. Brevity flatters and does better business; it gains by courtesy[99] what it loses by curtness. Good things, when short, are twice as good. The quintessence of the matter is more effective than a whole farrago of details. It is a well-known truth that talkative folk rarely have much sense whether in dealing with the matter itself or its formal treatment. There are that serve more for stumbling-stones than centrepieces, useless lumber in every one's way. The wise avoid being bores, especially to the great, who are fully occupied: it is worse to disturb one of them than all the rest. Well said is soon said.

cvi **Do not parade your Position**. To outshine in dignity is more offensive than in personal attractions. To pose as a personage is to be hated: envy is surely enough. The more you seek esteem the less you obtain it, for it depends on the opinion of others. You cannot take it, but must earn and receive it from others. Great positions require an amount of authority sufficient to make them efficient: without it they cannot be adequately filled. Preserve therefore enough dignity to carry on the duties of the office. Do not enforce respect, but try and create it. Those who insist on the dignity of their

---

[99] Orig. "gana por lo cortés lo que pierde por lo corto."

office, show they have not deserved it, and that it is too much for them. If you wish to be valued, be valued for your talents, not for anything adventitious. Even kings prefer to be honoured for their personal qualifications rather than for their station.

cvii Show no Self-satisfaction. You must neither be discontented with yourself—and that were poor-spirited—nor self-satisfied—and that is folly. Self-satisfaction arises mostly from ignorance: it would be a happy ignorance not without its advantages if it did not injure our credit. Because a man cannot achieve the superlative perfections of others, he contents himself with any mediocre talent of his own. Distrust is wise, and even useful, either to evade mishaps or to afford consolation when they come, for a misfortune cannot surprise a man who has already feared it. Even Homer nods at times, and Alexander fell from his lofty state and out of his illusions. Things depend on many circumstances: what constitutes triumph in one set may cause a defeat in another. In the midst of all incorrigible folly remains the same with empty self-satisfaction, blossoming, flowering, and running all to seed.

cviii The Path to Greatness is along with Others. Intercourse works well: manners and taste are shared: good sense and even talent grow insensibly. Let the sanguine man then make a comrade of the lymphatic, and so with the other temperaments, so that without any forcing the golden mean is obtained. It is a great art to agree with others. The alternation of contraries beautifies and sustains the world: if it can cause harmony in the physical world, still more can it do so in the moral. Adopt this policy in the choice of friends and defendants; by joining extremes the more effective middle way is found.

cix Be not Censorious. There are men of gloomy character who regard everything as faulty, not from any evil motive but because it is their nature to. They condemn all: these for what they have done, those for what they will do. This indicates a nature worse than cruel, vile Indeed. They accuse with such exaggeration that they make out of motes beams wherewith to force out the eyes. They are always taskmasters who could turn a paradise into a prison[100]; if passion intervenes they drive matters to the extreme. A noble nature, on the contrary, always knows how to find an excuse for failings, if not in the intention, at least from oversight.

cx Do not wait till you are a Sinking Sun. 'Tis a maxim of the wise to leave things before things leave them. One should be able to snatch a triumph at the end, just as the sun even at its brightest often retires behind a cloud so as not to be seen sinking, and to leave in doubt whether he has

---

[100] Orig. "galera," a sort of Bridewell

sunk or no. Wisely withdraw from the chance of mishaps, lest you have to do so from the reality Do not wait till they turn you the cold shoulder and carry you to the grave, alive in feeling but dead in esteem. Wise trainers put racers to grass before they arouse derision by falling on the course. A beauty should break her mirror early, lest she do so later with open eyes.

cxi **Have Friends.** 'Tis a second existence. Every friend is good and wise for his friend: among them all everything turns to good. Every one is as others wish him; that they may wish him well, he must win their hearts and so their tongues. There is no magic like a good turn, and the way to gain friendly feelings[101] is to do friendly acts. The most and best of us depend on others; we have to live either among friends or among enemies. Seek some one every day to be a well-wisher if not a friend; by and by after trial some of these will become intimate.

cxii **Gain Good-will.** For thus the first and highest cause foresees and furthers the greatest objects. By gaining their good-will you gain men's good opinion. Some trust so much to merit that they neglect grace, but wise men know that Service Road[102] without a lift from favour is a long way indeed. Good-will facilitates and supplies everything: is supposes gifts or even supplies them, as courage, zeal, knowledge, or even discretion; whereas defects it will not see because it does not search for them. It arises from some common interest, either material, as disposition, nationality, relationship, fatherland, office; or formal, which is of a higher kind of communion, in capacity, obligation, reputation, or merit. The whole difficulty is to gain good-will; to keep it is easy. It has, however, to be sought for, and, when found, to be utilised.

cxiii **In Prosperity prepare for Adversity.** It is both wiser and easier to collect winter stores in summer. In prosperity favours are cheap and friends are many. 'Tis well therefore to keep them for more unlucky days, for adversity costs dear and has no helpers. Retain a store of friendly and obliged persons; the day may come when their price will go up. Low minds never have friends; in luck they will not recognise them: in misfortune they will not be recognised by them.

cxiv **Never Compete.** Every competition damages the credit: our rivals seize occasion to obscure us so as to out-shine us. Few wage honourable war. Rivalry discloses faults which courtesy would hide. Many have lived in good repute while they had no rivals. The heat of conflict gives life, or even new life, to dead scandals, and digs up long-buried skeletons. Competition begins with belittling, and seeks aid wherever it can, not only where it ought.

---

[101] cf. xxxii, xl
[102] Orig. "Es grande el rodeo de solos los meritos sino se ayudan del favor."

And when the weapons of abuse do not effect their purpose, as often or mostly happens, our opponents use them for revenge, and use them at least for beating away the dust of oblivion from anything to our discredit. Men of good-will are always at peace; men of good repute and dignity are men of good-will.

cxv **Get used to the Failings of your Familiars**, as you do to ugly faces. It is indispensable if they depend on us, or we on them. There are wretched characters with whom one cannot live, nor yet without them. Therefore clever folk get used to them, as to ugly faces, so that they are not obliged to do so suddenly under the pressure of necessity. At first they arouse disgust, but gradually they lose this influence, and reflection provides for disgust or puts up with it.

cxvi **Only act with Honourable Men**. You can trust them and they you. Their honour is the best surety of their behaviour even in misunderstandings, for they always act having regard to what they are. Hence 'tis better to have a dispute with honourable people than to have a victory over dishonourable ones. You cannot treat with the ruined, for they have no hostages for rectitude. With them there is no true friendship, and their agreements are not binding, however stringent they may appear, because they have no feeling of honour. Never have to do with such men, for if honour does not restrain a man, virtue will not, since honour is the throne of rectitude.

cxvii **Never talk of Yourself**. You must either praise yourself, which is vain, or blame yourself, which is little-minded: it ill beseems him that speaks, and ill pleases him that hears. And if you should avoid this in ordinary conversation, how much more in official matters, and above all, in public speaking, where every appearance of unwisdom really is unwise. The same want of tact lies in speaking of a man in his presence, owing to the danger of going to one of two extremes: flattery or censure.

cxviii **Acquire the Reputation of Courtesy**; for it is enough to make you liked. Politeness is the main ingredient of culture,—a kind of witchery that wins the regard of all as surely as discourtesy gains their disfavour and opposition; if this latter springs from pride, it is abominable; if from bad breeding, it is despicable. Better too much courtesy than too little, provided it be not the same for all, which degenerates into injustice. Between opponents it is especially due as a proof of valour. It costs little and helps much: every one is honoured who gives honour. Politeness and honour have this advantage, that they remain with him who displays them to others.

cxix **Avoid becoming Disliked**. There is no occasion to seek dislike: it comes without seeking quickly enough. There are many who hate of their own accord without knowing the why or the how. Their ill-will outruns our readiness to please. Their ill-nature is more prone to do others harm than their cupidity is eager to gain advantage for themselves. Some manage to be on bad terms with all, because they always either produce or experience vexation of spirit. Once hate has taken root it is, like bad repute, difficult to eradicate. Wise men are feared, the malevolent are abhorred, the arrogant are regarded with disdain, buffoons with contempt, eccentrics with neglect. Therefore pay respect that you may be respected, and know that to be esteemed[103] you must show esteem.

cxx **Live Practically**. Even knowledge has to be in the fashion, and where it is not it is wise to affect ignorance. Thought and taste change with the times. Do not be old-fashioned in your ways of thinking, and let your taste be in the modern style. In everything the taste of the many carries the votes; for the time being one must follow it in the hope of leading it to higher things. In the adornment of the body as of the mind adapt yourself to the present, even though the past appear better. But this rule does not apply to kindness, for goodness is for all time. It is neglected nowadays and seems out of date. Truth-speaking, keeping your word, and so too good people, seem to come from the good old times: yet they are liked for all that, but in such a way that even when they all exist they are not in the fashion and are not imitated. What a misfortune for our age that it regards virtue as a stranger and vice as a matter of course! If you are wise, live as you can, if you cannot live as you would. Think more highly of what fate has given you than of what it has denied.

cxxi **Do not make a Business of what is no Business**. As some make gossip out of everything, so others business. They always talk big, take everything in earnest, and turn it into a dispute or a secret. Troublesome things must not be taken too seriously if they can be avoided. It is preposterous to take to heart that which you should throw over your shoulders. Much that would be something has become nothing by being left alone, and what was nothing has become of consequence by being made much of. At the outset things can be easily settled, but not afterwards. Often the remedy causes the disease. 'Tis by no means the least of life's rules: to let things alone.

cxxii [104]**Distinction in Speech and Action**. By this you gain a position in many places and carry esteem beforehand. It shows itself in everything, in talk, in look, even in gait. It is a great victory to conquer men's hearts: it does not arise from any foolish presumption or pompous talk, but

---

[103] Orig. "el que quiere hacer casa hace caso."
[104] *El Discreto*, c. ii

in a becoming tone of authority born of superior talent combined with true merit.

cxxiii **Avoid Affectation**. The more merit, the less affectation, which gives a vulgar flavour to all. It is wearisome to others and troublesome to the one affected, for he becomes a martyr to care and tortures himself with attention. The most eminent merits lose most by it, for they appear proud and artificial instead of being the product of nature, and the natural is always more pleasing than the artificial. One always feels sure that the man who affects a virtue has it not. The more pains you take with a thing, the more should you conceal them, so that it may appear to arise spontaneously from your own natural character. Do not, however, in avoiding affectation fall into it by affecting to be unaffected. The sage never seems to know his own merits, for only by not noticing them can you call others' attention to them. He is twice great who has all the perfections in the opinion of all except of himself; he attains applause by two opposite paths.

cxxiv **Get Yourself missed**. Few reach such favour with the many; if with the wise 'tis the height of happiness. When one has finished one's work, coldness is the general rule. But there are ways of earning this reward of goodwill. The sure way is to excel in your office and talents: add to this agreeable manner and you reach the point where you become necessary to your office, not your office to you. Some do honour to their post, with others 'tis the other way. It is no great gain if a poor successor makes the predecessor seem good, for this does not imply that the one is missed, but that the other is wished away.

cxxv **Do not be a Black List**. It is a sign of having a tarnished name to concern oneself with the ill-fame of others. Some wish to hide their own stains with those of others, or at least wash them away: or they seek consolation therein—'tis the consolation of fools. They must have bad breath who form the sewers of scandal for the whole town. The more one grubs about in such matters, the more one befouls oneself. There are few without stain somewhere or other, but it is of little known people that the failings are little known. Be careful then to avoid being a registrar of faults. That is to be an abominable thing, a man that lives without a heart.

cxxvi **Folly consists not in committing Folly, but in not hiding it when committed**. You should keep your desires sealed up, still more your defects. All go wrong sometimes, but the wise try to hide[105] the errors, but fools boast of them. Reputation depends more on what is hidden than on what is done; if a man does not live chastely[106], he must live cautiously.

---

[105] cf. Prov. xii. 16 "A fool's vexation is speedily known, but the prudent man concealeth shame."
[106] Orig. "Si no es uno casto, sea cauto"; Schop. turns neatly into Latin, *caute nisi caste*.

The errors of great men are like the eclipses of the greater lights. Even in friendship it is rare to expose one's failings to one's friend. Nay, one should conceal them from oneself if one can. But here one can help with that other great rule of life: learn to forget[107].

cxxvii[108] **Grace in Everything.** 'Tis the life of talents, the breath of speech, the soul of action, and the ornament of ornament. Perfections are the adornment of our nature, but this is the adornment of perfection itself. It shows itself even in the thoughts. 'Tis most a gift of nature and owes least to education; it even triumphs over training. It is more than ease, approaches the free and easy, gets over embarrassment, and adds the finishing touch to perfection. Without it beauty is lifeless, graciousness ungraceful: it surpasses valour, discretion, prudence, even majesty it-self. 'Tis a short way to dispatch and an easy escape from embarrassment.

cxxviii **Highmindedness.** One of the principal qualifications for a gentleman, for it spurs on to all kinds of nobility. It improves the taste, ennobles the heart, elevates the mind, refines the feelings, and intensifies dignity. It raises him in whom it is found, and at times remedies the bad turns of Fortune, which only raises by striking. It can find full scope in the will when it cannot be exercised in act. Magnanimity, generosity, and all heroic qualities recognise in it their source.

cxxix **Never complain.**[109] To complain always brings discredit. Better be a model of self-reliance opposed to the passion of others than an object of their compassion. For it opens the way for the hearer to what we are complaining of, and to disclose one insult forms an excuse for another. By complaining of past offences we give occasion for future ones, and in seeking aid or counsel we only obtain indifference or contempt. It is much more politic to praise one man's favours, so that others may feel obliged to follow suit. To recount the favours we owe the absent is to demand similar ones from the present, and thus we sell our credit with the one to the other. The shrewd will therefore never publish to the world his failures or his defects, but only those marks of consideration which serve to keep friendship alive and enmity silent.

cxxx **Do and be seen Doing.** Things do not pass for what they are but for what they seem. To be of use and to know how to show yourself of use, is to be twice as useful. What is not seen is as if it was not. Even the Right[110] does not receive proper consideration if it does not seem right. The observant are far fewer in number than those who are deceived by

---

[107] cf. cclxii
[108] *El Heroe*, c. xiii.
[109] "I make it a point never to complain," Mr. Disraeli once said in the House; cf. cxlv.
[110] cf. xcix.

appearances. Deceit rules the roast, and things are judged by their jackets[111], and many things are other than they seem. A good exterior is the best recommendation of the inner perfection.

cxxxi **Nobility of Feeling**. There is a certain distinction of the soul, a highmindedness prompting to gallant acts, that gives an air of grace to the whole character. It is not found often, for it presupposes great magnanimity. Its chief characteristic is to speak well of an enemy, and to act even better to-wards him. It shines brightest when a chance comes of revenge: not alone does it let the occasion pass, but it improves it by using a complete victory in order to display unexpected generosity. 'Tis a fine stroke of policy, nay, the very acme of statecraft. It makes no pretence to victory, for it pretends to nothing, and while obtaining its deserts it conceals its merits.

cxxxii **Revise your Judgments**. To appeal to an inner Court of Revision makes things safe. Especially when the course of action is not clear, you gain time either to confirm or improve your decision. It affords new grounds for strengthening or corroborating your judgment. And if it is a matter of giving, the gift is the more valued from its being evidently well considered than for being promptly bestowed: long expected is highest prized. And if you have to deny, you gain time to decide how and when to mature the No that it may be made palatable. Besides, after the first heat of desire is passed the repulse of refusal is felt less keenly in cold blood. But especially when men press for a reply is it best to defer it, for as often as not that is only a feint to disarm attention.

cxxxiii **Better Mad with the rest of the World than Wise alone**[112]. So say politicians. If all are so, one is no worse off than the rest, whereas solitary wisdom passes for folly. So important is it to sail with the stream. The greatest wisdom often consists in ignorance, or the pretence of it. One has to live with others, and others are mostly ignorant. "To live entirely alone one must be very like a god or quite like a wild beast," but I would turn the aphorism[113] by saying: Better be wise with the many than a fool all alone. There be some too who seek to be original by seeking chimeras.

cxxxiv **Double your Resources**. You thereby double your life. One must not depend on one thing or trust to only one resource, however pre-eminent. Everything should be kept double, especially the causes of success, of favour, or of esteem. The moon's mutability transcends everything and gives a limit to all existence, especially of things dependent on human will,

---

[111] Orig. merely "juzganse las cosas por fuera." TWC. It lit. says "Things are judged by their external appearance".
[112] cf. "In action wisdom goes by majorities," from "The Pilgrim's Scrip" in *Richard Feverel*.
[113] from Aristotle, *Pol*. i. s; also Heraclitus; cf. Grisebach, Schopenhauer's *Inedita*, 78. Also Bacon,*Essays*.

the most brittle of all things. To guard against this inconstancy should be the sage's care, and for this the chief rule of life is to keep a double store of good and useful qualities. Thus as Nature gives us in duplicate the most important of our limbs and those most exposed to risk, so Art should deal with the qualities on which we depend for success.

cxxxv **Do not nourish the Spirit of Contradiction**. It only proves you foolish or peevish, and prudence should guard against this strenuously. To find difficulties in everything may prove you clever, but such wrangling writes you down a fool. Such folk make a mimic war out of the most pleasant conversation, and in this way act as enemies towards their associates rather than towards those with whom they do not consort. Grit grates most in delicacies, and so does contradiction in amusement. They are both foolish and cruel who yoke together the wild beast and the tame.

cxxxvi **Post Yourself in the Centre of Things**. So you feel the pulse of affairs. Many lose their way either in the ramifications of useless discussion or in the brushwood of wearisome verbosity without ever realising the real matter at issue. They go over a single point a hundred times, wearying themselves and others, and yet never touch the all-important centre of affairs. This comes from a confusion of mind from which they cannot extricate themselves. They waste time and patience on matters they should leave alone, and cannot spare them afterwards for what they have left alone.

cxxxvii **The Sage should be Self-sufficing**. He that was all in all to himself carried all with him when he carried himself. If a universal friend can represent to us Rome and the rest of the world, let a man be his own universal friend, and then he is in a position to live alone. Whom could such a man want if there is no clearer intellect or finer taste than his own? He would then depend on himself alone, which is the highest happiness and like the Supreme Being. He that can live alone resembles the brute beast[114] in nothing, the sage in much and God in everything.

cxxxviii **The Art of letting Things alone**. The more so the wilder the waves of public or of private life. There are hurricanes in human affairs, tempests of passion, when it is wise to retire to a harbour and ride at anchor. Remedies often make diseases worse: in such cases one has to leave them to their natural course and the moral suasion of time. It takes a wise doctor to know when not to prescribe, and at times the greater skill consists in not applying remedies. The proper way to still the storms of the vulgar is to hold your hand and let them calm down of themselves. To give way now is to conquer by and by. A fountain gets muddy with but little stirring up, and

---

[114] See preceding note.

does not get clear by our meddling with it but by our leaving it alone. The best remedy for disturbances is to let them run their course, for so they quiet down.

cxxxix **Recognise unlucky Days**. They exist: nothing goes well on them; even though the game may be changed the ill-luck remains. Two tries should be enough to tell if one is in luck to-day or not. Everything is in process of change, even the mind, and no one is always wise: chance has something to say, even how to write a good letter. All perfection turns on the time; even beauty has its hours. Even wisdom fails at times by doing too much or too little. To turn out well a thing must be done on its own day. This is why with some everything turns out ill, with others all goes well, even with less trouble. They find everything ready, their wit prompt, their presiding genius favourable, their lucky star in the ascendant. At such times one must seize the occasion and not throw away the slightest chance. But a shrewd person will not decide on the day's luck by a single piece of good or bad fortune, for the one may be only a lucky chance and the other only a slight annoyance.

cxl **Find the Good in a Thing at once**. 'Tis the advantage of good taste. The bee goes to the honey for her comb, the serpent to the gall for its venom. So with taste: some seek the good, others the ill. There is nothing that has no good in it, especially in books, as giving food for thought. But many have such a scent that amid a thousand excellences they fix upon a single defect, and single it out for blame as if they were scavengers of men's minds and hearts. So they draw up a balance sheet of defects which does more credit to their bad taste than to their intelligence. They lead a sad life, nourishing themselves on bitters and battening on garbage. They have the luckier taste who midst a thousand defects seize upon a single beauty they may have hit upon by chance.

cxli **Do not listen to Yourself**. It is no use pleasing yourself if you do not please others, and as a rule general contempt is the punishment for self-satisfaction. The attention you pay to yourself you probably owe to others. To speak and at the same time listen to yourself cannot turn out well. If to talk to oneself when alone is folly, it must be doubly unwise to listen to oneself in the presence of others. It is a weakness of the great to talk with a recurrent "as I was saying" and "eh?" which bewilders their hearers. At every sentence they look for applause or flattery, taxing the patience of the wise. So too the pompous speak with an echo, and as their talk can only totter on with the aid of stilts, at every word they need the support of a stupid "bravo!"

cxlii **Never from Obstinacy take the Wrong Side because your Opponent has anticipated you in taking the Right One**. You begin the fight already beaten and must soon take to flight in disgrace. With bad weapons one can never win. It was astute in the opponent to seize the better side first: it would be folly to come lagging after with the worst. Such obstinacy is more dangerous in actions than in words, for action encounters more risk than talk. 'Tis the common failing of the obstinate that they lose the true by contradicting it, and the useful by quarrelling with it. The sage never places himself on the side of passion, but espouses the cause of right, either discovering it first or improving it later. If the enemy is a fool, he will in such a case turn round to follow the opposite and worse way. Thus the only way to drive him from the better course is to take it yourself, for his folly will cause him to desert it, and his obstinacy be punished for so doing.

cxliii **Never become Paradoxical in order to avoid the Trite.** Both extremes damage our reputation. Every undertaking which differs from the reasonable approaches foolishness. The paradox is a cheat: it wins applause at first by its novelty and piquancy, but afterwards it becomes discredited when the deceit is fore-seen and its emptiness becomes apparent. It is a species of jugglery, and in matters political would be the ruin of states. Those who cannot or dare not reach great deeds on the direct road of excellence go round by way of Paradox, admired by fools but making wise men true prophets. It argues an unbalanced judgment, and if it is not altogether based on the false, it is certainly founded on the uncertain, and risks the weightier matters of life.

cxliv **Begin with Another's to end with your Own.** 'Tis a politic means to your end. Even in heavenly matters Christian teachers lay stress on this holy cunning. It is a weighty piece of dissimulation, for the foreseen advantages serve as a lure to influence the other's will. His affair seems to be in train when it is really only leading the way for another's. One should never advance unless under cover, especially where the ground is dangerous. Likewise with persons who always say No at first, it is useful to ward off this blow, because the difficulty of conceding much more does not occur to them when your version is presented to them. This advice belongs to the rule about second thoughts [xiii], which covers the most subtle manœuvres of life.

cxlv **Do not show your wounded Finger**, for everything will knock up against it; nor complain about it, for malice always aims where weakness can be injured. It is no use to be vexed: being the butt of the talk will only vex you the more. Ill-will searches for wounds to irritate, aims darts to try the temper, and tries a thousand ways to sting to the quick. The wise never own to being hit, or disclose any evil, whether personal or hereditary. For even Fate sometimes likes to wound us where we are most tender. It always mortifies wounded flesh. Never therefore disclose the source of mortification or of joy, if you wish the one to cease, the other to endure.

cxlvi **Look into the Interior of Things.** Things are generally other than they seem, and ignorance that never looks beneath the rind becomes disabused when you show the kernel. Lies always come first, dragging fools along by their irreparable vulgarity. Truth always lags last, limping along on the arm of Time. The wise therefore reserve for it the other half of that power which the common mother has wisely given in duplicate. Deceit is very superficial, and the superficial therefore easily fall into it. Prudence lives retired within its recesses, visited only by sages and wise men.

cxlvii **Do not be Inaccessible.** None is so perfect that he does not need at times the advice of others. He is an in-corrigible ass who will never listen to any one. Even the most surpassing intellect should find a place for friendly counsel. Sovereignty itself must learn to lean. There are some that are incorrigible simply because they are <u>inaccessible</u>: they fall to ruin because none dares to extricate them. The highest should have the door open for friendship; it may prove the gate of help. A friend must be free to advise, and even to upbraid, without feeling embarrassed. Our satisfaction in him and our trust in his steadfast faith give him that power. One need not pay respect or give credit to every one, but in the innermost of his precaution man has a true mirror of a confidant to whom he owes the correction of his errors, and has to thank for it.

cxlviii **Have the Art of Conversation.** That is where the real personality shows itself. No act in life requires more attention, though it be the commonest thing in life. You must either lose or gain by it. If it needs care to write a letter which is but a deliberate and written conversation, how much more the ordinary kind in which there is occasion for a prompt display of intelligence? Experts feel the pulse of the soul in the tongue, wherefore the sage said, "Speak, that I may know thee." Some hold that the art of conversation is to be without art—that it should be neat, not gaudy, like the garments. This holds good for talk between friends. But when held with persons to whom one would show respect, it should be more dignified to answer to the dignity of the person addressed. To be appropriate it should adapt itself to the mind and tone of the interlocutor. And do not be a critic of words, or you will be taken for a pedant; nor a taxgatherer of ideas, or men will avoid you, or at least sell their thoughts dear. in conversation discretion is more important than eloquence.

cxlix **Know how to put off Ills on Others.** To have a shield against ill-will is a great piece of skill in a ruler. It is not the resort of incapacity, as ill-wishers imagine, but is due to the higher policy of having some one to receive the censure of the disaffected and the punishment of universal detestation. Everything cannot turn out well, nor can every one be satisfied:

it is well therefore, even at the cost of our pride, to have such a scapegoat, such a target for unlucky undertakings.

cl **Know to get your Price for Things**. Their intrinsic value is not sufficient; for all do not bite at the kernel or look into the interior. Most go with the crowd, and go because they see others go. It is a great stroke of art to bring things into repute; at times by praising them, for praise arouses desire at times by giving them a striking name, which is very useful for putting things at a premium, provided it is done without affectation. Again, it is generally an inducement to profess to supply only connoisseurs, for all think themselves such, and if not, the sense of want arouses the desire. Never call things easy or common: that makes them depreciated rather than made accessible. All rush after the unusual, which is more appetising both for the taste and for the intelligence.

cli **Think beforehand**. To-day for to-morrow, and even for many days hence. The greatest foresight consists in determining beforehand the time of trouble. For the provident there are no mischances and for the careful no narrow escapes. We must not put off thought till we are up to the chin in mire. Mature reflection can get over the most formidable difficulty. The pillow is a silent Sibyl, and it is better to sleep on things beforehand than lie awake about them afterwards. Many act first and then think afterwards—that is, they think less of consequences than of excuses: others think neither before nor after. The whole of life should be one course of thought how not to miss the right path. Rumination and foresight enable one to determine the line of life.

clii **Never have a Companion who casts you in the Shade**. The more he does so[115], the less desirable a companion he is. The more he excels in quality the more in repute: he will always play first fiddle and you second. If you get any consideration, it is only his leavings. The moon shines bright alone among the stars: when the sun rises she becomes either invisible or imperceptible. Never join one that eclipses you, but rather one who sets you in a brighter light. By this means the cunning Fabula in Martial[116] was able to appear beautiful and brilliant, owing to the ugliness and disorder of her companions. But one should as little imperil oneself by an evil companion as pay honour to another at the cost of one's own credit. When you are on the way to fortune associate with the eminent; when arrived, with the mediocre.

---

[115] "Tanto por mas, quanta por menos." Schop. takes it differently: "Sei es dadurch lass er über uns oder class er unter uns stehe."
[116] Martial, *Epigr.* viii. 79.

cliii Beware of entering[117] ***where there is a great Gap to be filled***. But if you do it be sure to surpass your predecessor; merely to equal him requires twice his worth. As it is a fine stroke to arrange that our successor shall cause us to be wished back, so it is policy to see that our predecessor does not eclipse us. To fill a great gap is difficult, for the past always seems best, and to equal the predecessor is not enough, since he has the right of first possession. You must therefore possess additional claims to oust the other from his hold on public opinion.

cliv Do not Believe, or Like, lightly. Maturity of mind is best shown in slow belief. Lying is the usual thing; then let belief be unusual. He that is lightly led away, soon falls into contempt. At the same time there is no necessity to betray your doubts in the good faith of others, for this adds insult to discourtesy, since you make out your informant to be either deceiver or deceived. Nor is this the only evil: want of belief is the mark of the liar, who suffers from two failings: he neither believes nor is believed. Suspension of judgment is prudent in a hearer: the speaker can appeal to his original source of in-formation. There is a similar kind of imprudence in liking too easily, for lies may be told by deeds as well as in words, and this deceit is more dangerous for practical life.

clv The Art of getting into a Passion. If possible, oppose vulgar importunity with prudent reflection; it will not be difficult for a really prudent man. The first step towards getting into a passion is to announce that you are in a passion. By this means you begin the conflict with command over your temper, for one has to regulate one's passion to the exact point that is necessary and no further. This is the art of arts in falling into and getting out of a rage. You should know how and when best to come to a stop: it is most difficult to halt while running at the double. It is a great proof of wisdom to remain clear-sighted during paroxysms of rage. Every excess of passion is a digression from rational conduct. But by this masterly policy reason will never be transgressed, nor pass the bounds of its own synteresis[118]. To keep control of passion one must hold firm the reins of attention: he who can do so will be the first man "wise on horseback[119]," and probably the last.

---

[117] The great Jewish teacher Hillel gave braver advice: "'Where there is no man, dare to be a man" (*Ethics of the Fathers*).
[118] *synteresis*; defined in Doctor and Student, Dial. I. ch. xiv., as: "The natural power of the soul set in the highest part thereof, moving it and stirring it to good and abhorring evil"; cf. Milton, *Common-place Book*, ed. Horwood, § 79; and cf. Saunder, transl. of Schopenhauer, *Aphorismen zur Lebensweisheit*, c. v. § 34.
[119] cf. "Nadie es cuerdo á caballo," Span. prov. quoted by Schop.

clvi **Select your Friends**. Only after[120] passing the matriculation of experience and the examination of fortune will they be graduates not alone in affection but in discernment. Though this is the most important thing in life, it is the one least cared for. Intelligence brings friends[121] to some, chance to most. Yet a man is judged by his friends, for there was never agreement between wise men and fools. At the same time, to find pleasure in a man's society is no proof of near friendship: it may come from the pleasantness of his company more than from trust in his capacity. There are some friendships legitimate, others illicit; the latter for pleasure, the former for their fecundity of ideas and motives. Few are the friends of a man's self, most those of his circumstances. The insight of a true friend is more useful than the goodwill of others: therefore gain them by choice, not by chance. A wise friend wards off worries, a foolish one brings them about. But do not wish them too much luck, or you may lose them.

clvii **Do not make Mistakes about Character**. That is the worst and yet easiest error. Better be cheated in the price than in the quality of goods. In dealing with men, more than with other things, it is necessary to look within. To know men is different from knowing things. It is profound philosophy to sound the depths of feeling and distinguish traits of character. Men must be studied as deeply as books.

clviii **Make use of your Friends**. This requires all the art of discretion. Some are good afar off, some when near. Many are no good at conversation but excellent as correspondents, for distance removes some failings which are unbearable in close proximity to them. Friends are for use even more than for pleasure, for they have the three qualities of the Good, or, as some say, of Being in general[122]: unity, goodness, and truth. For a friend is all in all. Few are worthy to be good friends, and even these become fewer because men do not know how to pick them out. To keep is more important than to make friends. Select those that will wear well; if they are new at first, it is some consolation they will become old. Absolutely the best are those well salted, though they may require soaking in the testing. There is no desert like living without friends. Friendship multiplies the good of life and divides the evil. 'Tis the sole remedy against misfortune, the very ventilation of the soul.

clix **Put up with Fools**. The wise are always impatient, for he that increases knowledge increase impatience of folly. Much knowledge is difficult to satisfy. The first great rule of life, according to Epictetus, is to put

---

[120] Orig. "Que lo han de ser á examen de la discretion y á prueba de la fortuna, graduados no solo de la voluntad sino del entendimiento."
[121] ; cf. Stevenson, Dr. Jekyll: "It is the mark of a modest man to accept his friends ready made at the hands of opportunity."
[122] the scholastic maxim running "Quodlibet ens est unum, verum, bonum."

up with things[123]: he makes that the moiety of wisdom. To put up with all the varieties of folly would need much patience. We often have to put up with most from those on whom we most depend: a useful lesson in self-control. Out of patience comes forth peace, the priceless boon which is the happiness of the world. But let him that bath no power of patience retire within himself, though even there he will have to put up with himself.

clx **Be careful in Speaking**.[124] With your rivals from prudence; with others for the sake of appearance. There is always time to add a word, never to withdraw one. Talk as if you were making your will: the fewer words the less litigation. In trivial matters exercise yourself for the more weighty matters of speech. Profound secrecy has some of the lustre of the divine. He who speaks lightly soon falls or fails.

clxi **Know your pet Faults**. The most perfect of men has them, and is either wedded to them or has illicit relations with them. They are often faults of intellect, and the greater this is, the greater they are, or at least the more conspicuous. It is not so much that their possessor does not know them: he loves them, which is a double evil: irrational affection for avoidable faults. They are spots on perfection; they displease the onlooker as much as they please the possessor. 'Tis a gallant thing to get clear of them, and so give play to one's other qualities. For all men hit upon such a failing, and on going over your qualifications they make a long stay at this blot, and blacken it as deeply as possible in order to cast your other talents into the shade.

clxii **How to triumph over Rivals and Detractors**. It is not enough to despise them, though this is often wise: a gallant bearing is the thing. One cannot praise a man too much who speaks well[125] of them who speak ill of him. There is no more heroic vengeance than that of talents and services which at once conquer and torment the envious. Every success is a further twist of the cord round the neck of the ill-affected, and an enemy's glory is the rival's hell. The envious die not once, but as oft as the envied wins applause. The immortality of his fame is the measure of the other's torture: the one lives in endless honour, the other in endless pain. The clarion of Fame announces immortality to the one and death to the other, the slow death of envy long drawn out.

clxiii **Never, from Sympathy with the Unfortunate, involve Yourself in his Fate**. One man's misfortune is another man's luck, for one cannot be lucky without many being unlucky. It is a peculiarity of the unfortunate to arouse people's goodwill who desire to compensate them for

---

[123] ἀνέχεσθαι καὶ ἀπέχεσθαι, the great Epicurean maxim.
[124] cf. Prov. xxix. 20. "Seest thou a man that is hasty in his words there is more hope of a fool than of him."
[125] "It's poor foolishness," says Adam Bede, "to run down your enemies", cf. Goethe.

the blows of fortune with their useless favour, and it happens that one who was abhorred by all in prosperity is adored by all in adversity. Vengeance on the wing is exchanged for compassion afoot. Yet 'tis to be noticed how fate shuffles the cards. There are men who always consort with the unlucky, and he that yesterday flew high and happy stands to-day miserable at their side. That argues nobility of soul, but not worldly wisdom.

clxiv **Throw Straws in the Air**[126], to find how things will be received, especially those whose reception or success is doubtful. One can thus be assured of its turning out well, and an opportunity is afforded for going on in earnest or withdrawing entirely. By trying men's intentions in this way, the wise man knows on what ground he stands. This is the great rule of foresight in asking, in desiring, and in ruling.

clxv **Wage War Honourably**. You may be obliged to wage war, but not to use poisoned arrows[127]. Every one must needs act as he is, not as others would make him to be. Gallantry in the battle of life wins all men's praise: one should fight so as to conquer, not alone by force but by the way it is used. A mean victory brings no glory, but rather disgrace. Honour always has the upper hand. An honourable man never uses forbidden weapons, such as using a friendship that's ended for the purposes of a hatred just begun: a confidence must never be used for a vengeance. The slightest taint of treason tarnishes the good name. In men of honour the smallest trace of meanness repels: the noble and the ignoble should be miles apart. Be able to boast that if gallantry, generosity, and fidelity were lost in the world men would be able to find them again in your own breast.

clxvi **Distinguish the Man of Words from the Man of Deeds**. Discrimination here is as important as in the case of friends, persons, and employments, which have all many varieties. Bad words even without bad deeds are bad enough: good words with bad deeds are worse. One cannot dine off words, which are wind, nor off politeness, which is but polite deceit[128]. To catch birds with a mirror is the ideal snare. It is the vain alone who take their wages in windy words. Words should be the pledges of work, and, like pawn-tickets, have their market price. Trees that bear leaves but not fruit have usually no pith. Know them for what they are, of no use except for shade.

clxvii **Know how to take your own Part**. In great crises there is no better companion than a bold heart, and if it becomes weak it must be strengthened from the neighbouring parts. Worries die away before a man who asserts himself. One must not surrender to misfortune, or else it would

---

[126] Orig. "Echar al ayre algunas cosas" merely refers to feigned blows; cf. xiii.
[127] rather an embellishment on the orig., which has merely "pero no mala (guerra)."
[128] cf. cxci

become intolerable. Many men do not help themselves in their troubles, and double their weight by not knowing how to bear them. He that knows himself knows how to strengthen his weakness, and the wise man conquers everything, even the stars in their courses.

clxviii **Do not indulge in the Eccentricities of Folly.** Like vain, presumptuous, egotistical, untrustworthy, capricious, obstinate, fanciful, theatrical, whimsical, inquisitive, paradoxical, sectarian people and all kinds of one-sided persons: they are all monstrosities of impertinence. All deformity of mind is more obnoxious than that of the body, because it contravenes a higher beauty. Yet who can assist such a complete confusion of mind? Where self-control is wanting, there is no room for others' guidance. Instead of paying attention to other people's real derision, men of this kind blind themselves with the unfounded assumption of their imaginary applause.

clxix **Be more careful not to Miss once than to Hit a hundred times.** No one looks at the blazing sun; all gaze when he is eclipsed. The common talk does not reckon what goes right but what goes wrong. Evil report carries farther than any applause. Many men are not known to the world till they have left it. All the exploits of a man taken together are not enough to wipe out a single small blemish. Avoid therefore falling into error, seeing that ill-will notices every error and no success.

clxx **In all Things keep Something in Reserve.** 'Tis a sure means of keeping up your importance. A man should not employ all his capacity and power at once and on every occasion. Even in knowledge there should be a rearguard, so that your resources are doubled. One must always have something to resort to when there is fear of a defeat. The reserve is of more importance than the attacking force: for it is distinguished for valour and reputation. Prudence always sets to work with assurance of safety: in this matter the piquant paradox holds good that the half is more than the whole.

clxxi **Waste not Influence.** The great as friends are for great occasions. One should not make use of great confidence for little things: for that is to waste a favour. The sheet anchor should be reserved for the last extremity. If you use up the great for little ends what remains afterwards? Nothing is more valuable than a protector, and nothing costs more nowadays than a favour. It can make or unmake a whole world. It can even give sense and take it away. As Nature and Fame are favourable to the wise, so Luck is generally envious of them. It is therefore more important to keep the favour of the mighty than goods and chattels.

clxxii **Never contend with a Man who has nothing to Lose**; for thereby you enter into an unequal conflict. The other enters without anxiety; having lost everything, including shame, he has no further loss to fear. He therefore re-sorts to all kinds of insolence. One should never expose a valuable reputation to so terrible a risk, lest what has cost years to gain may be lost in a moment, since a single slight may wipe out much sweat. A man of honour and responsibility has a reputation, because he has much to lose. He balances his own and the other's reputation: he only enters into the contest with the greatest caution, and then goes to work with such circumspection that he gives time to prudence to retire in time and bring his reputation under cover. For even by victory he cannot gain what he has lost by exposing himself to the chances of loss.

clxxiii **Do not be Glass in Intercourse, still less in Friendship**. Some break very easily, and thereby show their want of consistency. They attribute to themselves imaginary offences and to others oppressive intentions. Their feelings are even more sensitive than the eye itself, and must not be touched in jest or in earnest. Motes offend them[129]: they need not wait for beams. Those who consort with them must treat them with the greatest delicacy, have regard to their sensitiveness, and watch their demeanour, since the slightest slight arouses their annoyance. They are mostly very egoistic, slaves of their moods, for the sake of which they cast everything aside: they are the worshippers of punctilio. On the other hand, the disposition of the true lover is firm and enduring, so that it may be said that the Amant is half adamant.[130]

clxxiv **Do not live in a Hurry**. To know how to separate things is to know how to enjoy them. Many finish their fortune sooner than their life: they run through pleasures without enjoying them, and would like to go back when they find they have over-leaped the mark. Postilions of life, they increase the ordinary pace of life by the hurry of their own calling. They devour more in one day than they can digest in a whole life-time; they live in advance of pleasures, eat up the years beforehand, and by their hurry get through everything too soon. Even in the search for knowledge there should be moderation, lest we learn things better left unknown. We have more days to live through than pleasures. Be slow in enjoyment, quick at work, for men see work ended with pleasure, pleasure ended with regret.

clxxv **A Solid Man**. One who is finds no satisfaction in those that are not. 'Tis a pitiable eminence that is not well founded. Not all are men that seem to be so. Some are sources of deceit; impregnated by chimeras they give birth to impositions. Others are like them so far that they take more pleasure in a lie, because it promises much, than in the truth, because it

---

[129] Orig. "Ofendenla las motas que no son menester yá notas."

[130] This seems the only way of retaining the "conceit" and jingle of the orig.: "La condición del Amante tiene la mitad de diamante en el durar y en el resistir." TWC. Lit. The condition of lover, is like half a diamond both in durability and resistance."

performs little. But in the end these caprices come to a bad end, for they have no solid foundation. Only Truth can give true reputation: only reality can be of real profit. One deceit needs many others, and so the whole house is built in the air and must soon come to the ground. Unfounded things never reach old age. They promise too much to be much trusted, just as that cannot be true which proves too much.

clxxvi **Have Knowledge, or know those that have Knowledge**. Without intelligence, either one's own or another's, true life is impossible. But many do not know that they do not know, and many think they know when they know nothing. Failings of the intelligence are incorrigible, since those who do not know, do not know themselves, and cannot therefore seek what they lack. Many would be wise if they did not think themselves wise. Thus it happens that though the oracles of wisdom are rare, they are rarely used. To seek advice does not lessen greatness or argue incapacity. On the contrary, to ask advice proves you well advised. Take counsel with reason it you do not wish to court defeat.

clxxvii **Avoid Familiarities in Intercourse**. Neither use them nor permit them. He that is familiar, loses any superiority his Influence gives him, and so loses respect. The stars keep their brilliance by not making themselves common. The Divine demands decorum. Every familiarity breeds contempt. In human affairs, the more a man shows, the less he has, for in open communication you communicate the failings that reserve might keep under cover. Familiarity is never desirable; with superiors because it is dangerous, with inferiors because it is unbecoming, least of all with the common herd, who become insolent from sheer folly: they mistake favour shown them for need felt of them. Familiarity trenches on vulgarity.

clxxviii **Trust your Heart**, especially when it has been proved. Never deny it a hearing. It is a kind of house oracle that often foretells the most important. Many have perished because they feared their own heart, but of what use is it to fear it without finding a better remedy? Many are endowed by Nature with a heart so true that it always warns them of misfortune and wards off its effects. It is unwise to seek evils, unless you seek to conquer them.

clxxix **Reticence is the Seal of Capacity**. A breast without a secret is an open letter. Where there is a solid foundation secrets can be kept profound: there are spacious cellars where things of moment may be hid. Reticence springs from self-control, and to control oneself in this is a true triumph. You must pay ransom to each you tell. The security of wisdom consists in temperance in the inner man. The risk that reticence runs lies in the cross-questioning of others, in the use of contradiction to worm out secrets, in the darts of irony: to avoid these the prudent become more reticent than before. What must be done need not be said, and what must be said need not be done.

clxxx **Never guide the Enemy to what he has to do.** The fool never does what the wise judge wise, because he does not follow up the suitable means. He that is discreet follows still less a plan laid out, or even carried out, by another. One has to discuss matters from both points of view—turn it over on both sides. Judgments vary; let him that has not decided attend rather to what is possible than what is probable.

clxxxi **The Truth, but not the whole Truth.** Nothing demands more caution than the truth: 'tis the lancet of the heart. It requires as much to tell the truth as to conceal it. A single lie destroys a whole reputation for integrity. The deceit is regarded as treason and the deceiver as a traitor, which is worse. Yet not all truths can be spoken: some for our own sake, others for the sake of others.

clxxxii **A Grain of Boldness[131] in Everything.** 'Tis an important piece of prudence. You must moderate your opinion of others so that you may not think so high of them as to fear them. The imagination should never yield to the heart. Many appear great till you know them personally, and then dealing with them does more to disillusionise than to raise esteem. No one o'ersteps the narrow bounds of humanity: all have their weaknesses either in heart or head. Dignity gives apparent authority, which is rarely accompanied by personal power: for Fortune often redresses the height of office by the inferiority of the holder. The imagination always jumps too soon, and paints things in brighter colours than the real: it thinks things not as they are but as it wishes them to be. Attentive experience disillusionised in the past soon corrects all that. Yet if wisdom should not be timorous, neither should folly be rash. And if self-reliance helps the ignorant, how much more the brave and wise?

clxxxiii **Do not hold your Views too firmly.** Every fool is fully convinced, and every one fully persuaded is a fool: the more erroneous his judgment the more firmly he holds it. Even in cases of obvious certainty, it is fine to yield: our reasons for holding the view cannot escape notice, our courtesy in yielding must be the more recognised. Our obstinacy loses more than our victory yields: that is not to champion truth but rather rudeness. There be some heads of iron most difficult to turn: add caprice to obstinacy and the sum is a wearisome fool. Steadfastness should be for the will, not for the mind. Yet there are exceptions where one would fail twice, owning oneself wrong both in judgment and in the execution of it.

---

[131] cf. the opening of Bacon's Essay "Of Boldnesse," and Mrs. Poyser's aphorism, "It's them as take advantage that get advantage in this world, I think."

clxxxiv **Do not be Ceremonious**. Even in a king affectation in this was renowned for its eccentricity. To be punctilious is to be a bore, yet whole nations have this peculiarity. The garb of folly is woven out of such things. Such folk are worshippers of their own dignity, yet show how little it is justified since they fear that the least thing can destroy it. It is right to demand respect, but not to be considered a master of ceremonies. Yet it is true that a man to do without ceremonies must possess supreme qualities. Neither affect nor despise etiquette: he cannot be great who is great at such little things.

clxxxv **Never stake your Credit on a single Cast**; for if it miscarries the damage is irreparable. It may easy happen that a man should fail once, especially at first: circumstances are not always favourable: hence they say, "Every dog has his day." Always connect your second attempt with your first: whether it succeed or fail, the first will redeem the second. Always have resort to better means and appeal to more resources. Things depend on all sorts of chances. That is why the satisfaction of success is so rare.

clxxxvi **Recognise Faults, however high placed**. Integrity cannot mistake vice even when clothed in brocade or perchance crowned with gold, but will not be able to hide its character for all that. Slavery does not lose its vileness, however it vaunt the nobility of its lord and master. Vices may stand in high place, but are low for all that. Men can see that many a great man has great faults, yet they do not see that he is not great because of them. The example of the great is so specious that it even glosses over viciousness, till it may so affect those who flatter it that they do not notice that what they gloss over in the great they abominate in the lower classes.

clxxxvii **Do pleasant Things Yourself, unpleasant Things through Others**. By the one course you gain goodwill, by the other you avoid hatred. A great man takes more pleasure in doing a favour than in receiving one: it is the privilege[132] of his generous nature. One cannot easily cause pain to another without suffering pain either from sympathy or from remorse. In high place one can only work by means of rewards and punishment, so grant the first yourself, inflict the other through others. Have some one[133] against whom the weapons of discontent, hatred, and slander may be directed. For the rage of the mob is like that of a dog: missing the cause of its pain it turns to bite the whip itself, and though this is not the real culprit, it has to pay the penalty.

clxxxviii **Be the Bearer of Praise**. This increases our credit for good taste, since it shows that we have learnt elsewhere to know what is excellent,

---

[132] cf. cclxxxvi
[133] cf. Bacon, "Of Envy": "The wiser Sort of Great Persons bring in ever upon the Stage some Body upon whom to derive the Envy that would come upon themselves."

and hence how to prize it in the present company. It gives material for conversation and for imitation, and encourages praiseworthy exertions. We do homage besides in a very delicate way to the excellences before us. Others do the opposite; they accompany their talk with a sneer, and fancy they flatter those present by belittling the absent. This may serve them with superficial people, who do not notice how cunning it is to speak ill of every one to every one else. Many pursue the plan of valuing more highly the mediocrities of the day than the most distinguished exploits of the past. Let the cautious penetrate through these subtleties, and let him not be dismayed by the exaggerations of the one or made over-confident by the flatteries of the other; knowing that both act in the same way by different methods, adapting their talk to the company they are in.

clxxxix **Utilise Another's Wants**. The greater his wants the greater the turn of the screw. Philosophers say privation is non-existent, statesmen say it is all-embracing, and they are right. Many make ladders to attain their ends out of wants of others. They make use of the opportunity and tantalise the appetite by pointing out the difficulty of satisfaction. The energy of desire promises more than the inertia of possession. The passion of desire increases with every increase of opposition. It is a subtle point to satisfy the desire and yet preserve the dependence.

cxc **Find Consolation in all Things**. Even the useless may find it in being immortal. No trouble without compensation. Fools are held to be lucky, and the good-luck of the ugly is proverbial. Be worth little and you will live long: it is the cracked glass that never gets broken, but worries one with its durability. It seems that Fortune envies the great, so it equalises things by giving long life to the use-less, a short one to the important. Those who bear the burden come soon to grief, while those who are of no importance live on and on: in one case it appears so, in the other it is so. The unlucky thinks[134] he has been forgotten by both Death and Fortune.

cxci **Do not take Payment in Politeness**; for it is a kind of fraud. Some do not need the herbs of Thessaly for their magic, for they can enchant fools by the grace of their salute. Theirs is the Bank of Elegance[135], and they pay with the wind of fine words. To promise everything is to promise nothing: promises are the pitfalls of fools. The true courtesy is performance of duty: the spurious and especially the useless is deceit. It is not respect but rather a means to power. Obeisance is paid not to the man but to his means, and compliments are offered not to the qualities that are recognised but to the advantages that are desired.

---

[134] Orig. has a play upon the words "suerte" and "muerte."
[135] I have no excuse for this. Orig. simply "Hacen precio con la honra."

cxcii **Peaceful Life, a long Life.** To live, let live. Peacemakers not only live: they rule life. Hear, see, and be silent. A day without dispute brings sleep without dreams. Long life and a pleasant one is life enough for two: that is the fruit of peace. He has all that makes nothing of what is nothing to him. There is no greater perversity[136] than to take everything to heart. There is equal folly in troubling our heart about what does not concern us and in not taking to heart what does.

cxciii **Watch him that begins with Another's to end with his own.** Watchfulness is the only guard against cunning. Be intent[137] on his intentions. Many succeed in making others do their own affairs, and unless you possess the key to their motives you may at any moment be forced to take their chestnuts[138] out of the fire to the damage of your own fingers.

cxciv **Have reasonable Views of Yourself and of your Affairs**, especially in the beginning of life. Every one has a high opinion of himself, especially those who have least ground for it. Every one dreams of his good-luck and thinks himself a wonder. Hope gives rise to extravagant promises which experience does not fulfil. Such idle imaginations merely serve as a well-spring of annoyance when disillusion comes with the true reality. The wise man anticipates such errors: he may always hope for the best. but he always expects the worst, so as to receive what comes with equanimity. True, It is wise to aim high so as to hit your mark, but not so high that you miss your mission at the very beginning of life. This correction of the ideas is necessary, because before experience comes expectation is sure to soar too high. The best panacea against folly is prudence. If a man knows the true sphere of his activity and position, the can reconcile his ideals with reality.

cxcv **Know how to Appreciate.** There is none who cannot teach somebody something, and there is none so excellent but he is excelled. To know how to make use of every one is useful knowledge. Wise men appreciate all men, for they see the good in each and know how hard it is to make anything good. Fools depreciate all men, not recognising the good and selecting the bad.

cxcvi **Know your ruling Star**[139]. None so helpless as not to have one; if he is unlucky, that is because he does not know it. Some stand high in the favour of princes and potentates without knowing why or wherefore, except that good luck itself has granted them favour on easy terms, merely

---

[136] Orig. "No ay mayor desproposito que tomarlo todo de proposito." TWC note: "Despropósito" means something that makes no sense. The author says that there is nothing as senseless as making a "purpose" out of everything. In other words, be wise choosing your purpose.
[137] Orig. "Al intendido un buen entendedor.
[138] Orig. simply "Sacar del fuego el provecho ageno."
[139] There are some grounds for believing that great adventurers, like Napoleon, have a subjective star, hallucinatory of course, which appears to them at moments of great excitement; cf. Gallon, *Human Faculty*, 175-176

requiring them to aid it with a little exertion. Others find favour with the wise. One man is better received by one nation than by another, or is more welcome in one city than in another. He finds more luck in one office or position than another, and all this though his qualifications are equal or even identical. Luck shuffles the cards how and when she will. Let each man know his luck as well as his talents, for on this depends whether he loses or wins. Follow your guiding star and help it without mistaking any other for it, for that would be to miss the North, though its neighbour (the polestar) calls us to it with a voice of thunder.

cxcvii ***Do not carry Fools on your Back***. He that does not know a fool when he sees him is one himself: still more he that knows him but will not keep clear of him. They are dangerous company and ruinous confidants. Even though their own caution and others' care keeps them in bounds for a time, still at length they are sure to do or to say some foolishness which is all the greater for being kept so long in stock. They cannot help another's credit who have none of their own. They are most unlucky, which is the Nemesis of fools, and they have to pay for one thing or the other. There is only one thing which is not so bad about them, and this is that though they can be of no use to the wise, they can be of much use to them as signposts or as warnings.

cxcviii ***Know how to transplant Yourself.*** There are nations with whom one must cross their borders to make one's value felt, especially in great posts. Their native land is always a stepmother to great talents[140]: envy flourishes there on its native soil, and they remember one's small beginnings rather than the greatness one has reached. A needle is appreciated that comes from one end of the world to the other, and a piece of painted glass might outvie the diamond in value if it comes from afar. Everything foreign is respected, partly because it comes from afar, partly because It is ready made and perfect. We have seen persons once the laughing-stock of their village and now the wonder of the whole world, honoured by their fellow-countrymen and by the foreigners [among whom they dwell]; by the latter because they come from afar, by the former because they are seen from afar. The statue on the altar is never reverenced by him who knew it as a trunk in the garden.

cxcix ***To find a proper Place by Merit, not by Presumption***. The true road to respect is through merit, and if industry accompany merit the path becomes shorter. Integrity alone is not sufficient, push and insistence is degrading, for things arrive by that means so besprinkled with dust that

---

[140] cf. *contra* Galton, *Hered. Gen.*, 360 "As a rule the very ablest men are strongly disinclined to emigrate," and Prov. xxvii. 8.

the discredit destroys reputation. The true way is the middle one, half-way between de-serving a place and pushing oneself into it.

cc Leave Something to wish for[141], so as not to be miserable from very happiness. The body must respire[142] and the soul aspire. If one possessed all, all would be disillusion and discontent. Even in knowledge there should be always something left to know in order to arouse curiosity and excite hope. Surfeits of happiness are fatal. In giving assistance it is a piece of policy not to satisfy entirely. If there is nothing left to desire, there is everything to fear, an unhappy state of happiness. When desire dies, fear is born.

cci They are all Fools who seem so besides half the rest. Folly arose with the world, and if there be any wisdom it is folly compared with the divine. But the greatest fool is he who thinks he is not one and all others are. To be wise It is not enough to seem wise, least of all to oneself. He knows who does not think that he knows, and he does not see who does not see that others see. Though all the world is full of fools, there is none that thinks himself one, or even suspects the fact.

ccii Words and Deeds make the Perfect Man. One should speak well and act honourably: the one is an excellence of the head, the other of the heart, and both arise from nobility of soul. Words are the shadows of deeds; the former are feminine[143], the latter masculine. It is more important to be renowned than to convey renown. Speech is easy, action hard. Actions are the stuff of life, words its frippery. Eminent deeds endure[144], striking words pass away. Actions are the fruit of thought; if this is wise, they are effective.

cciii Know the great Men of your Age. They are not many. There is one Phœnix in the whole world, one great general, one perfect orator, one true philosopher in a century, a really illustrious king in several. Mediocrities are as numerous as they are worth-less: eminent greatness is rare in every respect, since it needs complete perfection, and the higher the species the more difficult is the highest rank in it. Many have claimed the title "Great," like Cæsar and Alexander, but in vain, for without great deeds the title is a mere breath of air. There have been few Senecas, and fame records but one Apelles.

---

[141] cf. lxxxii, ccxcix

[142] Orig. "Espira el cuerpo y anhela el espiritu."

[143] cf. Span. prov. "Palabras hembras son hechos machos." Howell, *Fam. Letters*, quotes the saying as Italian; cf. my edition, p. 270 and *n*. Herbert also gives it in his *Jacula Prudentum*.

[144] Schop. has characteristically expressed his dissent by annotating his own copy of the *Oráculo* at this point with a pithy "vale el contrario."

cciv *Attempt easy Tasks as if they were difficult, and difficult as if they were easy.* In the one case that confidence may not fall asleep, in the other that it may not be dismayed. For a thing to remain undone nothing more is needed than to think it done. On the other hand, patient industry overcomes impossibilities. Great undertakings are not to be brooded over, lest their difficulty when seen causes despair.

ccv *Know how to play the Card of Contempt.* It is a shrewd way of getting things you want, by affecting to depreciate them: generally they are not to be had when sought for, but fall into one's hands when one is not looking for them. As all mundane things are but shadows of the things eternal, they share with shadows this quality, that they flee from him who follows them and follow him that flees from them. Contempt is besides the most subtle form of revenge. It is a fixed rule with the wise never to defend themselves with the pen. For such defence always leaves a stain, and does more to glorify one's opponent than to punish his offence. It is a trick of the worthless to stand forth as opponents of great men, so as to win notoriety by a roundabout way, which they would never do by the straight road of merit. There are many we would not have heard of if their eminent opponents had not taken notice of them. There is no revenge like oblivion, through which they are buried in the dust of their unworthiness. Audacious persons hope to make themselves eternally famous by setting fire to one of the wonders of the world and of the ages. The art of reproving scandal is to take no notice of it, to combat it damages our own case; even if credited it causes discredit, and is a source of satisfaction to our opponent, for this shadow of a stain dulls the lustre of our fame even if it cannot altogether deaden it.

ccvi *Know that there are vulgar Natures everywhere*, even in Corinth itself, even in the highest families. Every one may try the experiment within his own gates. But there is also such a thing as vulgar opposition to vulgarity, which is worse. This special kind shares all the qualities of the common kind, just as bits of a broken glass: but this kind is still more pernicious; it speaks folly, blames impertinently, is a disciple of ignorance, a patron of folly, and past master of scandal; you need not notice what it says, still less what it thinks. It is important to know vulgarity in order to avoid it, whether it is subjective or objective. For all folly is vulgarity, and the vulgar consist of fools.

ccvii **Be Moderate.** One has to consider the chance of a mischance. The impulses of the passions cause

prudence to slip, and there is the risk of ruin. A moment of wrath or of pleasure carries you on farther than many hours of calm, and often a short diversion may put a whole life to shame. The cunning of others uses such moments of temptation to search the recesses of the mind: they use such thumbscrews as are wont to test the best caution. Moderation serves as a counterplot, especially in sudden emergencies. Much thought is needed to prevent a passion taking the bit in the teeth, and he is doubly wise who is wise on horseback. He who knows the danger may with care pursue his journey. Light as a word may appear to him who throws it out, it may import much to him that hears it and ponders on it.

ccviii **Do not die of the Fools' Disease**. The wise generally die after they have lost their reason: fools before they have found it. To die of the fools' disease is to die of too much thought. Some die because they think and feel too much: others live because they do not think and feel: these are fools because they do not die of sorrow, the others because they do. A fool is he that dies of too much knowledge: thus some die because they are too knowing, others because they are not knowing enough. Yet though many die like fools, few die fools.

ccix **Keep Yourself free from common Follies**. This is a special stroke of policy. They are of special power because they are general, so that many who would not be led away by any individual folly cannot escape the universal failing. Among these are to be counted the common prejudice that any one is satisfied with his fortune, however great, or unsatisfied with his intellect, however poor it is. Or again, that each, being discontented with his own lot, envies that of others; or further, that persons of to-day praise the things of yesterday, and those here the things there. Everything past seems best and everything distant is more valued. He is as great a fool that laughs at all as he that weeps at all.

ccx **Know how to play the Card of Truth**. 'Tis dangerous, yet a good man cannot avoid speaking it. But great skill is needed here: the most expert doctors of the soul pay great attention to the means of sweetening the pill of truth. For when it deals with the destroying of illusion it is the quintessence of bitterness. A pleasant manner has here an opportunity for a display of skill: with the same truth it can flatter one and fell another to the ground. Matters of to-day should be treated as if they were long past. For those who can understand a word is sufficient, and if it does not suffice, it is a case for silence. Princes must not be cured with bitter draughts; it is therefore desirable in their case to gild the pill of disillusion.

ccxi **In Heaven all is bliss**: in Hell all misery. On earth, between the two, both one thing and the other. We stand between the two extremes, and therefore share both. Fate varies: all is not good luck nor all mischance. This world is merely zero: by itself it is of no value, but with Heaven in Front of it, it means much. Indifference at its ups and downs is prudent, nor is there any novelty for the wise. Our life gets as complicated as a comedy as it goes on, but the complications get gradually resolved: see that the curtain comes down on a good *dénoûment*.

ccxii **Keep to Yourself the final Touches of your Art**. This is a maxim of the great masters who pride themselves on this subtlety in teaching their pupils: one must always remain superior, remain master. One must teach an art artfully. The source of knowledge need not be pointed out no more than that of giving. By this means a man preserves the respect and the dependence of others. In amusing and teaching you must keep to the rule: keep up expectation and advance in perfection. To keep a reserve is a great rule for life and for success, especially for those in high place.

ccxiii **Know how to Contradict**. A chief means of finding things out—to embarrass others without being embarrassed. The true thumbscrew, it brings the passions into play. Tepid incredulity acts as an emetic on secrets. It is the key to a locked-up breast, and with great subtlety makes a double trial of both mind and will. A sly depreciation of another's mysterious word scents out the profoundest secrets; some sweet bait brings them into the mouth till they fall from the tongue and are caught in the net of astute deceit. By reserving your attention the other becomes less attentive, and lets his thoughts appear while otherwise his heart were inscrutable. An affected doubt is the subtlest picklock that curiosity can use to find out what it wants to know. Also in learning it is a subtle plan of the pupil to contradict the master, who thereupon takes pains to explain the truth more thoroughly and with more force, so that a moderate contradiction produces complete instruction.

ccxiv **Do not turn one Blunder into two**. It is quite usual to commit four others in order to remedy one, or to excuse one piece of impertinence by still another. Folly is either related to, or identical with the family of Lies, for in both cases it needs many to support one. The worst of a bad case is having to fight it, and worse than the ill itself is not being able to conceal it. The annuity of one failing serves to support many others. A wise man may make one slip but never two, and that only in running, not while standing still.

ccxv **Watch him that acts on Second Thoughts**. It is a device of business men to put the opponent off his guard before attacking him, and thus to conquer by being defeated: they dissemble their desire so as to attain it. They put themselves second so as to come out first in the final spurt. This method rarely fails if it is not noticed. Let therefore the attention never sleep when the intention is so wide awake. And if the other puts himself second so to hide his plan, put yourself first to discover it. Prudence can discern the artifices which such a man uses, and notices the pretexts he puts forward to gain his ends. He aims at one thing to get another: then he turns round smartly and fires straight at his target. It is well to know what you grant him, and at times it is desirable to give him to understand that you understand.

ccxvi **Be Expressive**. This depends not only on the clearness but also on the vivacity of your thoughts. Some have an easy conception but a hard labour, for without clearness the children of the mind, thoughts and judgments, cannot be brought into the world. Many have a capacity like that of vessels with a large mouth and a small vent. Others again say more than they think. Resolution for the will, expression for the thought: two great gifts. Plausible minds are applauded: yet confused ones are often venerated just because they are not understood, and at times obscurity is convenient if you wish to avoid vulgarity; yet how shall the audience understand one that connects no definite idea with what he says?

ccxvii **Neither Love nor Hate, for ever** Trust the friends of to-day as if they will be enemies to-morrow, and that of the worst kind. As this happens in reality, let it happen in your precaution. Do not put weapons in the hand for deserters from friendship to wage war with. On the other hand, leave the door of reconciliation open for enemies, and if it is also the gate of generosity so much the more safe. The vengeance of long ago is at times the torment of to-day, and the joy over the ill we have done is turned to grief,

ccxviii **Never act from Obstinacy but from Knowledge**. All obstinacy is an excrescence of the mind, a grandchild of passion which never did anything right. There are persons who make a war out of everything, real banditti of intercourse. All that they undertake must end in victory; they do not know how to get on in peace. Such men are fatal when they rule and govern, for they make government rebellion, and enemies out of those whom they ought to regard as children. They try to effect everything with strategy and treat it as the fruit of their skill. But when others have recognised their perverse humour all revolt against them and learn to overturn their chimerical plans, and they succeed in nothing but only heap up a mass of troubles, since everything serves to increase their disappointment. They have a head turned and a heart spoilt. Nothing can be done with such monsters except to flee from them, even to the Antipodes, where the savagery is easier to bear than their loathsome nature.

ccxix **Do not pass for a Hypocrite**, though such men are indispensable nowadays. Be considered rather prudent than astute. Sincerity in behaviour pleases all, though not all can show it in their own affairs. Sincerity should not degenerate into simplicity nor sagacity into cunning. Be rather respected as wise than feared as sly. The open-hearted are loved but deceived. The great art consists in disclosing what is thought to be deceit. In the golden age simplicity flourished, in these days of iron cunning. 'The reputation of being a man who knows what he has to do is honourable and inspires confidence, but to be considered a hypocrite is deceptive and arouses mistrust.

ccxx *If you cannot clothe Yourself in Lionskin use Foxpelt*[145]. To follow the times is to lead them. He that gets what he wants never loses his reputation. Cleverness when force will not do. One way or another, the king's highway of valour or the bypath of cunning. Skill has effected more than force, and astuteness has conquered courage more often than the other way. When you cannot get a thing then is the time to despise it.

ccxxi *Do not seize Occasions to embarrass Yourself or Others*. There are some men stumbling-blocks of good manners either for themselves or for others: they are always on the point of some stupidity. You meet with them easily[146] and part from them uneasily. A hundred annoyances a day is nothing to them. Their humour always strokes the wrong way since they contradict all and every. They put on the judgment cap wrong side foremost and thus condemn all. Yet the greatest test of others' patience and prudence are just those who do no good and speak ill of all. There are many monsters in the wide realm of Indecorum.

ccxxii [147]*Reserve is proof of Prudence*. The tongue is a wild beast; once let loose it is difficult to chain. It is the pulse of the soul by which wise men judge of its health: by this pulse a careful observer feels every movement of the heart. The worst is that he who should be most reserved is the least. The sage saves himself from worries and embarrassments, and shows his mastery over himself. He goes his way carefully, a Janus for impartiality, an Argus for watchfulness. Truly Momus had better placed the eyes in the hand than the window in the breast.

ccxxiii *Be not Eccentric*, neither from affectation nor carelessness. Many have some remarkable and individual quality leading to eccentric actions. These are more defects than excellent differences[148]. And just as some are known for some special ugliness, so these for something repellant in their outward behaviour. Such eccentricities simply serve as trademarks through their atrocious singularity: they cause either derision or ill-will.

ccxxiv *Never take Things against the Grain*, no matter how they come. Everything has a smooth and a seamy side, and the best weapon wounds if taken by the blade[149], while the enemy's spear may be our best protection if taken by the staff. Many things cause pain which would cause pleasure if you regarded their advantages. There is a favourable and an

---

[145] . There may be here a reference to Lysander's saying in Plutarch: "If the lion's skin [of Hercules] is not long enough, we must stitch on to it a fox's skin

[146] Orig. "Encuentranse con gran facilidad y rompen con infelicidad."

[147] cf. clxxix

[148] Orig. "Que son mas defectos que diferencias."

[149] cf. lxxxiv

unfavourable side to everything, the cleverness consists in finding out the favourable. The same thing looks quite different in another light; look at it therefore on its best side and do not exchange good for evil. Thus it haps that many find joy, many grief, in everything. This remark is a great protection against the frowns of fortune, and a weighty rule of life for all times and all conditions.

ccxxv [150]**Know your chief Fault**. There lives none that has not in himself a counterbalance to his most conspicuous merit: if this be nourished by desire it may grow to be a tyrant. Commence war against it, summoning prudence as your ally, and the first thing to do is the public manifesto, for an evil once known is soon conquered, especially when the one afflicted regards it in the same light as the onlookers. To be master of oneself one should know oneself. If the chief imperfection surrender, the rest will come to an end.

ccxxvi **Take care to be Obliging**. Most talk and act, not as they are, but as they are obliged. To persuade people of ill is easy for any, since the ill is easily credited even when at times it is incredible. The best we have depends on the opinion of others. Some are satisfied if they have right on their side, but that is not enough, for it must be assisted by energy. To oblige persons often costs little and helps much. With words you may purchase deeds. In this great house of the world there is no chamber so hid that it may not be wanted one day in the year, and then you would miss it however little is its worth. Every one speaks of a subject according to his feelings.

ccxxvii **Do not be the Slave of First Impressions**. Some marry the very first account they hear: all others must live with them as concubines. But as a lie has swift legs, the truth with them can find no lodging. We should neither satisfy our will with the first object nor our mind with the first proposition: for that were superficial. Many are like new casks[151] who keep the scent of the first liquor they hold, be it good or bad. If this superficiality becomes known, it becomes fatal, for it then gives opportunity for cunning mischief; the ill-minded hasten to colour the mind of the credulous. Always therefore leave room for a second hearing. Alexander always kept one ear for the other side. Wait for the second or even third edition of news. To be the slave of your impressions argues want of capacity, and is not far from being the slave of your passions.

ccxxviii **Do not be a Scandal-monger**. Still less pass for one, for that means to be considered a slanderer. Do not be witty at the cost of others: it is easy but hateful. All men have their revenge on such an one by speaking

---

[150] cf. xxxiv
[151] cf. the Span. prov. "A la vasija nueva dura el resabio."

ill of him, and as they are many and he but one, he is more likely to be overcome than they convinced. Evil should never be our pleasure, and therefore never our theme. The backbiter is always hated, and if now and then one of the great consorts with him, it is less from pleasure in his sneers than from esteem for his insight. He that speaks ill will always hear worse.

ccxxix **Plan out your Life wisely**, not as chance will have it, but with prudence and foresight. Without amusements it is wearisome, like a long journey where there are no inns: manifold knowledge gives manifold pleasure. The first day's journey of a noble life should be passed in conversing with the dead: we live to know and to know our-selves: hence true books make us truly men. The second day should be spent with the living, seeing and noticing all the good in the world. Everything is not to be found in a single country. The Universal Father has divided His gifts, and at times has given the richest dower to the ugliest. The third day is entirely for oneself. The last felicity is to be a philosopher.

ccxxx **Open your Eyes betimes**. Not all that see have their eyes open, nor do all those see that look. To come up to things too late is more worry than help. Some just begin to see when there is nothing more to see: they pull their houses about their ears before they come to themselves. It is difficult to give sense to those who have no power of will, still more difficult to give energy to those who have no sense. Those who surround them play with them a game of blind man's buff, making them the butts of others, and be-cause they are hard of hearing, they do not open their eyes to see. There are often those who encourage such insensibility on which their very existence depends. Unhappy steed whose rider is blind: it will never grow sleek.

ccxxxi **Never let Things be seen half-finished**. They can only be enjoyed when complete. All beginnings are misshapen, and this deformity sticks in the imagination. The recollection of having seen a thing imperfect disturbs our enjoyment of it when completed. To swallow something great at one gulp may disturb the judgment of the separate parts, but satisfies the taste. Till a thing is everything, it is nothing, and while it is in process of being it is still nothing. To see the tastiest dishes prepared arouses rather disgust than appetite. Let each great master take care not to let his work be seen in its embryonic stages: they might take this lesson from Dame Nature, who never brings the child to the light till it is fit to be seen.

ccxxxii **Have a Touch of the Trader**. Life should not be all thought: there should be action as well. Very wise folk are generally easily deceived, for while they know out-of-the-way things they do not know the ordinary things of life, which are much more needful. The observation of higher things leaves them no time for things close at hand. Since they know not the very first thing they should know, and what everybody knows so well, they are either considered or thought ignorant by the superficial multitude. Let therefore the prudent take care to have something of the trader about him—enough to prevent him being deceived and so laughed at, Be a man adapted to the daily round, which if not the highest is the most necessary thing in life. Of what use is knowledge if it is not practical, and to know how to live is nowadays the true knowledge.

 ccxxxiii ***Let not the proffered Morsel be distasteful***; otherwise it gives more discomfort than pleasure. Some displease when attempting to oblige, because they take no account of varieties of taste. What is flattery to one is an offence to another, and in attempting to be useful one may become insulting. It often costs more to displease a man than it would have cost to please him: you thereby lose both gift and thanks because you have lost the compass which steers for pleasure. He who knows not another's taste, knows not how to please him. Thus it haps that many insult where they mean to praise, and get soundly punished, and rightly so. Others desire to charm by their conversation, and only succeed in boring by their loquacity.

 ccxxxiv ***Never trust your Honour to another, unless you have his in Pledge***. Arrange that silence is a mutual advantage; disclosure a danger to both. Where honour is at stake you must act with a partner, so that each must be careful of the other's honour for the sake of his own. Never entrust your honour to another; but if you have, let caution surpass prudence. Let the danger be in common and the risk mutual, so that your partner cannot turn king's evidence.

 ccxxxv ***Know how to Ask***. With some nothing easier: with others nothing so difficult. For there are men who cannot refuse: with them no skill is required. But with others their first word at all times is No; with them great art is required, and with all the propitious moment. Surprise them when in a pleasant mood, when a repast of body or soul has just left them refreshed, if only their shrewdness has not anticipated the cunning of the applicant. The days of joy are the days of favour, for joy overflows from the inner man into the outward creation. It is no use applying when another has been refused, since the objection to a No has just been overcome. Nor is it a good time after sorrow. To oblige a person beforehand is a sure way, unless he is mean.

 ccxxxvi ***Make an Obligation beforehand of what would have to be a Reward afterwards***. This is a stroke of subtle policy; to grant favours before they are deserved is a proof of being obliging. Favours thus granted beforehand have two great advantages: the promptness of the gift obliges the recipient the more strongly; and the same gift which would afterwards be merely a reward is beforehand an obligation. This is a subtle means of transforming obligations, since that which would have forced the superior to reward is changed into one that obliges the one obliged to satisfy the obligation. But this is only suitable for men who have the feeling of obligation, since with men of lower stamp the honorarium paid beforehand acts rather as a bit than as a spur.

ccxxxvii **Never share the Secrets of your Superiors**. You may think you will share pears[152], but you will only share parings. Many have been ruined by being confidants: they are like sops of bread used as forks, they run the same risk of being eaten up afterwards. It is no favour in a prince to share a secret: it is only a relief. Many break the mirror that reminds them of their ugliness. We do not like seeing those who have seen us as we are: nor is he seen in a favourable light who has seen us in an unfavourable one. None ought to be too much beholden to us, least of all one of the great, unless it be for benefits done him rather than for such favours received from him. Especially dangerous are secrets entrusted to friends. He that communicates his secret[153] to another makes himself that other's slave. With a prince this is an intolerable position which cannot last. He will desire to recover his lost liberty, and to gain it will overturn everything, including right and reason. Accordingly neither tell secrets nor listen to them.

ccxxxviii [154]**Know what is wanting in Yourself**. Many would have been great personages if they had not had something wanting without which they could not rise to the height of perfection. It is remarkable with some that they could be much better if they could he better in something. They do not perhaps take themselves seriously enough to do justice to their great abilities; some are wanting in geniality of disposition, a quality which their entourage soon find the want of, especially if they are in high office. Some are without organising ability, others lack moderation. In all such cases a careful man may make of habit a second nature.

ccxxxix **Do not be Captious**. It is much more important to be sensible. To know more than is necessary blunts your weapons, for fine points generally bend or break. Common-sense truth is the surest. It is well to know but not to niggle. Lengthy comment leads to disputes. It is much better to have sound sense, which does not wander from the matter in hand.

ccxl **Make use of Folly**. The wisest play this card at times, and there are times when the greatest wisdom lies in seeming not to be wise. You need

---

[152] Orig. "Pensará partir peras y partirá piedras." Schop. "Man glaubt Kirschen mit ihnen zu essen, wird aber nur die steine erhalten."
[153] cf. Span. prov. "A quien dizes poridad á esse tu das la liberdad," neither tell secrets nor listen to them—Eng. I. puts it rather neatly: "Tis a maxim for secrets Neither to hear them nor to tell them"; cf. the maxim of the Seven Sages, ap. Stobaeus, Flor. iii. 80: "Tell none a secret."
[154] cf. xxxiv, ccxxv

not be unwise, but merely affect unwisdom. To be wise with fools and foolish with the wise were of little use. Speak to each in his own language[155]. He is no fool who affects folly, but he is who suffers from it. Ingenuous folly rather than the pretended is the true foolishness, since cleverness has arrived at such a pitch. To be well liked one must dress in the skin of the simplest of animals.

ccxli **Put up with Raillery, but do not practise it**. The first is a form of courtesy, the second may lead to embarrassment. To snarl at play has something of the beast and seems to have more. Audacious raillery is delightful: to stand it proves power. To show oneself annoyed causes the other to be annoyed. Best leave it alone; the surest way not to put on the cap that might fit. The most serious matters have arisen out of jests. Nothing requires more tact and attention. Before you begin to joke know how far the subject of your joke is able to bear it.

ccxlii **Push Advantages**. Some put all their strength in the commencement and never carry a thing to a conclusion. They invent but never execute. These be paltering spirits. They obtain no fame, for they sustain no game to the end. Everything stops[156] at a single stop. This arises in some from impatience, which is the failing of the Spaniard, as patience is the virtue of the Belgian. The latter bring things to an end, the former come to an end with things. They sweat away till the obstacle is surmounted, but content themselves with surmounting it: they do not know how to push the victory home. They prove that they can but will not: but this proves always that they cannot, or have no stability. If the undertaking is good, why not finish it? If it is bad, why undertake it? Strike down your quarry, if you are wise; be not content to flush it.

ccxliii **Do not be too much of a Dove**. Alternate the cunning of the serpent with the candour of the dove. Nothing is easier than to deceive an honest man. He believes in much who lies in naught; who does no deceit, has much confidence. To be deceived is not always due to stupidity, it may arise from sheer goodness. There are two sets of men who can guard themselves from injury: those who have experienced it at their own cost, and those who have observed it at the cost of others. Prudence should use as much suspicion as subtlety uses snares, and none need be so good as to enable others to do him ill. Combine in yourself the dove and the serpent, not as a monster but as a prodigy.

ccxliv **Create a feeling of Obligation**. Some transform favours received into favours bestowed, and seem, or let it be thought, that they are

---

[155] cf. Prov. xxvi. 5, "Answer a fool according to his folly
[156] Orig. "Todo para en parar." Schop. omits.

doing a favour when receiving one. There are some so astute that they get honour by asking, and buy their own advantage with applause from others. They manage matters so cleverly that they seem to be doing others a service when receiving one from them. They transpose the order of obligation with extraordinary skill, or at least render it doubtful who has obliged whom. They buy the best by praising it, and make a flattering honour out of the pleasure they express. They oblige by their courtesy, and thus make men beholden for what they themselves should be beholden. In this way they conjugate "to oblige" in the active instead of in the passive voice, thereby proving themselves better politicians than grammarians. This is a subtle piece of *finesse*; a still greater is to perceive it, and to retaliate on such fools' bargains by paying in their own coin, and so coming by your own again.

ccxlv **Original and out-of-the-way Views** are signs of superior ability. We do not think much of a man who never contradicts us that is no sign he loves us, but rather that he loves himself. Do not be deceived by flattery, and thereby have to pay for it: rather condemn it. Besides you may take credit for being censured by some, especially if they are those of whom the good speak ill. On the contrary, it should disturb us if our affairs please every one, for that is a sign that they are of little worth. Perfection is for the few.

ccxlvi **Never offer Satisfaction unless it is demanded.** And if they do demand it, it is a kind of crime to give more than necessary. To excuse oneself before there is occasion is to accuse oneself[157]. To draw blood in full health gives the hint to ill-will. An excuse unexpected arouses suspicion from its slumbers. Nor need a shrewd person show himself aware of another's suspicion, which is equivalent to seeking out offence. He had best disarm distrust by the integrity of his conduct.

ccxlvii **Know a little more, live a little less.** Some say the opposite. To be at ease is better than to be at business. Nothing really belongs to us but time, which even he has who has nothing else. It is equally unfortunate to waste your precious life in mechanical tasks or in a profusion of important work. Do not heap up occupation and thereby envy: otherwise you complicate life and exhaust your mind. Some wish to apply the same principle to knowledge, but unless one knows one does not truly live.

ccxlviii **Do not go with the last Speaker.** There are persons who go by the latest edition, and thereby go to irrational extremes. Their feelings and desires are of wax: the last comer stamps them with his seal and obliterates all previous impressions. These never gain anything, for they lose everything so soon. Every one dyes them with his own colour. They are of

---

[157] Orig. "El escusarse antes de ocasion es culparse"; cf. Fr. prov. "Qui s'excuse s'accuse."

no use as confidants; they remain children their whole life. Owing to this instability of feeling and volition, they halt along cripples in will and thought, and totter from one side of the road to the other.

ccxlix ***Never begin Life with what should end it***. Many take their amusement at the beginning, putting off anxiety to the end; but the essential should come first and accessories afterwards if there is room. Others wish to triumph before they have fought. Others again begin with learning things of little consequence and leave studies that would bring them fame and gain to the end of life. Another is just about to make his fortune when he disappears from the scene. Method is essential for knowledge and for life.

ccl ***When to change the Conversation***. When they talk scandal. With some all goes contrariwise: their No is Yes, and their Yes No. If they speak ill of a thing it is the highest praise. For what they want for themselves they depreciate to others. To praise a thing is not always to speak well of it, for some, to avoid praising what's good, praise what's bad, and nothing is good for him for whom nothing is bad.

ccli ***Use human Means as if there were no divine ones, and divine as if there were no human ones***[158]. A masterly rule: it needs no comment.

cclii ***Neither belong entirely to Yourself nor entirely to Others***. Both are mean forms of tyranny. To desire to be all for oneself is the same as desiring to have all for oneself. Such persons will not yield a jot or lose a tittle of their comfort. They are rarely beholden, lean on their own luck, and their crutch generally breaks. It is convenient at times to belong to others, that others may belong to us. And he that holds public office is no more nor less than a public slave, or let a man give up both berth and burthen[159], as the old woman said to Hadrian. On the other hand, others are all for others, which is folly, that always flies to extremes, in this case in a most unfortunate manner. No day, no hour, is their own, but they have so much too much of others that they may be called the slaves of all[160]. This applies even to knowledge, where a man may know everything for others and nothing for himself. A shrewd man knows that others when they seek him do not seek *him*, but their advantage in him and by him.

---

[158] cf. "Human wit ought to be exhausted before we presume to invoke Divine interposition" (B. Disraeli, *Tancred*).
[159] Orig. "Renuncie el cargo con la carga." The story goes that an old woman met Hadrian with a petition. He repulsed her, saying he had no time. "Then give up your berth," retorted the beldam. Hadrian recognised the justice of the rebuke and decided the petition on the spot.
[160] cf. "Men in great Place are thrice servants" (Bacon, Essay "Of Great Place"). There is something like this in *El Criticon*, i. 7.

cccliii **Do not Explain overmuch**[161]. Most men do not esteem what they understand[162], and venerate what they do not see. To be valued things should cost dear: what is not understood becomes overrated. You have to appear wiser and more prudent than he requires with whom you deal, if you desire to give him a high opinion of you: yet in this there should be moderation and no excess. And though with sensible people common sense holds its own, with most men a little elaboration is necessary. Give them no time for blame: occupy them with understanding your drift. Many praise a thing without being able to tell why, if asked. The reason is that they venerate the unknown[163] as a mystery, and praise it because they hear it praised.

ccliv **Never despise an Evil, however small**, for they never come alone[164]: they are linked together like pieces of good fortune. Fortune and misfortune generally go to find their fellows. Hence all avoid the unlucky and associate with the fortunate. Even the doves with all their innocence resort to the whitest walls. Everything fails with the unfortunate—himself, his words, and his luck. Do not wake Misfortune when she sleeps[165]. One slip is a little thing[166]: yet some fatal loss may follow it till you do not know where it will end. For just as no happiness is perfect, so no ill-luck is complete. Patience serves with what comes from above; prudence with that from below.

cclv **Do Good a little at a time, but often**. One should never give beyond the possibility of return. Who gives much does not give but sells. Nor drain gratitude to the dregs, for when the recipient sees all return is impossible he breaks off correspondence. With many persons it is not necessary to do more than overburden them with favours to lose them altogether: they cannot repay you, and so they retire, preferring rather to be enemies than perpetual debtors. The idol never wishes to see before him the sculptor who shaped him, nor does the benefited wish to see his benefactor always before his eyes. There is a great subtlety in giving what costs little yet is much desired, so that it is esteemed the more.

cclvi **Go armed against Discourtesy**, and against perfidy, presumption, and all other kinds of folly. There is much of it in the world, and prudence lies in avoiding a meeting with it. Arm yourself each day before the mirror of attention with the weapons of defence. Thus you will

---

[161] cf. "Let the wise be warned against too great readiness of explanation" (G. Eliot,*Middlemarch*).
[162] cf.— "Was man nicht weiss, das eben brauchte man,
Und was man weiss kann man nicht brauchen."GOETHE, Faust, Th. I.
[163] cf. "Omne ignotum pro magnifico."
[164] cf. Span. prov. *ap. Don Quixote*, i. 28, "Un mal llama á otro," and Shakespeare, "When sorrows come, they come not single spies, But in battalions," *Hamlet*, iv. 5.
[165] cf. Span. prov. "Quando la mala Fortuna se duerme, nadie la despierte."
[166] cf. Stevenson, *Dr. Jekyll*.

beat down the attacks of folly. Be prepared for the occasion, and do not expose your reputation to vulgar contingencies. Armed with prudence, a man cannot be disarmed by impertinence. The road of human intercourse is difficult, for it is full of ruts which may jolt our credit. Best to take a byway, taking Ulysses as a model of shrewdness. Feigned misunderstanding is of great value in such matters. Aided by politeness it helps us over all, and is often the only way out of difficulties.

cclvii **Never let Matters come to a Rupture**, for our reputation always comes injured out of the encounter. Every one may be of importance as an enemy if not as a friend. Few can do us good, almost any can do us harm. In Jove's bosom itself even his eagle never nestles securely from the day he has quarrelled with a beetle. Hidden foes use the paw of the declared enemy to stir up the fire, and meanwhile they lie in ambush for such an occasion. Friends provoked become the bitterest of enemies. They cover their own failings with the faults of others. Every one speaks as things seem to him, and things seem as he wishes them to appear. All blame us at the beginning for want of foresight, at the end for lack of patience, at all times for imprudence. If, however, a breach is inevitable, let it be rather excused as a slackening of friendship than by an outburst of wrath: here is a good application of the saying about a good retreat.

cclviii **Find out some one to share your Troubles**. You will never be all alone, even in dangers, nor bear all the burden of hate. Some think by their high position to carry off the whole glory of success, and have to bear the whole humiliation of defeat. In this way they have none to excuse them, none to share the blame. Neither fate nor the mob are so bold against two. Hence the wise physician, if he has failed to cure, looks out for some one who, under the name of a consultation, may help him carry out, the corpse. Share weight and woe, for misfortune falls with double force on him that stands alone.

cclix **Anticipate Injuries and turn them into Favours**. It is wiser to avoid than to revenge them. It is an uncommon piece of shrewdness to change a rival into a confidant, or transform into guards of honour those who were aiming attacks at us. It helps much to know how to oblige, for he leaves no time for injuries that fills it up with gratitude. That is true *savoir faire* to turn anxieties into pleasures. Try and make a confidential relation out of ill-will itself.

cclx **We belong to none and none to us, entirely**. Neither relationship nor friendship nor the most intimate connection is sufficient to effect this. To give one's whole confidence is quite different from giving one's regard. The closest intimacy has its exceptions, without which the laws of friendship would be broken. The friend always keeps one secret to himself, and even the son always hides something from his father. Some things are kept from one that are revealed to another and *vice versâ*. In this way one reveals all and conceals all, by making a distinction among the persons with whom we are connected.

cclxi **Do not follow up a Folly**. Many make an obligation out of a blunder, and because they have entered the wrong path think it proves their strength of character to go on in it. Within they regret their error, while outwardly they excuse it. At the beginning of their mistake they were regarded as inattentive, in the end as fools. Neither an unconsidered promise nor a mistaken resolution are really binding. Yet some continue in their folly and prefer to be constant fools.

cclxii **Be able to Forget**. It is more a matter of luck than of skill. The things we remember best are those better for-gotten. Memory is not only unruly, leaving us in the lurch when most needed, but stupid as well, putting its nose into places where it is not wanted. In painful things it is active, but neglectful in recalling the pleasurable. Very often the only remedy for the ill is to forget it, and all we forget is the remedy. Nevertheless one should cultivate good habits of memory, for it is capable of making existence a Paradise or an Inferno. The happy are an exception who enjoy innocently their simple happiness.

cclxiii **Many things of Taste one should not possess oneself**. One enjoys them better if another's than if one's own. The owner has the good of them the first day, for all the rest of the time they are for others. You take a double enjoyment in other men's property, being without fear of spoiling it and with the pleasure of novelty. Everything tastes better for having been without it: even water from another's well tastes like nectar. Possession not alone hinders enjoyment: it increases annoyance whether you lend or keep. You gain nothing except keeping things for or from others, and by this means gain more enemies than friends.

cclxiv **Have no careless Days**[167]. Fate loves to play tricks, and will heap up chances to catch us unawares. Our intelligence, prudence, and courage, even our beauty, must always be ready for trial. For their day of careless trust will be that of their discredit. Care always fails just when it was most wanted. It is thoughtlessness that trips us up into destruction. Accordingly it is a piece of military strategy to put perfection to its trial when unprepared. The days of parade are known and are allowed to pass by, but the day is chosen when least expected so as to put valour to the severest test.

---

[167] D'Artagnan acts on this principle in keeping always on guard over the king during journeys. *Vicomte de Bragelonne*, c. xii.

cclxv **Set those under you difficult Task**, Many have proved themselves able at once when they had to deal with a difficulty, just as fear of drowning makes a swimmer of a man, In this way many have discovered their own courage, knowledge, or tact, which but for the opportunity would have been for ever buried beneath their want of enterprise. Dangers are the occasions to create a name for oneself; and if a noble mind sees honour at stake, he will do the work of thousands. Queen Isabella the Catholic knew well this rule of life, as well as all the others, and to a shrewd favour of this kind from her the Great Captain[168] won his fame, and many others earned an undying name. By this great art she made great men.

cclxvi **Do not become Bad from sheer Goodness**. That is, by never getting into a temper. Such men without feeling are scarcely to be considered men. It does not always arise from laziness, but from sheer inability. To feel strongly on occasion is something personal: birds soon mock at the mawkin. It is a sign of good taste to combine bitter and sweet. All sweets is diet for children and fools. It is very bad to sink into such insensibility out of very goodness.

cclxvii **Silken Words[169], sugared Manners**. Arrows pierce the body, insults the soul. Sweet pastry perfumes the breath. It is a great art in life to know how to sell wind. Most things are paid for in words, and by them you can remove impossibilities. Thus we deal in air, and a royal breath can produce courage and power. Always have your mouth full of sugar[170] to sweeten your words, so that even your ill-wishers enjoy them. To please one must be peaceful.

cclxviii **The Wise do at once what the Fool does at last[171]**. Both do the same thing; the only difference lies in the time they do it: the one at the right time, the other at the wrong. Who starts out with his mind topsyturvy will so continue till the end. He catches by the foot what he ought to knock on the head, he turns right into left, and in all his acts is but a child. There is only one way to get him in the right way, and that is to force him to do what he might have done of his own accord. The wise man, on the other hand, sees at once what must be done sooner or later, so he does it willingly and gains honour thereby,

cclxix **Make use of the Novelty of your Position**; for men are valued while they are new. Novelty pleases all because it is uncommon, taste

---

[168] Orig. "El gran Capitan," a reference to Gonsalvo de Cordova (1443-1515), who commanded the Spanish land forces against Chas. VIII. in Italy, and received his title "el gran Capitan" July 1496.

[169] Parysatis, mother of the younger Cyrus, advised one who was about to have an audience with a king to use words wrapped in fine linen; cf. Paley, *Greek Wit*, i. No. 152.

[170] cf. *contra* Spurgeon's *John Ploughman's Talk*, "Do not be all sugar, or the world will suck you down."

[171] cf. Span. prov. "Lo que hace el loco á la postre, hace sabio al principio (quoted by Trench,*Proverbs*5, 116).

is refreshed, and a brand new mediocrity is thought more of than accustomed excellence. Ability wears away by use and becomes old. However, know that the glory of novelty is short-lived: after four days respect is gone. Accordingly, learn to utilise the first fruits of appreciation, and seize during the rapid passage of applause all that can be put to use. For once the heat of novelty over, the passion cools and the appreciation of novelty is exchanged for satiety at the customary: believe that all has its season, which soon passes.

cclxx ***Do not condemn alone that which pleases all***. There must be something good in a thing that pleases so many; even if it cannot be explained it is certainly enjoyed. Singularity is always hated, and, when in the wrong, laughed at. You simply destroy respect for your taste rather than do harm to the object of your blame, and are left alone, you and your bad taste. If you cannot find the good in a thing, hide your incapacity and do not damn it straightway. As a general rule bad taste springs from want of knowledge. What all say, is so, or will be so.

cclxxi ***In every Occupation if you know little stick to the safest***. If you are not respected as subtle, you will be regarded as sure. On the other hand, a man well trained can plunge in and act as he pleases. To know little and yet seek danger is nothing else than to seek ruin. In such a case take stand on the right hand, for what is done cannot be undone. Let little knowledge[172] keep to the king's highway, and in every case, knowing or unknowing, security is shrewder than singularity.

cclxxii ***Sell Things by the Tariff of Courtesy***. You oblige people most that way. The bid of an interested buyer will never equal the return gift of an honourable recipient of a favour. Courtesy does not really make presents, but really lays men under obligation, and generosity is the great obligation. To a right-minded man nothing costs more dear that what is given him: you sell it him twice and for two prices: one for the value, one for the politeness. At the same time it is true that with vulgar souls generosity is gibberish, for they do not understand the language of good breeding.

cclxxiii ***Comprehend their Dispositions with whom you deal***, so as to know their intentions. Cause known, effect known, beforehand in the disposition and after in the motive. The melancholy man always foresees misfortunes, the backbiter scandals; having no conception of the good, evil offers itself to them. A man moved by passion always speaks of things differently from what they are; it is his passion speaks, not his reason. Thus each speaks as his feeling or his humour prompts him, and all far from the truth. Learn how to decipher faces and spell out the soul in the features. If a

---

[172] Orig. "A poco saber camino real."

man laughs always[173], set him down as foolish; if never, as false. Beware of the gossip: he is either a babbler or a spy. Expect little good from the misshapen: they generally take revenge on Nature, and do little honour to her, as she has done little to them. Beauty and folly generally go hand in hand.

cclxxiv **Be Attractive.** magnet of your pleasant qualities more to obtain goodwill than good deeds, but apply it to all. Merit is not enough unless supported by grace, which is the sole thing that gives general acceptance, and the most practical means of rule over others. To be in vogue is a matter of luck, yet it can be encouraged by skill, for art can best take root on a soil favoured by nature. There goodwill grows and develops into universal favour.

cclxxv **Join in the Game as far as Decency permits.** Do not always pose and be a bore: this is a maxim for gallant bearing. You may yield a touch of dignity to gain the general good-will: you may now and then go where most go, yet not beyond the bounds of decorum. He who makes a fool of himself in public will not be regarded as discreet in private life. One may lose more on a day of pleasure than has been gained during a whole life of labour. Still you must not always keep away: to be singular is to condemn all others. Still less act the prude—leave that to its appropriate sex: even religious prudery is ridiculous. Nothing so becomes a man as to be a man: a woman may affect a manly bearing as an excellence, but not *vice versâ*.

cclxxvi **Know how to renew your Character**, with the help both of Nature and of Art, Every seven years the disposition changes, they say. Let it be a change for the better and for the nobler in your taste. After the first seven comes reason, with each succeeding lustre let a new excellence be added. Observe this change so as to aid it, and hope also for betterment in others. Hence it arises that many change their behaviour when they change their position or their occupation. At times the change is not noticed till it reaches the height of maturity. At twenty[174] Man is a Peacock, at thirty a Lion, at forty a Camel, at fifty a Serpent, at sixty a Dog, at seventy an Ape, at eighty nothing at all.

cclxxvii[175] **Display yourself.** 'Tis the illumination of talents: for each there comes an appropriate moment; use it, for not every day comes a triumph. There are some dashing men who make much show with a little, a whole exhibition with much. If ability to display them is joined to versatile gifts, they are regarded as miraculous. There are whole nations given to

---

[173] Orig. "Conosca al que siempre rie por falto y al que nunca por falso."
[174] cf. the ages in *Ethics of the Jewish Fathers*, ed. C. Taylor, p. 111; L. Löw, *Die Lebensalter*, p. 22 and *n*.; and Shakespeare in *As You Like It*
[175] *El Discreto*, c. xii

display: the Spanish people take the highest rank in this. Light was the first thing to cause Creation to shine forth. Display fills up much, supplies much, and gives a second existence to things, especially when combined with real excellence. Heaven that grants perfection, provides also the means of display; for one without the other were abortive. Skill is however needed for display. Even excellence depends on circumstances and is not always opportune. Ostentation is out of place when it is out of time. More than any other quality it should be free of any affectation. This is its rock of offence, for it then borders on vanity and so on contempt: it must be moderate to avoid being vulgar, and any excess is despised by the wise. At times it consists in a sort of mute eloquence, a careless display of excellence, for a wise concealment is often the most effective boast, since the very withdrawal from view piques curiosity to the highest. 'Tis a fine subtlety too not to display one's excellence all at one time, but to grant stolen glances at it, more and more as time goes on. Each exploit should be the pledge of a greater, and applause at the first should only die away in expectation of its sequel.

cclxxviii **Avoid Notoriety in all Things**. Even excellences become defects if they become notorious. Notoriety arises from singularity, which is always blamed: he that is singular is left severely alone. Even beauty is discredited by coxcombry, which offends by the very notice it attracts. Still more does this apply to discreditable singularities. Yet among the wicked there are some that seek to be known for seeking novelties in vice so as to attain to the fame of infamy. Even in matters of the intellect want of moderation may degenerate into loquacity.

cclxxix **Do not contradict the Contradicter**. You have to distinguish whether the contra-diction comes from cunning[176] or from vulgarity. It is not always obstinacy, but may be artfulness. Notice this: for in the first case one may get into difficulties, in the other into danger. Caution is never more needed than against spies. There is no such countercheck to the picklock of the mind as to leave the key of caution in the lock.

cclxxx **Be Trustworthy**. Honourable dealing is at an end: trusts are denied: few keep their word: the greater the service, the poorer the reward: that is the way with all the world nowadays. There are whole nations inclined to false dealing: with some treachery has always to be feared, with others breach of promise, with others deceit. Yet this bad behaviour of others should rather be a warning to us than an example. The fear is that the sight of such unworthy behaviour should override our integrity. But a man of honour should never forget what he is because he sees what others are.

---

[176] cf. ccxiii

cclxxxi **Find Favour with Men of Sense**. The tepid Yes of a remarkable man is worth more than all the applause of the vulgar: you cannot make a meal off the smoke of chaff[177]. The wise speak with understanding and their praise gives permanent satisfaction. The sage Antigonus reduced the theatre of his fame to Zeus alone, and Plato called Aristotle his whole school. Some strive to fill their stomach albeit only with the breath of the mob. Even monarchs have need of authors, and fear their pens more than ugly women the painter's pencil.

cclxxxii **Make use of Absence to make yourself more esteemed or valued**. If the accustomed presence diminishes fame, absence augments it. One that is regarded as a lion in his absence may be laughed at when present as the ridiculous result of the parturition of the mountains. Talents get soiled by use, for it is easier to see the exterior rind than the kernel of greatness it encloses. Imagination reaches farther than sight, and disillusion, which ordinarily comes through the ears, also goes out through the ears. He keeps his fame that keeps himself in the centre of public opinion. Even the Phoenix uses its retirement for new adornment and turns absence into desire.

cclxxxiii **Have the Gift of Discovery**. It is a proof of the highest genius, yet when was genius without a touch of madness? If discovery be a gift of genius, choice of means is a mark of sound sense. Discovery comes by special grace and very seldom. For many can follow up a thing when found, but to find it first is the gift of the few, and those the first in excellence and in age. Novelty flatters, and if successful gives the possessor double credit. In matters of judgment novelties are dangerous because leading to paradox, in matters of genius they deserve all praise. Yet both equally deserve applause if successful.

cclxxxiv **Do not be Importunate**, and so you will not be slighted. Respect yourself if you would have others respect you. Be sooner sparing than lavish with your presence. You will thus become desired and so well received. Never come unasked and only go when sent for. If you undertake a thing of your own accord you get all the blame if it fails, none of the thanks if it succeeds. The importunate is always the butt of blame; and because he thrusts himself in without shame he is thrust out with it.

cclxxxv **Never die of another's Ill-luck[178]**. Notice those who stick in the mud, and observe how they call others to their aid so as to console themselves with a companion in misfortune. They seek some one to help them to bear misfortune, and often those who turned the cold shoulder on

---

[177] Orig. "Porque regueldos de aristas no alientan." Schop. omits.
[178] Schop. adds to his copy "y mucho menos de necedad y ruindad agena."

them in prosperity give them now a helping hand. There is great caution needed in helping the drowning without danger to oneself.

cclxxxvi **Do not become responsible for all or for every one**, otherwise you become a slave and the slave of all. Some are born more fortunate than others: they are born to do good as others to receive it. Freedom is more precious than any gifts for which you may be tempted to give it up. Lay less stress on making many dependent on you than on keeping yourself independent of any. The sole advantage of power is that you can do more good[179]. Above all do not regard responsibility as a favour, for generally it is another's plan to make one dependent on him.

cclxxxvii **Never act in a Passion**. If you do, all is lost. You cannot act for yourself if you are not yourself, and passion always drives out reason. In such cases inter-pose a prudent go-between who can only be prudent if he keeps cool. That is why lookers-on see most of the game, because they keep cool. As soon as you notice that you are losing your temper beat a wise retreat. For no sooner is the blood up than it is spilt, and in a few moments occasion may be given for many days' repentance for oneself and complaints of the other party.

cclxxxviii **Live for the Moment**. Our acts and thoughts and all must be determined by circumstances. Will when you may, for time and tide wait for no man. Do not live by certain fixed rules, except those that relate to the cardinal virtues. Nor let your will subscribe fixed conditions, for you may have to drink the water to-morrow which you cast away to-day. There be some so absurdly paradoxical that they expect all the circumstances of an action should bend to their eccentric whims and not *vice versâ*. The wise man knows that the very polestar of prudence lies in steering by the wind[180].

cclxxxix **Nothing depreciates a Man more than to show he is a Man like other Men**. The day he is seen to be very human he ceases to be thought divine. Frivolity is the exact opposite of reputation. And as the reserved are held to be more than men, so the frivolous are held to be less. No failing causes such failure of respect. For frivolity is the exact opposite of solid seriousness. A man of levity cannot be a man of weight even when he is old, and age should oblige him to be prudent. Although this blemish is so common it is none the less despised.

ccxc **'Tis a piece of good Fortune to combine Men's Love and Respect**. Generally one dare not be liked if one would be respected. Love is more sensitive than hate. Love and honour do not go well together. So that one should aim neither to be much feared nor much loved. Love introduces

---

[179] cf. clxxxvii; cf. "Power to doe good is the true and lawfull end of Aspiring" (Bacon, "Of Great Place").
[180] The derangement of metaphors is mine; orig. has simply "En portarse à la ocasion."

confidence, and the further this advances, the more respect recedes. Prefer to be loved with respect rather than with passion, for that is a love suitable for many.

ccxci **Know how to Test**. The care of the wise must guard against the snare of the wicked[181]. Great judgment is needed to test that of another. It is more important to know the characteristics and properties of persons than those of vegetables and minerals. It is indeed one of the shrewdest things in life. You can tell metals by their ring and men by their voice. Words are proof of integrity, deeds still more. Here one requires extraordinary care, deep observation, subtle discernment, and judicious decision.

ccxcii **Let your personal Qualities surpass those of your Office**, Let it not be the other way about. How-ever high the post, the person should be higher. An extensive capacity expands and dilates more and more as his office becomes higher. On the other hand, the narrow-minded will easily lose heart and come to grief with diminished responsibilities and reputation. The great Augustus thought more of being a great man than a great prince. Here a lofty mind finds fit place, and well-grounded confidence finds its opportunity.

ccxciii **Maturity**. It is shown in the costume, still more in the customs. Material weight is the sign of a precious metal; moral, of a precious man. Maturity gives finish to his capacity and arouses respect. A composed bearing in a man forms a *façade* to his soul. It does not consist in the insensibility of fools, as frivolity would have it, but in a calm tone of authority. With men of this kind sentences are orations and acts are deeds. Maturity finishes a man off, for each is so far a complete man according as he possesses maturity. On ceasing to be a child a man begins to gain seriousness and authority.

ccxciv **Be moderate in your Views**. Every one holds views according to his interest, and imagines he has abundant grounds for them. For with most men judgment has to give way to inclination. It may occur that two may meet with exactly opposite views and yet each thinks to have reason on his side, yet reason is always true to itself and never has two faces. In such a difficulty a prudent man will go to work with care, for his decision of his opponent's view may cast doubt on his own. Place yourself in such a case in the other man's place and then investigate the reasons for his opinion. You will not then condemn him or justify yourself in such a confusing way.

ccxcv[182] **Do not affect what you have not effected**. Many claim exploits without the slightest claim. 'With the greatest coolness they make a

---

[181] Orig. "Compita la atencion del juyzioso con la detencion del recatado."
[182] *El Discreto*, c. xix

mystery of all. Chameleons of applause they afford others a surfeit of laughter. Vanity is always objectionable, here it is despicable. These ants of honour go crawling about filching scraps of exploits. The greater your exploits the less you need affect them: content yourself with doing, leave the talking to others. Give away your deeds but do not sell them. And do not hire venal pens to write down praises in the mud, to the derision of the knowing ones. Aspire rather to be a hero than merely to appear one.

ccxcvi **Noble Qualities**. Noble qualities make noblemen[183]: a single one of them is worth more than a multitude of mediocre ones. There was once a man who made all his belongings, even his household utensils, as great as possible. How much more ought a great man see that the qualities of his soul are as great as possible. In God all is eternal and infinite, so in a hero everything should be great and majestic, so that all his deeds, nay, all his words, should he pervaded by a transcendent majesty.

ccxcvii **Always act as if your Acts were seen**. He must see all round who sees that men see him or will see him. He knows that walls have ears and that ill deeds rebound back. Even when alone he acts as if the eyes of the whole world were upon him. For as he knows that sooner or later all will be known, so he considers those to be present as witnesses who must afterwards hear of the deed. He that wished the whole world might always see him did not mind that his neighbours could see him over their walls.

ccxcviii **Three Things go to a Prodigy**. They are the choicest gifts of Heaven's prodigality—a fertile genius, a profound intellect, a pleasant and refined taste. To think well is good, to think right is better: 'tis the understanding of the good. It will not do for the judgment to reside in the backbone: it would be of more trouble than use. To think aright is the fruit of a reasonable nature. At twenty the will rules; at thirty the intellect; at forty the judgment. There are minds that shine in the dark like the eyes of the lynx, and are most clear where there is most darkness. Others are more adapted for the occasion: they always hit on that which suits the emergency: such a quality produces much and good; a sort of fecund felicity. In the meantime good taste seasons the whole of life.

ccxcix **Leave off Hungry**. One ought to remove even the bowl of nectar from the lips. Demand is the measure of value. Even with regard to bodily thirst it is a mark of good taste to slake but not to quench it. Little and good is twice good. The second time comes a great falling off. Surfeit of pleasure was ever dangerous and brings down the ill-will of the Highest Powers. The only way to please is to revive the appetite by the hunger that

---

[183] Orig. "Las primeras hazen los primeros hombres."

is left. If you must excite desire, better do it by the impatience of want than by the repletion of enjoyment. Happiness earned gives double joy.

ccc ***In one word, be a Saint.*** So is all said at once. Virtue is the link of all perfections, the centre of all the felicities. She it is that makes a man prudent, discreet, sagacious, cautious, wise, courageous, thoughtful, trustworthy, happy, honoured, truthful, and a universal Hero. Three HHH's make a man happy—Health, Holiness, and a Headpiece.[184]

Virtue is the sun of the microcosm, and has for hemisphere a good conscience. She is so beautiful that she finds favour with both God and man. Nothing is lovable but virtue, nothing detestable but vice. Virtue alone is serious, all else is but jest. A man's capacity and greatness are to be measured by his virtue and not by his fortune. She alone is all-sufficient. She makes men lovable in life, memorable after death.

About the NOTES

ORIG. refers to the Spanish original, generally from the Barcelona edition of 1734, though I have occasionally referred to the Madrid edition of 1653, and at times used the text of the *Biblioteca de autores epañoles*. This may have occasioned some inconsistencies, especially with regard to accentuation. Schop. refers to Schopenhauer's translation; I have used Grisebach's edition in the Reclam series. M.G.D. is prefixed to quotations from Sir M. Grant Duff's renderings in Fort. Rev., March 1877; Eng. I. and II. refer to the English translations of 1694 and Savage's of 1902 respectively.

THE END

---

[184] Orig. "Tres eses hazen dichoso, Santo, Sano y Sabio." Schop. "Drei Dinge die in Spanischen mit einem S anfangen machen glücklich —Heiligkeit, Gesundheit, and Weisheit." M.G.D. "Three SSS render a man happy, Sanctity, Soundness of body, and Sageness."

BOOK TWO
THE CRITICK

Translated by Sir Paul Rycaut

Sir Paul Rycaut (1629-1700): An author and diplomat, Rycaut was the leading authority of his day on the Ottoman Empire. Rycaut spent seventeen years in Turkey first (1661) as secretary to the English Ambassador in Constantinople, then English Consul for the Levant Company in Smyrna (1667-1678). This was followed by a brief spell as chief secretary in Ireland under James II, and eleven years as British resident at the Hanse Towns for William and Mary. He wrote *The Present State of the Ottoman Empire* (1665) and *The History of the Turkish empire (1623-1677)*. Besides translating Gracián's work, Rycaut also translated (1685) the 1479 *Historia B. Platinae de Vitis Pontificum Romanorum* [Lives of the Popes] of Bartolomeo Platina, Vatican Librarian.

The Epistle dedicatory

To the KING.

May it please your most excellent majesty,

This little treatise, which was written in my youth, was the first fruits of my travels, and ought to have been offered in the years of my minority, when perhaps it had looked much more like myself than it does at present: but because the words only are mine, and the sense and scope the thoughts and contrivance of a serious don; the subject will be liable to no other incongruity, than that which is now common in the world, where we see men of years and gravity dressed in the hair and fashion of the youthful. But be the attire what it will, I am sure the subject, which is morality, giving rules for a virtuous and prudent life, is seasonable in all ages; and much more conducing to the common good of your majesties' kingdoms, than the swarms of libels, and seditious pamphlets, which fill the press; and are the entertainments of men who are wanton and at ease. It is want of true morality which makes men censurers of others actions, neglecting in the meantime to pry into their own: It makes them proud, high-minded, and boasters, and gives them confidence to arraign princes, and their cabinet counsels of government; whilst in the mean time they are so far from ruling their own little world within them, that they are not able to subdue a passion, or moderate that little, or untowardly member of their tongue. But our *CRITICK*, which suggests better things, does with that humility which he teaches, appear before your majesty, being conducted to your royal presence by the interpreter, who having received encouragement by the gracious eye, your majesty has been pleased to bestow on his other writings, does with greater boldness, and yet with due reverence, tender this at your royal feet, praying always for the long life of your sacred majesty, in which the peace, prosperity, and welfare of your people is bound up; and that God Almighty may ever bless your majesty with increase of honour, triumph, and greater exaltation of glory, are the unfeigned, and fervent prayers of,

most *dread* *sovereign,*
your MAJESTY'S
most dutiful subject, and
most humble servant,

PAUL RYCAUT.

THE TRANSLATOR TO THE READER.

When I was about the age of twenty, of which I had spent five in the University of Cambridge, my good father, who was desirous to bestow on me a liberal education (though the youngest of his ten sons) and to improve me in all the languages which are common to Europe, thought fit to send me to the Court of Spain in company with my eldest brother, whose principal business there was to recover a debt of one hundred thousand pieces of eight, which his Catholic majesty owed unto my father:

The demand was unquestionable, for the account was liquid, and clearly stated by the Council of the exchequer, and the King upon their report, was pleased to give his own royal firm for confirmation of it, and to make several decrees for the payment; but as the proceedings in Spain are always dilatory, and the King's revenue most commonly anticipated, so our private pretensions were forced to give place to the more importunate necessities of the public, and after a year and half's solicitation, we were dispatched thence with a poor Auyda de costas, or something under the name of a largess, to bear our expenses, paid in vellion, or the base copper money of Spain. Since which the interest has increased without either payment of it, or of the principal, though our King of Great Britain (whom God preserve) has been graciously pleased often to recommend our case to his ambassadors sent to Madrid, and to make it one particular in their Instructions: but all this being without effect, gave me often cause to conclude, that it was much better, and of more Security to have a mortgage on good Farms and Tenements in England, than of honour to be a creditor of the most mighty and Potent monarch of both the Indies.

But I, who in the gaiety of my youth, little regarded the interest of wealth, leaving that care to the incumbence of my pious parents, attended wholly to the improvements of my mind; and to that end, not to lose time, I studied awhile at Alcala de Henares, called in Latin, Collegium Complusense, where I had the honour to be esteemed more for my skill in the Latin tongue, and my faculty in poetry, than ever I had a reputation for in my own university; I there applied myself especially to learn the Spanish tongue, in gaining of which I had something more than an ordinary advantage, by having no conversation with English; and than this book of the Critick being newly published and recommended to me for being wrote by one of the best wits and pens of Spain; I was easily persuaded to read it over; the style being smooth and pleasant in the beginning, gave me an easy introduction to it; but the remainder being more harsh, and crabbed, I forced myself with some difficulty to understand the sense and humour of the author, fancying in the mean time, that I was entered into those steep and thorny ways of virtue, which Critilo teaches, and from which no difficulties ought to divert, or discourage a wise and a resolved person. When I had once read it, I was so pleased with the subject, that I was willing to try how it would run in English; which being finished, I was infinitely pleased with the work, both for the argument, which is virtue, & morality, and for my own improvement by the translation; for it had almost made me a master of the Spanish tongue. Howsoever, as our greatest enjoyments, and things which please our minds most at first, grow dull, and disrelishing with time; so these beloved papers were neglected, and thrown by me whilst I had occasion to travel the world; for I was afterwards in Italy, and there I embarked on the fleet under command of General Blake, and was present at the burning of nine Turkish ships, and battering the castles at Porta Farina, near Tunis; I also spent about two years in the Low Countries, when his majesty resided at Brussels; after which having the employment of Secretary to the Earl of Winchilsea at Constantinople for seven years, and subsequent to that of consul at Smyrna, for the space of eleven more, I was so taken up with the thoughts and business of that country, that I had no leisure to remember, or reflect upon my little Critick. But now, being by God's providence returned to a more quiet, and reposed life in my own country, and tumbling one day over my old memoirs, these papers casually offered themselves to my hands, torn and worm-eaten with bad ink, and in every manner ill- treated. When I saw them, I presently knew and owned them, recalling them to my mind and acquaintance, and with much eagerness and delight I read them over, because they lively represented to my memory and fancy the verdures of my youth, which I found to be over affectionate to words, and romantic expressions; howsoever I observed, that I kept close to the sense, and that I was as faithful even in those years to the author whom I translated, as I was to the charge, and interest which I afterwards undertook. And though in my late perusal of this book, I have suffered it to pass with little alteration, that so it might appear more like to a product of my youth; yet having now ruminated with more serious, and mature reflections, on the subject of its discourse, than I was capable to do formerly, my judgment tells me that this treatise is neither misbecoming my present years, nor unseasonable to the present times. It begins like a Spanish novel, placing the scene of discourse in the ocean, and in the Isle of St. Helen, where a man is strangely figured to have been enclosed in the darkness of a cave, and fed by beasts, until he arrived to some maturity of age; which is purposely designed to introduce the notions, which a man may by the mere light of his immaterial soul, without sight, or conversation, conceive of a deity, and of his own being. Than he fancies, a whirl-wind or hurricane to break open the cavern of this natural man, and all on a sudden to represent a new scene to him of Heaven, and Earth, and sea; and than he strives to express the ecstasies of his soul, and the strange conceptions he must entertain upon the view of such different objects: Thance he descends from the natural to the moral world, drawing a scheme of the follies and vanities of it, in order to a true regulation of life, built on the foundation of morality, and virtue. I am of opinion, that the author of this book might originally have deduced his fancy from the History of *Hai Ebn Yokdhan*, wrote in Arabic by Ebn Tophail, and translated into Latin by Dr. Pocock; and though there is much difference in the relation of one, and the other, yet the design of both is almost the same, being only to show how far the spiritual and immortal soul of man, is able in its natural capacity, and by its own reflex acts to consider its proper being, and the existence of something above it; and by degrees, and steps of exterior objects to proceed unto rules for conservation of its own well-being, and that of others. The subject of this fancy being much affected and enlarged by Arabians, it is probable that from them it was derived to the moors, who have the same language with little diversity of dialect, and accent common together: and the Spaniards, who for the space of 600 years had the same country and manners with moors, easily received their fashions, learning, proverbs, and every thing but their religion: So that as their customs and way of living are different to other nations of Europe, and most resemble that of the eastern countries; so their way of writing in dialogues and novels is much after that manner, and is as well pleasant and diverting in itself, as it is curious to us, who follow another form, and manner in all our books, and treatises of philosophy. And thus, reader, having given thee some intimation concerning the substance of this book; the occasion on which it was translated; and the reasons, why after so many years, it came to be published. I leave thee to a perusal of it, which I beseech thee to do, with the same candour, which is to be allowed to the works of youthful fancies. Farewell.

The Spring of Childhood, and the Summer of Youth.

The First Crisis

Now both worlds had kissed the feet of Catholic Philip their universal monarch: and the circle of his royal crown, the greatest stage the sun runs both in the one and the other hemisphere: within whose crystalline centre lies enamelled a small isle, or pearl of the sea, or emerald of the land: to which the august empress gave it her own name, that it might be queen of all other isles, and crown of the ocean. This isle of St. Helena (for so it is called) in the passage from one world to the other, yields refreshment to the grand cargason of Europe, and has always been a free-port, preserved by divine providence between those immense gulfs to afford entertainment for the Eastern Catholic Fleet.

To this place a shipwrecked person endeavoured to make his port, who striving with the waves, and contending with the winds, but more with his own sad disasters, a monster of Nature, and of fortune, a swan in his hoariness, and voice, sinking on his plank, between the fatal medium of life, and death, thus complained.

"O Life! thou shouldst never have begun, but since thou hast, thou shouldst never end: there is nothing more desired, nor yet nothing more frail, than thou art, and he, who once looseth thee, too late seeks to recover thee; for ever after I esteem thee for lost: Nature has showed herself a stepmother to man, denying him a sense to rejoice at his birth, and yet to fill him with sad apprehensions at his death: to make him insensible of the good he receives at his beginning, and yet to affright and torment him with a combination of mischiefs at his end. O tyrant! a thousand times more cruel than humane Nature is capable to be, who first through a scandalous temerity trusted his life to this inconstant element on no better support than a frail vessel; They say his breast was covered with steel, but I think it was doubled with iron. In vain has the supreme providence separated nations with seas and mountains, since human boldness has found a bridge to transport its malice. Whatsoever humane industry has invented, has been unfortunately retorted to its own destruction. Gun-powder, that horrible devourer of lives, has been an instrument of greatest ruin; and what other is a ship, but a coffin to anticipate the solemnities of death. The land seemed too narrow a theatre to act the tragedies of death, until man found ways to triumph on the seas, and find a passage to his fatal destiny through both elements. By what other means needs unfortunate man seek to perish, than in the hull of his own ship, which like a scaffold seems erected for punishment of his boldness: With Reason did Cato esteem amongst the three Follies of his Life, his embarking to have been the greatest. O fate! O heavens! O fortune! though I would persuade myself that I were something, yet so dost thou pursue me, that when thou beginnest, thou knowest no end but mine. O! that now it were possible for me to be nothing, that I might disclaim that being, which is confined with eternity."

In this manner he beat the air with sighs, whilst his arms rowed the waters, accompanying his art with industry, he seemed to rise above the reach of danger; for perils do both fear and respect great persons, whom death itself is sometimes ambitious to spare, and fortune seeks occasions to advantage. Thus the serpents spared Alcides, the tempests Caesar, the sword great Alexander, and bullets had no commission for Charles the Fifth. But alas! how misfortunes are enwreathed, one is but the introduction, or but the parent to another; for when he thought to reach the secure bosom of our common mothers, he than began to apprehend new fears, lest the enraged waves should dash him against the rocks, which were as hard, as his fortune was cruel; the earth too caught at by his hands, crumbled between them, and tantalized his hopes, when his life seemed almost secured; there being neither water in the seas, nor earth on the land, to assist the miserable. Thus floated he between both elements, in the medium between life, and death, made a sacrifice of his own fortune: when a sprightly youth, an angel in his appearance, but much more in his actions, stretched forth his arms to enclose him, attracting him as the secret virtue of the loadstone does the iron, and securing his happiness together with his life: and being now in safety on the shore, he first kissed the earth, and casting his eyes up to heaven, he gave thanks for his deliverance; and than returning to the restorer of his life, with open arms, endeavoured to gratify him with embraces, and acknowledgments; but he, that had thus obliged him by deeds, could not answer him with words, but only gave demonstrations of the grand satisfaction he received at this accident, and of an astonished admiration, to see one so like himself. The grateful naufrague repeated the expressions of his thanks, and seconded his embraces, asking him of his health and fortune; to all which the astonished islander was silent; wherefore he varied his idioms, and tried him with some other languages, with which he was acquainted; but in vain, since he was a person void of speech; so that turning all into signs and actions, he ceased not to behold, and admire him, mixing the extremes of wonder with contentment. One might reasonably have believed him to have been some incult product of those woods, but that this island being uninhabited by mankind, could not be the native soil of human race; besides the fairness and length of his hair, and the equal proportion of his mouth, was an argument that he was an European; the fashion of his clothes, or garments, could yield no light to any conjectures, being no other than nakedness the livery of innocence. The intelligent naufrague reasoned with himself, whether he was destitute of those two servants of the soul, hearing, and speech; but his experience soon revolved him in that, for he listened to the least noise, and by his ready attention could so aptly imitate the voices of beasts, and chirping of birds, with such natural propriety, that he seemed better to understand brutes than men, so prevalent is the force of custom, and education. From these sensitive actions the vivacity of his spirit darted forth certain rays, as through the twilight of reason, the soul labouring to show, that where education is wanting, Nature of itself is wholly rude and unpolished.

The desire of knowing each others fortunes, and lives, increased equally in both; but the want of a common idiom, was that which envied them this enjoyment; for speech is the grand effect of rationality, and he that cannot discourse, cannot converse. "Speak," saith the Philosopher, "that I may know you;" for the soul does in a noble manner communicate itself, by producing the images of what it conceives in the mind of him that hears, which is properly to converse: there is no presence where there is not discourse, nor can they be termed absent, who communicate by writing. Those wise sages live still, though dead, and discourse with us daily by their immortal volumes, and illuminate posterity with a continued source, and spring of knowledge. Speech is both necessary, and pleasant, which two, wise Nature always conjoined in the functions of life: conversation is ever attended with pleasure, and thance is immediately derived the important affair of knowing, which speech only can administer. Wise men by speaking beget others like themselves, and by converse knowledge is gently instilled into the soul. Hence it is, that men cannot live happily without some common language, both in respect of their necessity, and of their pleasure. For should two infants be cast purposely into an island, they would invent a language to communicate, and converse with each other; so that noble conversation is the daughter of discourse, the mother of wisdom, the ease of the soul, the commerce of hearts, the bond of amity, the food of contentment, and the employment of humanity.

The experienced naufrague being well assured of the truth hereof, began immediately to teach this ignorant youth to exercise speech, who being both desirous and docible, was very apt to improve the flexibility of his tongue: He began by the names of them both, calling himself Critilo, and the other Andrenio, which fitted the ripe judgment of the one, and of the other, in his natural principles. The desire of bringing those conceptions unto light, which had so long inwardly been suppressed, and the curiosity of knowing the truth of what lay clouded, and confused: in his understanding, were strong incitements to the docility of Andrenio: so that now he began to pronounce, than to ask, than to answer, and endeavouring at length to discourse, accompanied his words with action, that sometimes where his words began, his gestures supplied the want of other expressions in the conclusion. The account he gave of his life, was in short and abrupt speeches, so much the more strange, by how much the less understood; and oftentimes, where the improbability of the matter could not gain belief with Critilo, there he pretended to want a true conception of what he related; but when he had learned to continue his discourse, and the number of his words were equal to the greatness of his thoughts, at the earnest desires of Critilo, who afforded him also somewhat of his assistance, began to satisfy him in this manner.

"I," saith he, "neither know who I am, nor who has given me this being, nor to what end he has given it me: which question I often, without words proposed to myself, being as ignorant, as curious; but since queries are caused by ignorance, I had little means to resolve myself: yet so would I prove myself with argument, that I might, if possible, exceed myself; for as yet no affectation to any particular good had so possessed me, but that withdrawing my soul out of ignorance, I might reach the limits of my desires. Thou, Critilo askest who I am, and I desire to know that of thee; for thou art the first man that until this day I have seen, in whom I find myself more perfectly delineated, than in the silent crystals of a fountain, which oftimes my curiosity carried me unto, and my ignorance applauded; but if you would be informed of the most material success of my life, I shall relate that to you, which is more strange than long, or tedious."

"The first time that I could take knowledge of myself, and form conceptions of my being, I found myself immured within the bowels of that mountain, which though it hangs out beyond the rest, yet its height asserts its honour and eminency above the other rocks. There it was that I received my first nourishment from one of those which you call brutes, but I call mother, believing myself to have been born from her, and that she had given me the being I am endued with."

"It is very agreeable," replied Critilo, "to natural ignorance to style men fathers, and women mothers, from whom we receive beneficence, in which manner, until now, you esteemed a beast for such; so the world in its infancy called every creature which was profitable, and beneficial, by the name of father, and at length improved that to the title of God."

"So I," proceeded Andrenio, "believed that beast to be my mother, which nourished me at her breasts, and bred me up amongst her young ones, which I esteemed for my brethren, and as a brute amongst the brutes, we played and slept together. She often gave me milk from her own teats, shared me part of her fruits, and prey which she brought for them. At first I was not so sensible of that tedious imprisonment, whilst the interior darkness of my mind accorded with the exterior of my body; and the want of knowledge alleviated the deprivation of light, though some confused glimmerings appeared, which Heaven dispensed at times, through the top of that unhappy cavern."

"But at length arriving at a certain term of growth and life, I was on a sudden surprised with such an extraordinary force of knowledge, with so bright a radiancy of light, and advertency, that I began to make several reflexions upon my own proper being. 'What is this,' said I? 'am I, or am I not? for since I live, and know, and observe, I must have a being: but if I am, who am I? and who has given me this being? And to what end has he given it me? If it be to remain here, it were a high infelicity! Am I a brute like these? No, for I observe most apparent differences between us; for they are covered with hair, but I, as less favoured of him, who gave me this being, am naked, and unclothed; besides, I observed my whole body otherwise proportioned than theirs; I laugh, and weep, they howl, and cry. I walk strait, raising my face upwards, when they move bending with their heads towards the earth.' These were palpable differences, and which observation administered to my understanding. my desire to come out from hence increased daily, and the endeavours to see, and know, as they are natural to every one, so they were in me more than ordinarily violent, and impatient; but that which troubled me most, was to see the brutes my companions, with a strange nimbleness to trip over the indigested heaps, entering out, and returning in at their own pleasure; which I not being able to do, was soon sensible, that that privilege and liberty was denied only unto me."

"I assayed often times to follow those beasts, and crawl over the rocks after them, which I appayed with the blood, that started from my fingers; and I would have helped myself likewise with my teeth, but all in vain, and to my prejudice; for I commonly tumbled to the next bottom, which I left wetted with my blood, and tears: at my voice and cries the compassionate beasts came running to my succour, and dividing me a share of their fruits, and prey, moderated my grief, and in part eased me of my discontent. The want of my outward speech was supplied by my inward thoughts, and soliloquies, and the doubts, and difficulties my observation and curiosity encountered, not being capable of being resolved by my judgment, ended in wonder and admiration; but the confused noise of these seas, was a subject of my continued trouble, whose waves beat more violently against my breast, than these rocks; but what should I think of those affrighting claps of thunder, those encounters in the air, whose clouds dissolved into rain, as my eyes into tears? But that which reduced me from a perplexity of mind, and pangs of soul even to the very agonies of death, were certain voices which I heard from without, somewhat like yours, which at a distance seemed more confused, but afterwards came by little and little more distinct and articulate, which so naturally affected me, that they left me not without strong impressions in my mind. I well observed the difference of them from those of beasts, and from the usual sounds with which I was formerly acquainted, which begot in me a vehement passion, to see, and know from whence they proceeded; but being not able to attain thereunto, I languished in the extremes of despair, and death; and though there were but few things into which I could dive with my thoughts, yet I have neither wanted of them discourse, nor meditation: one thing I can assure you, that I have often, and a thousand times entertained thoughts of the manner and disposition, situation, variety, and composure of these things according to the meanness of my capacity, yet never could attain to the least apprehension of the manner, and order of this various composition, which we now see, and admire."

"This is not much," answered Critilo, for if the wits of all those men, which have been, or shall be hereafter, should unite in one, to trace the artifice of this world's composure, and to consider of its government, their consultations would come short of that providence, which is required in its direction. But why do I instance in the universe? since their art reaches not to the formation of the least flower, or fly; only that supreme creator has found a way, and order to make a harmony in beauty and changeable Variety."

"But tell me, that which I so greatly desire to know, and hear from you, in what manner you came forth from that tedious prison, that untimely grave of your habitation, but especially (if it be possible for you to express) what thoughts, and notions, your admirable spirit conceived, at your first entrance into light, when you discovered, saw and admired the applauded theatre of the universe."

"Hold," said Andrenio, "I had here need to take breath to prosecute a relation so strange and pleasant.

The Second Crisis

They say, that as soon as the supreme artificer had accomplished the composure of the worlds fabric; his next work was to dispose unto every one his order, and apart all kinds in their several and most natural stations. So he summoned all creatures from the elephant to the fly, and showing them the several distinct regions, and elements, left the choice of all to their free and voluntary election. The elephant answered, that he would content himself with a wood, the horse with a meadow, the eagle with one of the regions of the air, the whale in the ocean, the swan in a fishpond, the barbel in the river, and the frog in a pool. The last of all came man, though the first in dignity, who to the question propounded, answered, that he could not content himself with less than all, and that too seemed but little for his enlarged desires. This exorbitant ambition struck no small wonder to those present, though it was soon applauded by a flattering sycophant, as a demand agreeable to the greatness of his mind; though by one with better judgment termed the defect of his depraved corporeal composition. The superficies of this globe seemed too narrow a confinement for his enlarged desires, until in quest of gold, and silver, he found a way to undermine, and rip up the bowels of the Earth. His pride makes him climb to possess the air by the lofty pinnacles of his edifices, lest his ambition should be suffocated, and stifled in the lower region. He compasses the seas, sounds the ocean, dives for pearls, amber, and coral to nourish his folly, and swell his vanity. He taxes each element according to its quality to pay him tribute, the air her birds, the sea her fish, the Earth her beasts, the fire its heat, to entertain, not to satisfy his luxury. And yet, as if all this were insufficient, nothing can appease his complaints of a penurious portion. O monstrous covetousness of man! The supreme creator took him by the hand, "See," said he, "and know, that I have formed man by my own hands, for my servant, and your lord, and like a king, as he is, pretends to govern all. But understand, O man, that this is to be with your mind, and not with your belly, as a man, not as a beast. You ought to be lord of all creatures, and not a slave to them, they ought to follow you, and not you attracted by them. You ought to possess all with knowledge, and acknowledgement, that is contemplating in all these created mirrors the divine perfections, making a step of the creature to pass unto the creator." This relation of prodigies, though a lesson amongst us common to the meanest and most vulgar capacities, was yet strange, and unheard of to Andrenio, who recovering himself from his deep contemplations thereon, and passionate aspirations towards the divine essence, began to proceed in this manner.

"my sleep," said he, prosecuting his former discourse, "was the ordinary pastime of my hours, and the chiefest ease of my melancholy, and solitariness: to that I inclined as a remedy of my discontent, when one night (for all to me were such) a more than ordinary deadness of sleep possessed me, an infallible presager of evil; and so it was, for startling from my slumber, awakened by the vehemency of a gust, burst from the deepest caverns of yonder mountain, which shook the whole fabric, and firm pillars which support it; and whistling through the breach it made, diffused itself into a general tempest with so much rage and violence, as to shake the foundation of the neighbouring rocks, as if its force had been sufficient to have shattered this grand machine into their first nothing."

"Hold," said Critilo, "the mountains themselves are not exempted from change, but exposed to earthquakes, and thunder, their power of resistance being the cause of their subversion."

"But if these Rocks shook," said Andrenio, "what should I? All the joints of my body seemed to be loosed, and dissolved, my heart ready to break with throbs, my senses failed me, that I found myself half dead, and almost buried between the rocks and my own fears; whilst this eclipse of my soul remained, the parenthesis of my life, neither can I know, nor can any other inform me concerning it, at length, I know not how, nor when, I returned by little and little to recover myself from this total dereliction of my spirits; I unclosed my eyes to the dawnings of the day, a day clear, great, and happiest that ever my life has seen, a day which I have noted on the stones and engraved on the rocks. I instantly perceived the doors of my tedious prison broke open, a comfort so transporting me, that I delayed no time to unbury myself, and as one new-born in the world, to leap into it, through that gap, in which appeared the rays, and light of the cheerful heaven: at first, not fully satisfied of the reality, I went round the rock, still suppressing with what power I could the strong rebulliency of my passions: but at length, well assured, I returned to the confused balcony of my life, and prospect, diffusing my eyes in a general view over this grand theatre of heaven and Earth: the whole vigour of my soul applying itself to the windows of my eyes with that contentment, and curiosity, that it disabled the rest of my senses to perform their function, that for a whole day I remained immoveable, insensible, and dead, being overwhelmed by over-powering of too strong a life. I would here express, but it is impossible, the intense violence of my affections, the extravagant raptures of my soul; I can only tell you, that there still remain impressions thereof upon me; and the wonder, and amazement I than conceived, are not so clearly forgotten, but that the sense thereof, do strongly affect me."

"I believe," said Critilo, "that when the eyes see what they never espied, the heart feels, what it was never sensible of."

"I beheld," proceeded Andrenio, "the sea, the land, the heaven, and each severally, and altogether, and in the view of each I transported myself without thoughts of ever ending, admiring, enjoying, and contemplating a fruition which could never satiate me."

"O! How much I envy thee," said Critilo, this unknown happiness of thine, the only privilege of the first man, and you, the faculty of seeing all at once, and that with observation, the greatness, beauty, harmony, stability, and variety of this created fabric. Familiarity in us takes off admiration, and novelty affects little those, who have neither knowledge, nor advertency to enjoy it. For we enter into the world with the eyes of our understanding shut, and when we open them unto knowledge the custom of seeing has rendered the greatest wonders, neither strange, nor admired at the judgment's disclosure. Therefore the wise worthies have repaired much of this defect by reflections, looking back again as it were to a new birth, making everything, by a search and examination into its nature, a new subject of astonishment; admiring, and criticizing on their perfections. Like those, who walk in a delicious garden, diverted solely with their own thoughts, not observing at first the artificial adornments, and variety of flowers; yet afterwards return back to view each plant, and flower with great curiosity: So we enter into this garden of the universe walking from our birth, until our death, without the least glance on the beauty, and perfection of it: unless some wiser heads chance to turn back, and renew their pleasure by a review, and contemplation."

This Andrenio considered to be his greatest happiness, in that he arrived to that height of perfection, which he had so long expected and desired.

"Your happiness," said Critilo, "was your restraint, since afterwards you knocked off your bolts, and arrived at a full fruition both of your own desire, and them; for things that are worth our wishes, and obtained, are twice enjoyed: the greatest wonders, if familiar, and common, soon loose their repute, and an easy access, and a free use makes but a toy of the greatest prodigy; The sun has done us a courtesy in absenting himself at night, that his return may be the more grateful in the morning. What a conjunction of affections must you needs feel? What over-flowings of your senses? How must your soul have been ravished, and employed in its attention on those objects? 'Twas much, you were not over- bourn with a contemplation so violent, and admirable."

"I believe," answered Andrenio, "that whilst my attention was busied in seeing, and observing, it was so fixed on the present object, that it found no force nor power to communicate unto another. But those cheerful emanations of the grand-monarch of light, which you call the sun, crowned with his own beams, and encircled with rays, stroke an awfulness to eyes to render him the reverence, and admiration: at the glory of his throne, at the sovereignty and silence of his majesty, which triumphs in the crystalline waves, and fills all creatures with his bright presence; I was wholly swallowed up in amazement, envying the eagle should be more intent, than myself."

At his naming the sun, Critilo could contain no longer, but instantly cried out, and applauded the comfort, the bliss, the happiness enjoyed in that immortal and glorious light the sun.

"my admiration still increased," said Andrenio, "until my attention grew dim, and amazed, because I desired him at a distance, to whom I feared to approach near, my reason telling me, what I observed that no other light but his could dim my eyes, and that no nearer access could be to him, but only by contemplation."

"The sun," said Critilo, "is that creature, which is the most lively effigies, and abstract of the creator's majesty and greatness. He is called, Sol, because he solely runs the compass of the heavens, his presence outshining the glory of the other luminaries: his situation is in the midst of the celestial orbs, as the centre and heart of Light, the perpetual fountain of rays, a constant and an unchangeable essence, whose virtue assisted us to see other things, and yet covers and hides his own beauty with the veil of his brightness: his influence concurs with more immediate causes to the production of all creatures: nor can man deny him to be the author, and parent of his life. His light is most effectual in being communicated; for diffusing itself into all parts, and piercing the very bowels of the Earth, does with an admirable virtue, strengthan, foment, rejoice, and nourish: his influence is not partial, but common, all having need of him, and he of none. In fine, he is a creature of the greatest pomp and glory, the most resplendent beam of the divine majesty."

"A whole day," said Andrenio, "I was employed in beholding him, sometimes in himself, and sometimes his reflections in the waters being forgetful of my time and self."

At this Critilo remembered what the Philosopher said, that he was born to behold the sun; which was well said, though ill understood; for his meaning was, that in this material sun, he did contemplate the divine glory, for if but an emission, and shadow of him be so bright, what must be the true light of that infinite, and uncreated beauty?

"But alas," said Andrenio, "how soon, like the inconstancy of this world, was the height of my comfort changed into displeasure, the joy of my birth into the horror of my death, the throne of the morning into the grave of the night, the Sun being descended through the waters into another world, left me drowned in a sea of my own tears; but whilst the apprehensions of never seeing him again, did grievously affect me, behold on a sudden a new wonder diverted my thoughts, the appearance of a heaven adorned with stars, changed the scene, and renewed my contentment. This prospect was no less welcome than the other, the variety, and strangeness of the objects affording me an entertainment to busy my attention."

"O that immense wisdom of God!" said Critilo, "which has found a means to make the night no less beautiful and admirable than the day. Absurdly has vulgar ignorance imposed the epithets of drowsy, dark, and uncomely upon the twinklings, and serenity of the night: those descriptions of being the repose of labour, the refreshments and diversion of cares, are but reproaches of its sluggishness and melancholy: but better is it expressed by a person of wisdom, who calls it the time of contemplation and thoughts: and for that reason, was the owl at Athans celebrated as the hieroglyphic of knowledge. The night is not so proper for the ignorant to sleep, as for the wise and studious to watch, the night being to prepare that which the day must execute. In this entertainment my thoughts were soon engaged in a labyrinth of numbering the stars, some whereof only twinkled, others shined clearly, observing their various magnitudes, degrees, motions, and colours, whilst some appeared, others withdrew: all resembling," said Critilo, "human fortune, which is no sooner up, but inclines to his setting."

"But what I much considered," said Andrenio, with small satisfaction, "was that disorderly, and yet admirable disposition of them; for seeing the superior artificer had adorned, and sealed the convexity of the heavens with stars, why he did not dispose them with order and method, interweaving them with pretty knots, and flowery circles: I know not how to declare or express myself."

"I already understand you," said Critilo, "your meaning is, that the stars should have been disposed in order, and rank, like some rich embroidery, or the flowers of some delicious garden, or studded like rows of diamonds, that the lustre of one, might with an artificial correspondency have set off the beauty of another."

"Yes," said he, "for besides that the disposition of this resplendent artifice, would have been a prospect more delicious to the sight, so it would have cleared that fond imagination of some, who suppose chance to have been framer of this universe, and by a foolish profaneness hoodwink the providence of the almighty."

"Your query," said Critilo, "is not from the purpose, for you must know that the divine wisdom directing, and disposing of them in this manner, had more sublime reason, than is easily conceivable, placing their harmony, and rule not so much in their situation, as the conveniency of their motion, and temperature: for there is not a star in heaven, which has not his different nature, and influence; as herbs and plants of the Earth have their distinct virtues, some predominate in heat, others in cold, some are dry, others moist; so that their extreme qualities being equally mixed, produce a just and moderate temperature in all. That artificial order that you speak of, is but an idle toy, and fond invention of art affected, and procured only to entertain the vanity of human folly. In this manner, every night represents us a new scene of heaven, nor is our sight, nor our humour though inconstant, ever wearied to behold it. Every person according to his fancy, entertains a distinct conception, and idea of their proportions, the variety and well ordered confusion make the vulgar to imagine them innumerable, and the appearance of disorder is to them a riddle of providence, though wise men have the knowledge to search out, and discover their order and government."

"I was much pleased," said Andrenio, "with the diversity, and variety of their colours, some were pale, others ruddy, some of a gold, others of a silver colour, there only, methoughts, wanted green, that acceptable and grateful object of the sight."

"That," said Critilo, "partakes too much of an earthly quality, greenness being a symptom, or badge of hope, is more agreeable to the future wishes, and growing expectation of the Earth, than to that sublimer region, which is swallowed up wholly in a happy possession. This colour also is contrary to the nature of the celestial luminaries, and is a sign of humidity, and corruption. Did you never observe that star which makes a point in the globe of heaven, the object to the which the load- stone tends, and the blank to which it darts all its emissions? To that the compass of our attention fixes one point, and thereby measures other circles, which running round encompasses our lives."

"I must confess," said Andrenio, "with no less curiosity was my attention taken up in admiring that beautiful queen of the stars the governess of the night, the sun's substitute, and little inferior to him in dignity, that which you call the moon; though at this light I found not those refreshments, nor alacrity, as at the other; yet the varieties of its increasing, and decreasing was no less subject of my admiration."

"It is the second president of time," said Critilo, "an equal colleague with the Sun in government, if one governs the day, the other rules the night, if one is the almanac of the year, the other is of the months, if the Sun heats and dries the Earth by day, the moon refreshes, and bedews it at night; if the Sun cherishes, and ripens the fruitful fields, the moon swells, and overflows the fountains, so that both perform their several functions, and are the two scales and balances of the times and seasons. But that which is best worth your observation is, that as the Sun is a clear mirror, and emblem to represent unto us the perfection of the divine attributes; so the moon is the glass wherein to discover the uncertainty of humane frailty; for her condition, like the inconstancy of his, is never settled, or permanent, but is sometimes in the increase, than in the decrease; sometimes in the first point of its appearance, anon in the last term of its decrease; sometimes at the full, anon in an unperceivable nothing: whose light being totally communicated by the Sun, is eclipsed of her glory by an interposition of the Earth; when she is brightest, she discovers most of her spots; she is the lowest of all the planets in situation, and dignity; her power is more predominant on Earth, than in heaven: so that all those epithets of changeable, defective, spotted, inferior, poor, sad, and the like, are all derived from her too near vicinity with the Earth."

"All this night," said Andrenio, "and many more I spent in this pleasant entertainment, making myself as many eyes, as the heaven had stars, and all too little to view this prospect. But by this time the notes of the birds were alarms of the mornings approach tuning their Salve to his second entrance, giving notice to the stars to retire, and to the flowers to awake. The Sun began again to arise, and I to revive with his sight, whom I cheerfully saluted, but methoughts, with something more cool affections.

"The Sun," said Critilo, "at the second view does not amaze, nor at the third strike admiration. my curiosity began by this time to abate, as my stomach became more sharp; so after I had repeated some applauses, and praises in his honour, I descended lower by the direction of his light (which I perceived was a creature, and an instrument to serve my use) for the strengthaning of the mind is subject to the necessities of the body, and sublime contemplations cannot be continued but by new supplies made to the decays of nature. So that, I say, I descended by that dangerous ladder which those confused ruins had rudely and casually digested, which yet I acknowledge to the providence of heaven; for otherwise there had been no means for my safe descent. But before I tread the least step on the bottom, I must tell you, that both my voice and words fail me; and therefore I must entreat the supply of your expressions to recount the number of my thoughts, and so the second time I invite you to new wonders, though terrene.

The Third Crisis

The variety of Nature is one part of its comely adornment, and affords us matter to busy our heads in contemplation, and our tongues in praises: our souls are naturally propense to observe the effects of Nature: The wisest man called it the worst employment, and indeed so it is, when our considerations arrest themselves in satisfaction of our own vanity, not proceeding to such sublime raptures as may serve to raise in us the returns gratitude and glory to the supreme creator. Though admiration be the daughter of ignorance, yet it is the mother of content; to admire in small things is folly, and to stand unstruck at more miraculous prodigies, is inadvertency. Admiration is the highest expression of praise, we can attribute to any object, and especially if it proceeds like expressions of flattery, which pretend those excesses of perfection that are better evidenced by silence, than words. But it is a vulgar saying, that not the greatness of a wonder, but the novelty affects us; for we are not studious to behold those superior wonders, because they are known but because they are strange; by which means we beg for trifling novelties to entertain our inconstant humour, and pacify our curious solicitude with extravagancies. So much has novelty bewitched us, that the staleness of ancient wonders, is oppressive, and tedious to our inconstancy, which our brains are forced to remedy by the arts and toys of new inventions. That which yesterday struck admiration to the beholders, is to day slighted, and undervalued, not that it has lost its perfection, but our estimation; therefore the wiser sages excuse this former clownery by the civility of new addresses, reflecting on those ancient perfections with delight and admiration. If therefore a pearl brought from another world affects us more, than our own diamond, because extraordinary, what advantage must it than be to Andrenio to see on a sudden the heaven, the stars, the moon, the Sun, the Earth decked with Flowers, and the sky enamelled with stars? Let him relate this himself, and with that he prosecuted his discourse.

"In this conjunction of beautiful rarities, which I never before apprehended, I found the motion of my soul more active, and vigorous than my body, moving my eyes more than my feet, every object retarded my progress, and found me matter to admire and applaud. Whilst yesterday I admired the heaven, I had only opportunity to exercise my sight, but in this nearer approach, had I had a hundred eyes, and as many hands, all would have been too feeble, and exhausted in the diffusion they made of themselves through all the variety of these objects. I unweariedly beheld the multitude of creatures, their different proprieties their essences, forms, colours, affections, and motions: with one hand I gathered a rose, considering the beauty of it, and smelt its fragrant odour, with the other I plucked some fruit to please my taste, and satisfy my appetite: That in a short time I found myself so embarked in such a diversity of prodigies, that I was forced to leave one, to consider the other, still filled with delight, and admiration. But that which with most delight I considered, was, that amongst the multitude of creatures, there should be so great diversity, and difference, that not one leaf of a plant, nor of a sparrow, should have a resemblance of another species."

"In this," said Critilo, "the wise creator determined not only to supply the mere necessities, and wants of man, for whose sake all was created, but bountifully to extend his hand in a various plenty, that so he, who had been thus liberal in his gifts, might well expect man should nor be sparing or niggardly in his returns of service."

"I soon knew," proceeded Andrenio, "some sorts of those fruits, which the courtesy of the beasts had brought unto my enclosure: but especially I observed the manner of their growing, the extension of their boughs, the twining of their roots, which as they were of no small delight to me to behold, so the reason, and nature thereof was too high for my young and unpolished understanding to comprehend: the crudity of the unripe fruits, which I gathered, offended my teeth and taste, not knowing as yet how to distinguish their times and seasons."

"This is another rule," said Critilo, "and disposition of divine providence, to prolong the ripening of some fruits, till the necessity of animals require them. Some not only budded, but ripened in the spring, are first fruits and sacrifices more devoted to our taste, than nourishment, and would rather be early than seasonable: the cool refreshments of others are fitted to temper the summer's heat, and others of a more dry, and durable quality are heaped up for the winter's store, both for provision of the barren season, and by their innate heat to fortify men's stomachs against the winter's cold. The cool herbs of summer abate, and attemper July's heat, and hot plants revive our benumbed coldness in December's frosts: so that one fruit being gone, another comes in, observing their appointed times, and seasons, so as to supply our wants with abundance, and convenience. O that provident bounty of the creator! who appears so expressly manifest, that none can in words deny him, but his inward thoughts and conscience will immediately check, and accuse him."

"I was involved," proceeded Andrenio, "in so delightful a labyrinth of natures twining, that I committed myself to the mercy of my own insatiable curiosity, and to the astonishment, and confusion, which every new object had power to inculcate. I gathered this and t'other flower, feasted with its fragrancy, flattered its beauty; nor was I ever wearied with its smell, or sight;

I plucked each leaf particularly, making a prolix lecture thereon, anatomatizing its artificial composure, deducing conclusions from thance of the general comeliness of the whole universe. For thus I reasoned, if one flower be so beautiful, what must be the whole garden? if one star, so bright, and glorious, what must be that transparent clearness of the whole heavens? Who does not admire this glory, and celebrate the praises of so comely, and profitable a fabric?"

"I commend your fancy," said Critilo, "but take care, that the intentness of your outward sense obstruct not the operations of your inward thoughts; that you walk not like those in this garden of the world, whose eyes are fixed downwards, and decline with souls no more elevated than their animal senses: but do you raise your contemplation to that infinite perfection of the creator; other things being but a ray, and glimpse of him: and thus argue, if the shadow be such, what must be the cause and the reality which it follows; if such be the dead, what must be the living? if such be the image, what is the original? For as a cunning artist, designing to build a palace, intends not only to make it strong and convenient, but stately also, and excellent in its symmetrical proportions, which may please the sight, which is one of the most noble of our senses. Even to the divine architect of this palace of the world, has not only fixed the foundation, and pillars of it firm, and stable, but adorned it with the excellency of proportion: so that trees do not yield their fruit before they are first decked with blossoms, making beauty subservient unto profit. From the flagrant flowers the bees collect both substance for their combs, and honey; and from the thin leaves are distilled sweet, and medicinal waters, to revive our spirits, and please our senses."

"But alas," replied Andrenio, "as at first the beauty and odour of those flowers delighted my fancy, so was I no less troubled to see that flourishing estate so soon changed, and faded."

"This," said Critilo, "is a lively emblem of humane frailty, for beauty begins in ostentation, the year smiles amongst the flowers of a cheerful spring, and the day dawns with beams of a blushing Aurora, and man begins to live with the smiles of infancy, and wantonness of youth; but all ends in sadness, and corruption, when the apprehension of being laid in the dust, and paying the tribute of Nature, affrights us with horror; whilst the uncertain time of destiny in general serves to elude men's expectation thereof in particular."

"After I had in this pastime entertained my sight," said Andrenio, "there wanted not the harmony, and musical notes of birds to content my ears: their tuned throats ravished my senses, their quavers, stops, and sweet airs kept time with the woods, and valleys which were instruments of their louder sounds, and by echo bore part with them in the same music; the shrubs also, and twigs dancing at the noise, seemed to salute the Sun at his first arise. I observed here, and that with no small admiration, that nature had bestowed the gift of melody in voice, which is the recreation of our lives, on birds only; beasts with an ungrateful voice offended my ears, and the sound they made was more of horror, than harmony."

"The reason is," said Critilo, "because birds as inhabitants of the air are of more refined spirits in that subtle region, and therefore have the advantage of other creatures, and only can imitate the words of men, through the purity of that place they live in, and abiding in a region of nearer vicinity unto Heaven, have need of sweeter voices to resound continually divine praises. Another thing I would have you to observe, that amongst all the diversity of birds, none is affected with a venomous quality, like those animals, who crawling on the earth, suck in noxious qualities, which should admonish man to avoid the dangers of this region, and retire from the filth of this infection."

"I was much taken," said Andrenio, "to see them so neat, and so pretty in their variety of colours." "But here observe," said Critilo, "that the male has more variety in his colours, than the female, resembling the like in man, whom Nature itself has so sufficiently decked, that he needs no other foils to set him off; but women being subtle in their inventions, know ways to deceive with the snare of their dresses, and to cover their defects with counterfeited feathers."

"That which I much observed," said Andrenio, "was that admirable correspondence, and rule by which the distinct multitudes of creatures were distinguished, and disposed, without one being troublesome unto the other, but rather every one in their several natures, like a well- ordered commonwealth, helpful and assistant amongst themselves."

"This is another effect," said Critilo, "of divine wisdom, the balance of all things in weight number, and measure; for every creature has its centre, his natural place of residence, his duration in time, his proper end both in being, and operation: by this you may see the link and chain of creatures, their orderly situation, and the due degree of their perfection. Of the elements the meanest servants of nature are composed mixed bodies, and the inferiors are subordinate to the superiors: herbs, and plants, which are in the lowest order and degree, of life, are vegetables, moving and increasing until they arrive at the full point, and period of their perfection. In the second order of life are sensitives, the animals of the Earth, which prey on the vegetables, making them food, and nourishment for their own sustenance; and these are the beasts of the field, the fishes of the sea, and the birds of the air; these feed on the grass, people the trees, peck the buds, build in the branches, and make the leaves their defence, and security: but both these, one, and the other are bound to obey a third sort of Nature, viz. the vegetable, and the sensitive are made servants to a higher master, reason, and understanding, which is man, and he subordinated to a greater sovereign which is God, whom he ought to know, love, and serve. In this wonderful order, and harmony, all things are disposed, one creature being made helpful to assist the wants and necessities of another. The water has need of the earth to support it, the earth of the water to bedew it; the water in rarefaction becomes air, and the air food to nourish, and foment the fire: every part being ordained mutually to maintain the other, all generally concur to the preservation of the whole. Besides, it is worth observation to consider those ways, and means the divine providence has invented for the preservation of that being, which he has given to every creature, especially to the sensitive, as the most considerable, which is a natural instinct to know the good, and avoid the bad: whence we may better admire, than relate, the apt ability some have to deceive, and that others have to escape and fly the danger."

"Though all this diversity of prodigies," said Andrenio, "was but as one continued series of novelty: yet my wonder was still dilated with the sight and survey of that immense ocean. The sea seemed as envious of the earth to form tongues in the water to chide my sluggishness, and by the noise of its waves to invite my curiosity to a new admiration. Thus wearied with my walks, but not with my thoughts, I sat me down, on one of yonder cliffs, oppressed with as many fits of astonishment, as the sea has waves. I contemplated much on those slight bounds that imprison the sea, and the obedience of that furious monster to the gentle curb of the unstable sand. Is it possible," said I, "there should be no stronger wall, than that of dust, to limit the violence of this furious enemy?"

"Hold," said Critilo, "divine Providence has with much lenity circumscribed the rage of two boundless enemies, which being let loose, would have destroyed the world, and its inhabitants. The sea he has terminated with the limits of the sands, and the fire he has imprisoned in the hard entrails of the flint, which being called by two strokes only comes forth, and serves our occasions: when we have no farther need of it, it retires or is extinguished; if this were not, two days could not pass, before the Earth were consumed by the fire, or drowned with the waters."

"I could not satiate myself," said Andrenio, "in beholding the transparent clearness of the waters, and my eyes were hydropically thirsty to view the constant motion of those liquid crystals."

"They say," answered Critilo, "that the eyes being composed of those two humours waterish, and crystalline, are so much pleased with beholding waters, that they are never wearied in beholding them.

"Above all," said Andrenio, "when I saw so many fishes within the bowels of the sea, so differently formed from birds, and beasts, it was here, that I can properly say, my admiration was at a stand, and being wholly exhausted was reduced to a *ne plus ultra*. Upon this rock being set alone, without other admonition than my own weak meditations, I began to consider the rare harmony of the universe, which being composed of contraries, one would think in so near a conjunction should like irreconcilable enemies, as they are, combat both to their own, and the world's destruction: This held me for some time in contemplation; for who would think a league could be made to compose things so contrary, and opposite?"

"It is true," answered Critilo, "the world is compounded of contraries, and agreement of discords; as the philosopher saith, 'there is nothing, but has an enemy with whom to combat,' either with victory, or subjection, all is with action, and passion, none assaults, but his blows are returned by his enemy. The elements command the vanguard, by whose example the mixed compositions are encouraged to battle, one destroying the other, evils waiting to entrap our goods, and malice to ruin, and overthrow our fortunes. Sometimes even the stars have their dissentions, and quarrels, and though there is no weapons, or power in fight capable to hurt those invulnerable bodies; yet the damage of the war, like that of sovereign princes, redounds to the affliction of their sublunary vassals, and their natural discords are converted to moral oppositions: so that none on Earth, is so peaceable and quiet, but finds some whom he may hate, or emulate, for corrupt nature is pregnant with the innate seeds of dissention. Thus in age the old are opposers of the young, in complexion the phlegmatic are averse to the choleric, in estate the rich unsociable with the poor, in climate the Spaniard unpleasing to the French: thus in all forts of qualities, and conditions, some are contrary, or in opposition unto others. But what if I should tell you, that within the very gates of man himself, within the small compass of that earthly cottage, the fire of dissention should be kindled, and he as an enemy oppose himself? For he as a little world is compounded of all contraries: the humours begin the quarrel, the moisture resists the radical heat, still endeavouring to abate, and quench it; the inferior parts are always offensive to the superior, contradicting their designs, and intentions, and the appetite subdues, and tramples on reason. The soul, that immortal spirit, is not free from this calamity, the passions quarrel amongst themselves; Fear endeavours to abate valour, melancholy mirth; sometimes we desire, and than we abhor, sometimes vices triumph, and anon virtues, all consists of arms and war, and the life of man on Earth is nothing but a continued warfare. But O! that wonderful and infinite wisdom of the creator, who has so moderated, and attempered the contrarieties of creatures, as to make their discords their stay, support, and conservation, and thereby to unite, and sustain the whole fabric of the universe."

"This," said Andrenio, "was none of my meanest contemplations, observing so much change in so much permanency, all things seemed to move in a continual progress to their natural end, and yet the world as the stage of the tragedy to remain the same constant, and immutable."

"The supreme artificer," said Critilo, "has so ordained, that nothing should end, but another should begin, that from the ashes, or ruin of the one should arise another, that the corruption of one should be the generation of another: when all things seem to be at an end, a new offspring begins, Nature peoples again the world, and older ages cast their bill, and grow young with a new generation, in all which is to be admired, and adored the wisdom of divine providence."

"But here," said Andrenio, "did not my thoughts, and observation rest, but still proceeded to consider the variety of times, and seasons, the exchange of day with night, of summer with winter, by the moderate and gradual intervention of the temperate spring; Nature proceeding by degrees never makes so long a step as from one extreme to another."

"In this again," said Critilo, "appears the divine government, not only in appointing unto all creatures, their orders and situation, but in accommodating fit times and opportunities agreeable to all occasions. The day serves for labour, and the silence of the night for quietness and repose: the frosts of winter fix and extend the roots of plants, and the spring with a reviving warmth causes the branches to blossom, and the summer appears in plentiful hopes, and the autumn crowns our labours with the fruits we reap, and gather into our barns. But what do you think of the strange miracle of the rains?"

"This too I admired very much," said Andrenio, to see those sweet dews distil on the earth with gentleness, and divided streams, for a common refreshment."

"And so seasonable," added Critilo, "in the two months of October and April, which are productive of fruit, and serve the plow, and seed, with a kindly moisture. The changes also of the moon contribute unto plenty, and favour by a wholesome influence the health of creatures; for some months are cold, others hot, some moist, and blustering, others dry, and serene, according to the different seasons: the waters cleanse, and fructify, the winds purge, and animate; the Earth immovably supports the descending gravity of bodies, the air is pliable not to hinder their motion, and diaphanous not to obstruct and cloud the sight. Whence we may see, that it is, that divine omnipotence, that eternal providence, and that only immense bounty, which alone knows how to erect this vast fabric, which we can never sufficiently admire, contemplate and applaud."

"These are certain truths," said Andrenio, "which I have often observed, and yet ill conceived in my rude understanding. It was no unpleasant entertainment to me, to traverse all the day from one place unto another, from one prospect to another, continuing to admire, and view the heaven, the earth, the seas, the fields, and all with an insatiable fruition. But that point, on which I much insisted, was that admirable art of the divine wisdom, which with so much facility has performed a labour so difficult, and in the first invention proceeded to the very height and top of all perfection, and accomplishment: How much art was there in fixing the Earth firmly on its basis to be a secure foundation for the following superstructure? Nor less admirable are those perennal streams of fountains, which swell with an inexhaustible increase, whose continued inundation is no more than a necessary plenty. How much power is there in forming the tempests, and those still whisperings of wind, which steal from unknown places, and as much unknown the stages to which they tend? How much power was there in digesting those useful heaps of mountains, the ribs of this composure, the bay and harbour for the Earth to shroud itself under? These, as they are additions to the beauty of the world's variety, so are they the treasuries of the snows the mines from which metals are extracted, are the dissolvers, or breakers of the clouds, the head and original of fountains, and the dens of beasts; from them fall the lofty pines to build our ships, and houses; in them we have refuge from the over- flowings of waters, in them we remain secure, as in towers, or bull-works from the sudden assaults, or surprizal of our enemies: all which miracles, and wonders, what but an infinite wisdom could storm, and dispose with reason, therefore must we confess that were all the best heads, and judgments of the world united in one, and all their reasons, and discourses, squeezed, and distilled to the purest quintessence of rationality, it were not capable to amend the least circumstance, or make an addition to the least atom of Nature's perfection. And if that king, for only knowing four stars, was so highly commended by one of his parasites (so much is wisdom esteemed in a prince) and with that extravagant applause, saying, that if he had been counsellor to the divine workman, at that time when he created, and ordered these things, that his human wisdom would have outdone the divine, and better contrived the composure of his fabric. But this saying proceeded not from an effect of reason, but from a defect of judgment, incident to the nature of the Spanish nation; which in the swellings of their boasting humour cannot moderate their ostentation though with God himself."

"Hear me," said Andrenio, "this last truth the greatest, and most sublime of any, that I have yet declared. I confess, that though I have admired four strange prodigies in this universe, The multitude and variety of creatures, the harmony and agreement in contraries, their beauty and ornament mixed with profit, and convenience, and their mutations with permanency. Yet above all, I remained confused in the knowledge of the creator, who is so manifest in his creatures, and yet hid in himself; whose attributes are imprinted on every step, and action of his work, as his omnipotence in the execution, his providence in the government, his beauty in the perfection, his bounty in the communication; and so the rest of his attributes; of which as none were unemployed at the beginning, so in succeeding ages are maintained, and conserved by the existence and operation of his power. And notwithstanding this great God is hid, though known, not seen, though manifest, far distant, though near; this is that riddle which has confused my understanding, and left me in an ecstasy of love, and adoration."

"Man," said Critilo, "is naturally inclined to love his maker, as the beginning, and end he tends unto. Nor is there any nation so barbarously ignorant, in whom the light of Nature has not infused the awe, and reverence of a deity, sufficient to curb the most audacious profaneness, and convince them of the divine essence, omnipresence. Nature having made nothing but to some end, the inclinations and propensities of every creature are useful in their several operations. If the loadstone turns unto the North, it denotes a sympathy between them, and its trembling till it returns unto its point, shows that a violence is offered to its nature, whilst it remains in the state of separation. If the plant turns with the Sun, the fish to the water, the stone to the centre, and man to God, there must be a God, who is his attracting North, his centre, and Sun, to which his head bends, and with whose vigour, and heat the deadness of his soul receives vigour to revive. From this great sire do all creatures acknowledge to have received their being: he only is from himself, and therefore is infinite in all kind of perfection, whose being none is able to circumscribe with place, or time. Though he is not seen, yet he is known, and like a sovereign prince keeps a distance agreeable to his majestic greatness, not admitting, unless rarely, his vassals to a familiar audience, and yet is familiarly present with all by the representation of his creatures. So that a philosopher defines this world to be the grand looking-glass of God. Philon Ebreus terms it 'the invitation of the soul, and the only nourishment which feeds minds.' Pythagoras calls it 'a tuned-harp, whose measure, and harmony wraps up our contemplations, and thoughts with uncontainable ravishments.' Tertullian names it 'the pomp of increated majesty.' And Trismegistus 'the musical consonancy of the divine attributes.'"

"These are," and so concluded Andrenio, "the first rudiments of my life, better conceived than related; for where the thoughts are screwed beyond their natural power, there must consequently want words to utter them. That which I must now desire of you is, that you would satisfy my longing expectation to know what you are, and from whence you came, and how you passed the rolling waves of this ocean, tell me if there be more worlds, or more people than this, to all which my curiosity will render me as attentive as you can desire."

To which relation Critilo willingly consented, being the great tragedy of his life declared in the following Crisis.

The Fourth Crisis

Critilo Relates the misfortunes of his Love in the time of his Youth; and the occasion of his Shipwreck.

They say that Cupid complained of the injuries he had received from fortune, in that she had slighted and undervalued the power of his mother, by not appealing, as she was want, to her arbitrement and judicature.

"What want you blind boy?" said Fortune, and he again, replied, "this is agreeable to those reproaches and scorn, which envy and dissention have cast upon me."

Fort. With whom have you this enmity?

Cupid. With all the world.

Fortune. I am sorry you should contend with so powerful an enemy, and that the justice of your cause should invite none to defend it.

Cupid. Had I but only you on my side, I should be sufficiently defended, and this my mother daily tells me, and often preaches to me, that I should get you to my friendship and party.

Fort. But do you not revenge yourself?

Cupid. Yes, both of young and old.

Fort. Well, but what is the occasion, and reason for your anger?

Cupid. The cause is as great, as just.

Fort. Perhaps those ordinary reproaches of having been born in the family of a mechanic, or your education to be no other than amidst the anvil, and hammers of a smooty forge.

Cupid. No, not these, for never was I so disingenuous as to deny truth.

Fort. Nor should it trouble you to be called the son of your mother.

Cupid. This less; for I triumph and glory rather to proceed from the race of so divine a progeny; neither can I be without her, nor she without me; neither Venus without Cupid, nor Cupid without Venus.

Fort. Now I know your distaste, you are vexed to be thought the heir of your grandfathers defects, or to imitate the sea, that troubled and inconstant element.

Cupid. No, for these are but fables.

Fort. If these be fables, what are truths?

Cupid. That which unquiets me is, that they impose upon me false aspersions, unseemly epithets, and slanders.

Fort. I understand you now; without doubt it is, that they say, you have changed your bow with death, and are not called amor from amare, but from mori, as if love, and death were both one, your profession being to destroy life, to unrip the heart, and lodge it in another; rather where it loves, than where it animates.

Cupid. This is all true.

Fort. If this be true, what other reproach can you complain of, as false, or injurious?

Cupid. Are those true, that speak me blind, and whose malice would pluck out my eyes? If I am blind, let those well-shot arrows declare, or those marks hit, be mended by the shafts of a more quick- sighted shooter. They paint me also with a fillet bound about my eyes; not only *Apelles*, whose fancy guides his pencil, nor the poets, whose obligation is to feign, and their trade to invent fabulous fancies; but also the wise and understanding philosophers; These are they which move my patience, and make me angry to think their better judgments should style me such, and like the rest be seduced with a vulgar error. Prithee tell me, Fortune, what passion is there, that does not blind? Is not the angry blinded with his own choler? The covetous with his interest? The desperate with his confidence? The idle with his sleep? Is not the vain a mole in his gallantry, and the hypocrite blinded with the beams of his eyes? And do not the proud, gluttonous, and drunkards group in the darkness of their own passions? Why than do they impose this ignominy on me only, and so deprive me of my sight, that by a metonymy of blindness they describe me? which is the more strange, because this deprivation is contrary to my nature; and sight gives me the first being. By seeing I begin, and thereby my passion is nourished and formed, and like an eagle at the Sun, am never wearied with beholding beauty. This is the quarrel, and injury I complain of; what think you, have not I reason?"

"The same," said Fortune, "is my grievance; and since we both lie under the same abuse, let our equal misfortune comfort, and content us both; but that which has chiefly imposed this name upon you, is the too raised conceit of your own sight, as if only enamoured spirits knew how to delight their eyes; and that others had only light to serve their necessity, and not their curiosity, which causes you to accuse them of blind ignorance, and upbraid your defects in return of their affronts: He that will see this philosophy compared with experience, let him attend to this following discourse of Critilo, which he dedicates to the years of flourishing youth."

"Your demand," said he, "renews my ancient grief, which my mind already better feels, than my tongue relates: as your discourse was pleasant and delightful, so the troubles, and misfortunes of my life convert our former content into extremes of melancholy: happy art thou who wast born among the beasts, and unhappy I who was born and educated amongst men, whose cruelty exceeds that of ravenous wolves; for every one is to the other such, and to be a man is to be more inhumane than they. You have given me an account how you came into the world, and I shall tell you, how I came out of it; the sense of which has so altered, and changed my humour, and condition, that I know not so well to tell you who I am, as who I was. They say I was born at sea, and indeed the inconstancy of my fortune persuades me the same."

The word, sea, was no sooner out of his mouth, but turning his eyes towards it, on a sudden started up, and distrusting his sight at first, stood a while in suspense, but at length calling to Andrenio, and pointing with his Finger, "dost thou not see," said he, "yonder afar off?"

"What is it you see?"

"I see," said he, "some wandering mountains, or winged sea- monsters, or else some clouds."

"No," said Critilo, "they are ships, though you have said aptly in calling them clouds; for they rain gold into Spain."

Andrenio was much pleased to see them come in with such full swelled Sails; for he admired a sight so unusual, being naturally desirous to enter into human society; but Critilo began to sigh, and lament the trouble and inconvenience of the present occasion.

"What is the matter," said Andrenio, "is not this the desired fleet of which you told me?"

"Yes."

"Are not those men that come?"

"Yes."

"Why than are you so sad?"

"For this only reason," said Critilo, "for know, Andrenio, that we are already lodged within the power of our enemies; now we must be circumspect over all our actions, be provident in seeing, cautious in hearing, but especially speaking; we must bridle our tongues, and before we begin our speech, we must premeditate what inconvenience may ensue. The professions you make may to credulous ears insinuate affection and friendship, but be so provident as to arm against the assaults of enemies."

This new lecture seemed strange to Andrenio, whose Judgment not being improved by experience, made him to reprove Critilo, wondering that he did not rather advise him of the dangers of the woods, and cruelty of beasts, than with so much inveterate hatred to inveigh against man.

"Was not our danger greater," said he, "whilst our want of habitation drove us to the dens of tigers, nor did you fear them, much less should your courage abate with the sight of men."

"Yes," sighing, answered Critilo, "for if men be not beasts, it is because their inhumanity exceeds theirs, whose irrational soul is not capable to invent such extravagant iniquities. Never was our danger greater than with the approach of these; which truth is confirmed by the example of a king, who to protect his favourite from the violent hands of his own courtiers, enclosed him within the den of his lions, esteeming him more secure there, than within the reach, or power of his malevolent prosecutors."

"I shall refer that to your own confession, after that your better experience has acquainted you with the same."

"Hold," said Andrenio, "are they not all like you?"

"Yes, and yet are not, for every one is the son of his mother, wedded to his own humour, and opinion, and affected with a diversity both of fancy and gesture. There are some who but pigmies in growth, have yet their souls elevated to the skies, and others, giants in bodies, have yet their thoughts levelled with the earth: you shall meet others of a revengeful, and malicious spirit, whose rage dies not with time, and whose rancour infects others; as poisonous as the scorpion's tail, having its venom sublimated by age, and long durance. You shall hear, but let it be your care to avoid the impertinent discourses of the talkative, which are often vain, and idle, and neither profitable to him that speaks, or hears them. You will please yourself with the conceits of some, whose quicker genius comments on the actions of others, imitating in a jesting scorn their words, their manners, and behaviour; but these men reflect not on the looseness of their own lives, nor how obnoxious they are to the censures of a scrutinous judge; others there are foolishly inquisitive, whose impertinent questions may puzzle the answers of a good resolver. You shall see others, whose long discourses conclude in nothing, in all things aggravating and enlarging; for though they be men more short in stature than one of Navarre, and corpulent also, are yet without substance. In fine, you shall find few men that are so, brutes they may be, and monsters of the world, having no substance but their own flesh and skin, and the rest but a mere shadow or apparition of mankind."

"But tell me, how is man capable of doing so much mischief, since Nature as seemingly negligent of him, has denied him those weapons with which, she has armed, and defended beasts? He has no claws like the lion, or tiger, no trunk like the elephant, no horns like the bull, no tusks like the boar, no teeth like the dog, nor mouth like the wolf, how than is that unarmed malice able to wage such continual war?"

"For this very reason," said Critilo, "has provident Nature not delivered weapons into the hands of an enemy dangerous to himself, and the rest of her Product; whose hate knows no bounds, for being let loose, would destroy even Nature herself, notwithstanding all which, his malice has found means to convert those parts which Nature has given him for necessary uses into more bloody and cruel weapons than those of beasts, his tongue is more sharp than the lions claws, by which he shatters the reputation of others, and wounds them in their name, and honour. His bad intentions are more perverse, and crooked than the bulls horns, hurt at random, and hit those it never aimed at: his bowels are more poisonous than the vipers, his breath blasts more than the dragons, his eyes are more envious, and dart more deadly emissions, than the basilisks, his teeth are more sharp than the fangs of the boar, and his nose like the elephants trunk, wrings and turns itself into a thousand forms, and shapes of derision; so that all those offensive arms which are sparingly delivered to other creatures, are not given to, but usurped by man, and in him found as the store and magazine of them all. And that you may understand this the better, know that lions, and tigers are capable of no other damage, than what touches their bodies; but man is liable to what misery, fraud, deceit, treason, theft, homicide, adultery, envy, injuries, detractions, and falsities can throw on his honour, and cast on his peace, estate, content, happiness, conscience, nay and to a malice, which would proceed to the very ruin, and destruction of his soul. Believe me, there is no wolf, nor lion, nor tiger so inhumane, as man; which is sufficiently verified, if true, what is reported. That a malefactor being condemned to die upon a legal trial, was by sentence of justice to be cast into a deep cave to be there devoured by ravenous beasts: it fortuned that a stranger passing by, and hearing the sighs, and groans of the condemned person, and yet ignorant of the punishment, was moved by compassion to relieve him out of misery; to which end opening the cave suddenly, with extraordinary nimbleness leaped out the tiger, which contrary to its nature, and the expectation of the traveller, by way of salute and gratefulness, kindly kissed and licked his hands; next followed the snake, which twined about his legs, not to wound, but to embrace them; in like manner did all the rest most gratefully join to give him thanks not only for saving their lives, but for rescuing them from a death accompanied with the loathsome society of a wicked man; in recompense of which they seemed to advise him to fly and be gone, least when that miscreant came forth, he should endanger his own life, by saving his the passenger, though much amazed, yet desired to see him whom he had so much obliged, expecting some acknowledgements for so great a benefit, instead of which the malefactor coming forth, and supposing that the traveller carried some wealth and riches with him, killed him, and despoiled him of all, a kind return of his charity and compassion. And now judge, which are most cruel, men, or beasts."

"I am more astonished, and amazed," said Andrenio, to hear this, than the day I beheld the world."

"You cannot fully conceive their malice," said Critilo, "and yet women are worse, and more dangerous."

"If they be worse, what must they be than?"

"In short they are devils, hereafter I will tell you more of them: but above all I conjure you, that by no means you tell, who we are, nor how I came hither, nor how you proceeded to light, for by that means you may loose your liberty, and I my life. And though I distrust not your faithfulness, and secrecy, yet I am glad, that I have not finished the relation of my misfortunes, which in this only are fortunate, that being as yet untold, are not subject to that discourse which may sometimes inconsiderately fall from you. Here therefore we will double down the leaf, until the next occasion, which cannot want in so long a voyage."

By this time the near approach of the fleet made their voices more distinct and audible, which they raised with greater acclamations with the joy conceived at their arrival: men always grow more wanton, when their success promises fairest, and their enterprises have the face of a happy issue; being come into the road, they furled their sails, and cast their anchors, and the passengers began to land on the desired shore: The meeting was as strange to the new-come guests, as to the two inhabitants; who in the relation they gave of themselves, declared, that having been asleep, or negligent at the departure of the last fleet, they were left behind on that island, which account reconciled both their pity, and their courtesy. Having thus for some days entertained themselves in hunting, and furnished their vessels with fresh water, and wood, they set to sea, directing their course to desired Spain. Critilo and Andrenio embarked together on the same galleon, which sort of vessel is a terror to its enemies, the opposer of the winds, and a yoke of subjection to the ocean. The voyage was as dangerous as long, but the relation which Critilo made of the many tragedies his life had passed, was a good entertainment for tedious hours, which he prosecuted in this manner.

"I was born, (as I have already told you) amidst of this immense gulf, and of the dangers and continual motions of this turbulent element. The reason was, that my parents being spaniards, by consent, and favour of Philip the Great, the most universal and mighty monarch, embarked for the Indies with no small wealth to improve their fortunes. my mother at that time suspecting herself with child, carried me in her womb; and before the tedious voyage was ended, brought me forth, whose untimely birth was hastened by the terrors of that tempest, in which I came to light, that so the raging of the seas, might add pains to the pangs of her travail: my being born amidst this confusion, was a bad omen of my future infelicities, so early began fortune to play with my life, hurrying me from one part of the world to the other. At last we arrived at that rich and famous city of Goa, which is the court of the Catholic empire in the east, the imperial and august seat of its vice-kings, and universal emporium of the Indies, and its richness. At this place lived my father, whose stock, which he brought with him, directed with prudence, and industry, advanced suddenly both his fame, and fortune. But I, being educated amidst the happiness of a plentiful condition, and being the only son of my parents, was tenderly nurtured with too much care, and indulgence, whose fondness to me in my childhood, produced the fruits of an exorbitant youth. For being now entered into the green champions of springing years, made wanton with delights, loose and uncurbed by the reigns of reason, I fell into gaming, impairing my estate, and abusing the industry of my parents, whose cares obtained that with trouble, which my folly squandered in pastime. From this vice I passed to the vain toys of gallantry, and fashions, dressing my body with borrowed feathers, whilst I neglected the true adornments and virtues of the soul. This vanity of mine was incited forward, by the evil conversation of some pretended friends, flatterers, and braves, the vile moths of an estate, honour, and conscience. The wisdom of my father prognosticated the ruin of me his unfortunate son, and family, from whose rigour I appealed to the indulgent tenderness of my mother, whose protection defended me not, but destroyed me."

"But at that time my father gave an end unto his days, seeing but little hopes to recover me from my desperate condition, especially as than being blindly entangled within the labyrinth of love, For I had cast my affections upon a lady, though noble, beauteous, and as perfect as Nature could make her, yet wanting the endowments of fortune, she shined not in that lustre to the world as to be adored, and courted for them: only I alone idolized her person, and my devotion grew more zealous by the correspondence of her favours: and though her parents desired to admit me into their family, yet mine refused to admit her into theirs, endeavouring by all means to wean my affections, which they stilled my ruin, and by proposing another match more fitted to their convenience, than my content, thought to distract, or divert my love, which was so firm, and blindly constant, that nothing could overcome: I thought, I spake, I dreamed of nothing but Felisinda (for so she was called) esteeming no small portion of my happiness to consist in the repetition of her name. This, and many other discontents were heavy troubles of my aged father (the ordinary punishment of paternal indulgence) which sat so heavily on him, as to deprive him of his life, and me of my protection; but yet the ignorance of my youth knew not how to make that estimate of my loss as the importance of so great damage ought to have affected me. my tender natured mother bewailed, and performed the obsequies of the dead with tears sufficient for us both; but with that excess, that her own life lasted not long after, leaving me more free, and less sad. The undoubted hopes of obtaining my mistress, were now by the removal of those obstacles, some remedy of my grief, and recompense of my loss; but those filial respects I owed to the memory of my dead parents, and my desires to comply with the censures of the world, made me for some days to retard my intentions, which seemed years, and ages to my longing hopes. In which interim my inconstant fortune so changed the condition of these present affairs, that the death of my parents, which at first seemed to facilitate my desires, was that at last which put the obstacle. and reduced them to an estate of almost impossible. For it fortuned, that in a short time the brother of my mistress died, a gentleman well accomplished, and noble, the sole heir of the family, leaving my Felisinda inheritrix of all, and phoenix in all ornaments, whose beauty now joined with riches, made her glory to shine in the highest magnitude; her fame was greatly spread in one day, being become a person that suited with the most aspiring ambition of that court. This unexpected accident intervening, things had a strange change, and the face of my affairs looked different, to what they formerly promised; only the constancy of Felisinda was stable, and changed in nothing but in greater kindness; her friends and parents aspiring now unto higher mmatches, were the first who by cold entertainments discountenanced my pretensions, which they had formerly invited: this neglect proceeded afterwards to affronts, and endeavours to move in her a hatred of my person; but she advised me of all that might disadvantage me, made me of a lover to become her councillor. many other rivals as powerful as numerous declared themselves; but lovers who were wounded more by those arrows which were shot from the quiver of her portion, than from the bow of love;

yet of all I was timorous and suspicious, love being naturally jealous, and like an effeminate passion apt to be foiled with the least disappointment, but that which gave me the greatest blow, was the pretensions of a new rival, who, besides that he was comely, rich, and youthful, he was kinsman of the vice-king, which is there as much as to be allied to a deity, or to be a branch of divinity, whose will is his law, and whose intentions are as soon executed, as conceived; he, I say, began to declare himself a pretender to my mistress, being as confident, as powerful; we both stood at open defiance, he encouraged by the strength of his authority, and I enabled with the passion of love: but his own, and the reason of others assured him, that this long rooted affection of mine, completed with time, and conversation, was not easily eradicated, unless diverted; to which effect, he promised his best assistance, and favour to the industry, and malice of my enemies; whose plot was by law to pretend upon my estate, and thereby either to scare me out of the fits of love, or at least to affright the parents of Felisinda from matching her with me, over whom hanged an apparent ruin. I soon perceived myself entangled within two dangerous toils, of interest, and love; but love being that which most prevailed, the fear of loosing my estate was not strong enough to contend with the valour of my affection, which like the palm grew more under the heavy pressure. But what this plot wanted to avail with me, it worked in the parents of my mistress, who considering most the conveniences of interest, and honour, contrived - I know not how to proceed, it will be better to leave off..." - but Andrenio, still pressing him to proceed - "Well," said he, "in fine, they resolved to kill me, and to deliver that life to my adversary which was already consecrated, and devoted to my mistress; but she acquainted me with the design that night from her balcony, and according to her custom consulted with me concerning the remedy; with which she let fall such a flood of tears, as kindled in my breast a sire, and hell of despair, and fury, so that the next day, not considering the inconveniencies, nor dangers of honour or life, but guided by the blindness of my passion, armed with my sword, or rather thunderbolt, pierced through the quiver of love, and whetted with anger and jealousy, I went in pursuit of my enemy; and now remitting disputes to works, and our tongues to our hands, we unsheathed our swords without remorse, and having made some few passes each at the other, I soon pierced his heart, depriving him both of love, and life; so that now I lay exposed to the sentence of justice; whose ministers, desirous to content the vice- king, and covetous to engross my estate, were ready at hand to execute their office. I was presently sentenced to imprisonment in a dark dungeon, laden with bolts, and irons, the natural fruit of my foolish rashness. The sad news soon came to the ears of my rival's parents, who melted in their sighs and tears, and resolving to revenge the injury, continually thundered out threats against me. The vice-king also moved with the death of his kinsman, designed to prosecute justice to the utmost extremity. The report of our combat was soon bruited abroad, and as men's affections led them, they either condemned, or defended me; but all were generally sorry, that our reason guided us not better than so unfortunately to ruin each other. Only my mistress was she alone, that triumphed in my valour, and celebrated the faithfulness of my affection, and constancy. The charge was strongly prosecuted against me, of which being convicted, my estate became their prey, and my riches a sacrifice to their revenge, venting their malice thereupon, as the angry bull does on the cloak of his escaped enemy. The sole support which remained unto me, were some jewels, which providently I had entrusted within the sacred walls of a monastery, the only relic of my shipwrecked fortune. The violence of this storm stopped not at the ruin of my estate, but proceeded to a condemnation of my life; and having lost my goods, I lost also my friends, which are companions inseparable each from the other; but all this had not yet abated my courage, had not something more unhappy augmented my misfortunes: For the parents of Felisinda discontented at the accidents and disgraces lately past, resolved to leave the Indies, and seek more quietness, and preferment in Spain, which they hoped to procure by the favour, and recommendations of the vice-king. So that having converted their estate into money, they embarked on the first fleet, leaving me -"

With that his sighs interrupted his speech, and his tears gave a full stop unto his discourse: "at last," said he, "they carried with them two pledges of my soul, which doubled my grief, and made it more fatal; one was Felisinda herself, and the other was, the burden which she bore in her womb, miserable only for being mine. They being in this manner set to sea, had their wind increased by the storms of my breast, whom whilst I leave engulfed in the ocean, I was drowned in the sea of my tears, remaining eternally condemned to darkness, and a dungeon, poor and forsaken, forgotten of all, but the malice, and hatred of my enemies."

"As he who falling from a mountain, scatters his spoils on every stone, here his hat, there his cloak, there his eyes, and hands, till at last he looses his life, and bursts in pieces at the bottom. Even so, I sliding from the dangerous cliffs of this ivory rock, more to be feared, because delightful, rolled myself from one misfortune to another, left on every stone testimonies of my ruin, in goods, honour, health, parents, friends, and liberty, till I arrived at this grave, and prison, the abyss and pit of my miseries. Yet I may truly say, that though wealth corrupted my happiness, and raised enemies to throw troubles on me; yet poverty restored me to a better condition; for here I found wisdom, unto which, till now, the extravagance of youth had made me a stranger; here I undeceived myself, and gained experience and health both of body and soul: and being abandoned of all living society, I conversed with the dead, and by reading I began to understand, and to become rational, having only before led the sensitive life; so that having extracted some knowledge, my understanding was enlightened, and my will was obedient to the dictates of it, one being replete with wisdom, and the other with virtue: and so I opened my eyes when there was nothing to see, and so it happens often. I studied the noble arts, and sublime sciences, devoting myself with great affection to moral philosophy, which is the food of the judgment, the centre of reason, and the life of discretion. I reformed myself from the vain society of my companions; instead of a wanton youth, I chose a severe Cato, in place of a shallow wit, a wise Seneca; sometimes I perused Socrates, anon divine Plato, easing in this manner my tedious hours, and recreating myself in that grave of the living, and labyrinth of liberty. Years passed, and vice-kings, but still continued the rigour of my adversaries; for they prolonged the hearing of my cause, and since they could arrive no higher, they resolved to linger out my days in prison, and convert my dungeon into my grave. But at the end of some years miseries, came an order from Spain, obtained by the secret negotiation of my mistress, that my cause and person should be remitted thither. The new vice-king being less my enemy, and more favourable, put it in execution, and dispatched me away in the first fleet, committing me a prisoner to the charge of the captain of the ship. Thus parted I from the Indies, the first from that place, poor, and necessitous, to whom the dangers of the seas seemed entertainments and pleasures. my affable disposition soon gained me friends, and those, that were delighted with truth, were attentive auditors of my lectures of morality; but above all, the captain of the admiralship made me his confident, a favour which I much esteemed, and verified the truth of that common saying, that fortune often changes with the place; and that our designs can never be prosperous, whilst we live under the influence of *a malevolent star*. But here sit, and admire a prodigy of humane fraud, an extremity of malice, the spite, and quarrel of a contrary fortune, and the full point and period to which the preamble of my miseries tended; for this captain being a gentleman obliged in all points of honour to treat me civilly and fairly, yet puffed with ambition, and infected with the same rancour, and malice which the former vice-king my enemy, and his kinsman bore me, or rather incited with a covetous desire to inherit the small remainder of my estate, which I had saved from the storms of my late shipwreck, was induced to put in execution the lowest, and most inhumane of all unworthiness; for standing together with him one day, on the quarter-deck, entertaining each other with discourse, and with the prospect of the seas, he surprised me unawares, and threw me into the sea: and that he might cover this treachery, he called out too late for assistance to save my life; at his call came his mariners, and my friends, who desirous to help me, threw out their cables and ropes, but all in vain; for my slow arms not being able to follow the swift sails of the flying ship, I was left striving with the waves, and death: but one of those planks which they threw out, as the last hopes, and means to preserve me, was my sacred anchor, and support, which the compassionate waves presented to my innocence, the desperate, yet welcome refuge of my lost hopes, the which I kissing, said, 'On thee will I lay myself, the coffin of this body.' Having thus small hopes to reach the ship, I suffered myself to be carried by the waves, and my own fortune; which not contented to reduce me unto this point of extremity, but venting the rest of her tyranny, called all the elements to conspire against me in such a tempest, as if her intent was not only to destroy me, but first to exercise on me all the train, and solemnity of miseries. The waves sometimes tossed me so high, that I feared to be dashed against the points of the moon, or bruised against the heavens; anon I descended to the centre of the Earth, and again raised to that height, that I feared more to be burned with the heat of heaven, than drowned in the waters of the sea. But as these rigours, of which I have so much complained, have graciously been converted into favours, so the blustering storms have sometimes broke up in a mild calm: for miseries often times have so exceeded, and so over-acted, and strained their part, that misfortunes themselves have passed into blessings. I tell you this because the fury of the tempest, and current of the waters so violently carried me, that in a few hours I came to the sight of this little isle, for otherwise it had been impossible for me, before I had perished with cold, and hunger to have steered my vessel without oars or sails, or rudder, unto this place, which is your country, and my heaven: but in the bad consisted the good, my courage helping me more than my strength, I sheltered myself in the port of your arms, in which I desire a thousand times more to be embraced, and to confirm our friendship to all eternity."

In this manner Critilo gave an end to his relation, and embracing each other, they renewed their first enjoyment, finding within themselves a mutual sympathy of love, and contentment. They passed the rest of their voyage in profitable exercises, and besides, their pleasing discourses, which were all but a continued lecture of Iinstructions, he taught him some knowledge of the world, and the rudiments of those arts which inspire and enrich the soul; as history, cosmography, the sphere, and chiefly that which most becomes a man, namely moral philosophy; but that to which Andrenio was most intent, and studious in, was to learn the tongues, as Latin, that eternal treasury of wisdom, Spanish, as universal as its empire; the courtly French, and eloquent Italian, which he made use of as keys to open that treasure which is enclosed in them; and sometimes for his convenience, and use, to pass over the various countries of the world. The curiosity Andrenio had, was as great as his docility; so that he was always conferring, and asking concerning the provinces, republics, monarchies, and cities, and of their kings, and governors, still improved himself with as much delight, as novelty, desiring to arrive at the highest point of wisdom, and understanding. In this pleasant employment they contentedly passed the tediousness of this voyage, who at their usual time arrived in this part of the world. Whose various successes, and events are related in the following crisis.

The Fifth Crisis

Nature has dealt subtly, if not fraudulently with man, by decoying him into the world in a condition of ignorance: for he enters in obscurity, and blindness, and begins to live before he is sensible of his life, or knows, what it is to live; his fond childishness is hushed with every trifle, and lulled asleep with a toy. She makes him believe, that she has led him into a kingdom of felicities, which prove but miseries to enslave him, which when the eyes of man's judgment discovers, he finds himself defrauded, and engaged without remedy, placed in that dirt out of which he was formed, and can now only trample on it, and endeavour on the best conditions to escape. I am persuaded were it not for this universal policy, none would upon such hard conditions adventure to tread this deceitful world, were they forewarned of those difficulties they were to undergo. For who being first acquainted with these infallible inconveniencies, would rashly precipitate himself into this feigned kingdom, and true prison, wherein to suffer both multitudes, and varieties of punishments, as in the body, hunger, thirst, cold, heat, nakedness, grief, infirmities; in the mind, deceits, persecutions, envies, contempts, dishonours, melancholy, fear, anger, desperation; and at the end of all to escape out by the passage of a miserable death, with the loss of our goods, houses, honours, friends, parents, nay of life itself, which than flies from us, when we most pursue it. Nature knew well what she proffered, and what evil man accepted. For he who were aware of this condition, would rather than pass these miseries, step at once from his cradle to his urn, or from his marriage-bed into his grave. The tears which he drops at his birth, are common presages of his succeeding miseries. The happiest that are born to great Inheritance, enter but on a sad possession, and the music which welcomes this king man into the world, is composed of his own cries, and tears, which fore-run his troubles, and denote the future unhappiness of his kingdom. For what can that life be to which the groans of his mother give a being, and the weepings of the child, which receives it; though he has no knowledge to conceive his misfortunes, has yet a prophetic spirit to divine them.

"We are now," said the wise Critilo, to the inexperienced Andrenio, "arrived in the world," when they first disembarked and stepped on the sands of Spain; "I am sorry that your understanding so ripe enters into this country, for thereby you must needs be most sensible of the dissatisfaction, and emptiness of things; whatsoever the supreme artist has undertaken to perform, has been completed in the greatest height, and measure of perfection; but the invention of man has begun what he can never be capable to perfect. What God has orderly disposed, the unquietness of man to the farthest extent of his power has strained itself to trouble, and confound, and what through his inability he could not reach, his working fancy has endeavoured to disorder. You have seen hitherto the works of nature, admired and contemplated on them; now observe those of art, the artificial skill of men, and comparing those of men, and God together, your own reason will distinguish one from the other. Oh what a vast distance and difference you will find between the civil, and the natural world, between the human, and the divine; this I thought fit to advise you, that you may not admire whatsoever it is, you see, nor be discouraged by any accidents that befall you."

Thus being entered upon their journey, they reasoned themselves into a path plain and beaten, the first they met with, wherein Andrenio observed that in all the ways and paths of men, the footsteps seemed to bend forward, and none backwards, a sign that those who followed them, never returned. Not far had they passed before there offered a strange encounter, yet very pleasing and diverting, namely, a disordered band of childish infantry, a squadron of children made up of different conditions and nations, a Babylonish confusion both of fashions, and languages: the governess, and protectress of these was a woman, of a courteous aspect, cheerful countenance, kind words, pious care, who diligently over-eyed, and watched her charge, with the greatest caresses and love, that could be expressed from a most indulgent mother. The servants which she had procured to be assistant to her, were of the same good disposition, and nature like her, who still attended to this helpless board; those that could not go, they carried in their arms, and such as could walk they led by the hand. It was wonderful to observe the tender bowels of this common mother, whose sole thoughts and desires were to pacify their unreasonable complaints, which she hushed with a thousand toys, and baubles, which she had provided for them, together with comfits, and sweetmeats, with which no sooner any cried, than immediately she applied herself to pacify it; but a more special care she took of some of greater finery and bravery than the rest, which seemed the sons, and offspring of more noble families, which she so indulgently contented, as in nothing to restrain their desires, such was the care, and embraces of this pious mother, that the natural parents would resign their trust into her arms, in whose they esteemed them more secure, than in their own. Andrenio was much pleased to see the marches of this tender infantry, admiring, and contemplating on the childish age of man, and taking one into his arms, wrapped in his mantles, said to Critilo, "is it possible this should be a man? who would believe it? is it likely this almost senseless creature, this unprofitable member of the world should with time put on the gravity of Cato, and his babbling tongue persuade with the eloquence of a Seneca, or of a Count monterrey?"

"Now you may see," said Critilo, "what it costs to become a man: for to be so, is not the work of a moments space; brutes soon attain their perfection, and with agility and strength of body live, and move; but man's accomplishments are of a higher value than naturally to grow upon him, or to surprise him at unawares."

"I did much admire," said Andrenio, "this fond affection of this rare woman, and the unnatural bowels of mothers in comparison of hers: So that I who was born within the hard bowels of the rocks, and nurtured among beasts, began to envy this felicity, and to wish a recall of my years, only to deliver my helpless age to the protection of her arms; for I have been exposed to hunger, cold, nakedness, and all has seemed to stop their ears unto my cries, nothing endeavouring to pacify my tender peevishness, or to comply with the weak simplicity of my humour."

"Do not envy," said Critilo, "that which as yet you know not, nor style that a happiness whose end and event is uncertain; for there are many things in the world which bear a different face to what really they are, as you will find by experience; being now come into the world to live, see, and observe: this youthful crowd travelled, without stay, or refreshment, traversing the country, but still descending downward; it was wonderful to see this pigmy band march so stoutly, and that for all the weary steps they fetched, none tired, nor desired repose: they always gave them meat, which for being all the day, may be called but once."

At length, after they had traversed much ground, they found themselves in a deep valley, fortified about with high mountains, the highest of this universal road; by this time it was night, and than the deep profundity of the place made the darkness more horrible: this deceitful woman, the greatest impostor of humane kind, and traitoress to this tender nursery, made her sign; upon which rushed out from the wood, and dismal dens, an army of lions, tigers, bears, wolves, serpents, and dragons, which mercilessly set on this unresisting force, and disarmed bands of innocents, who in a horrible massacre burst themselves, with draughts of their blood, for some they dragged, others they tore in pieces; the blood of some they sucked; and when their ravenous stomachs were satiated, they sported themselves with the plenty of their feast; there was one monster that swallowed down two at once, and not sufficiently filled with these, extended his paws to enclose others: another beast chewed one in his teeth, whilst his claws were preparing another for his palate; and the rest ran furiously about this tragic theatre, drivelling out the overflowing blood, and laden with two of three apiece, the relics of their plenteous fare, they carried to feed their savage-whelps; great was the confusion, and sad, and cruel was the spectacle of these innocents. And yet such was the fond simplicity, and humour of the infants, that they esteemed this destruction and ruin to be a pastime, and a delight, or sport to be devoured, with nods to invite their cruelty, and with open arms to meet half way the approach of death.

Andrenio was much astonished at the horrid treason of such an unexpected cruelty, and being by the diligence of Critilo retired to a secure place, thus sighed, and said, "O traitorous, barbarous, and sacrilegious woman, more cruel and inhumane than the beasts themselves! is this the fruit of so much care, and were these toils, and indulgencies for no intent, or end but this? O innocent lambs! how soon were you made a victim, and sacrifice of your misfortunes? how soon were you betrayed to an untimely ruin? O deceitful world, is this the fruit you bear, and do you protect those who dare to attempt such horrid cruelties? my own hands shall revenge this sin;" with that he furiously arose to destroy the tyrant-mother, whose known guilt hastened her flight, and with the rest of her assistants, went in pursuit of more, which she had already sold to the cruelty of those destroyers, so that she still supplied the hunger of these beasts, whose stomachs continually craved; whilst Andrenio lamented this irreparable damage.

Amidst of this horrid confusion, and cruel massacre appeared on the other side of the valley, over the top of the highest mountain, with the dawning of the day, another woman of a different nature, who encompassed with light, and attended with a train of servants, which winged flew to the speedy delivery of these perishing infants, her countenance was cheerful, though majestic, and being dressed with rows of pearls, and diamonds, sent forth such emissions and rays of light, that she might well stand in competition with, or supply the place, and absence of Aurora: she was beautiful above measure, and with her more glorious light outshone the beauty of her attending ministers. O fortunate accident! for at the same instant that these murdering beasts perceived her approach, they left their prey, and betaking themselves to their legs, with yells and cries retired to their dens; than she began with singular diligence to collect the scattered relics, which were few, and those gored, and lanced with gaping wounds. The rest of her attendants, with the like care searched their obscure dens; and wresting some from the very jaws and mouths of monsters, saved and protected those in whom they saw the least breath, or pantings of life; but Andrenio observed, that these were those of the meanest rank and condition, and most neglected by that cursed mother, which the beasts esteemed of a more coarse diet, having already made their feast of the more delicious dish of her pampered care; when she had collected them altogether, she made no stop, nor delay to clear them from danger; nor did she stay, till she had conducted them to the top of the mountain, as being most secure. From thence she placed them in the view, and by the rays of light she had infused into them, making them sensible of their rescued condition, and of that danger, to which their ignorance had betrayed them. They being thus secured, she presented to every one those precious stones, which were oreservatives against any danger, and which darted forth such rays of light, that they made the night, day, and were the more estimable, because they were not obnoxious to corruption, or decay. She recommended them to the tuition of wise governors, who should direct, and lead them still upwards, till they arrived to the grand city and metropolis of the world; at the same instant they were again alarmed by the cries of more perishing Infants, in the same fatal, and dismal valley; which this valiant and pious queen no sooner heard, but with the rest of her Amazons she marched to defend and succour. Andrenio was greatly astonished at this sight, and wondered to see the variety of fortune, and the successive exchanges of happiness and miseries of this life?

"What two women are these," said he, "and what strange visions are these of different apparitions. Tell me Critilo, who was the first, that I may hate, and abhor her, and who is the second, that I may honour and adore her."

"What do you think, said Critilo, of this entrance into the world, is it not agreeable to those many admonitions and relations I have already delivered you? Observe well the passages, and state of things here, and if such be the beginning, tell me what you conceive may be the progress and conclusion; that so you may always live awake, and be readily provided against the assaults of enemies. You desire to know, who was the first unnatural and cruel mother, whom you at the first sight so much applauded, hereafter be not so rash in your censures, but see the conclusion before you either undertake to commend, or disprise any; know than that this first tyrant is our own bad inclination, and propensity to evil, this is she, that takes advantage on the unripe understanding of infancy, rages, and triumphs in the spoils, to that degree, that the fond impertinency of the parents, would rather suffer their son to live in his folly, than to displease his palate with the bitter pills and remedies of correction; so that they commit him to his own will, and rather not contradict his humour, than that he should cry or be displeased. And in this manner vice, choler, gluttony, deceit, fraud, and peevishness get ground upon him, and he becomes swelled with ignorance, and self-conceit. And thus the passions having gained strength, are seconded by paternal connivance, whereby the evil of depraved nature prevailing, allures the tender infant into the valley of beasts to be made a prey unto vice, and a slave to passions."

"But when Reason breaks forth, which is the queen of light, the mother of undeceived judgment, with the virtues her companions she rescues our depraved wills from the jaws of vice, and heals those wounds which are almost incurable. She finds no small resistance, and opposition to withdraw them from the claws of their evil inclinations, and greater difficulty to direct their steps to the top, and secure habitations of virtue; but the way being steep and difficult, many are discouraged in the journey, and return again to opprobrious vice, most whereof are rich, the sons of monarchs and princes, whose smiling prosperity, and plentiful fare, is the Food, and Nourishment for Vice: but others, who are born poor, and under the rigours of a severe step-mother, do most usually prevail, and like a Hercules, strangle their serpent passions in the very cradle."

"But what was that precious stone," demanded Andrenio, "that she has recommended to us with so much earnestness. Know, answered Critilo, that what some have fabulously reported of the virtue of certain stones, is verified in these; for this is the true carbuncle whose rays and light scatter the clouds of ignorance, and vice; this is the true diamond which resists the hammer of vice; and amidst the fires, and heats of passion, comes forth more pure, and refined. This is the touchstone to examine the good, and bad: This is the lodestone which is always attentive to the North of virtue. In fine, this is the jewel of all virtues, which the philosophers call the dictate of reason, the most faithful and true friend in whom we may confide. Thus they went on conferring, and discoursing together, till they came to a crossway, where the paths were divided, and the diversities of life distinguished, it was a notable knot of difficulty, yet not so much discernable by the understanding, as by the choice and election of the will. But here their doubt was the more increased, by that common tradition of being but two ways, one plain and smooth, on the left hand, with a deep descent, and the other on the right hand, rugged and stony, of a steep ascent; but with no small admiration, Critilo observed that here were three ways, which did the more confound him in his election:

"Heavens guide me now," said he, "is not this the difficult Bivium, where Hercules himself lost his way;" he looked behind, and before, and privately demanded of himself, "Is not this the letter by which Pythagoras described, and ciphered wisdom, which hitherto proceeds equal, and afterwards divides itself into two branches, one broad, which is vice, and the other narrow, which is virtue, but the ends are differently distinguished, one concludes in punishment, and the other honoured, and rewarded with a crown. Hold," said he, "where are those bound marks of Epictetus, the Abstine in the way of delight, and the Sustine in the path of virtue. Well," said he, "we are come to such times of change, that the very kings highways are altered."

"What is that heap of stones," demanded Andrenio, "which stops up the middle of the way?"

"Let us go thither," said Critilo, "for this is the sign of the gold vial, by which he calls and directs us. This is the mysterious heap of mercury, in which our wise ancestors made a hieroglyphic of wisdom, standing with a stretched out hand to point us out the way, or as the clue of thread to guide us out of this labyrinth into heaven."

"But to what purpose," replied Andrenio, "is this unprofitable direction of the way, which serves only to confound or make the unwary traveller to stumble?"

"These are," answered Critilo sighing, "the stones which pilgrims cast up, in tribute, and reward to the instructors of truth and virtue; for such is the envy and malice to piety, that the very stones are raised in opposition against them. Let us go round this pillar, and see if the oracle can give us light in this difficulty.

Critilo read the inscription, which said, "in all things there is a mean, depart not to the extremes." This pillar was from the top to the bottom carved with great artifice, and rarity, and the groundworks and materials not unworthily refined with that curiosity of art. In it were engraved many sententious aphorisms, and allusive histories, which Andrenio admired, and Critilo commented on with much perspicuity, and clearness. Hereon was represented that rash and inconsiderate youth, who mounted the chariot of the sun, and his grave father admonishing him to keep the middle way in which he should drive secure.

"This was," said Critilo, "a youth who ambitiously entering into government, and not observing that mean of prudence, according to the rule, and example his experienced predecessors had instructed him, lost the reigns and bounds of reason, and by immoderate imposition of tributes, contracted such clouds and vapours of envy, that he consumed all, and lost both the world, and his command; on the other side was falling the unwinged Icarus, passing from one extreme unto another, from the fire, into the water, being deaf to the cries of D'dalus, who admonished him to keep the middle. This is another," commented Critilo, who not contented with a convenient knowledge, but endeavouring to soar too high in ungrounded subtleties, and aerious motions, his wings failing him, tumbled down with all his chimeras into the brinish sea of tears, and miseries. This is famous Cleobulus, who in answer to three epistles in which a king had demanded his advice, in three more only wrote modus, as being a most secure way and rule for his government. Observe well one of those seven worthies of Greece, who is eternally chronicled, for that one sentence, 'in all things avoid excess;' as if to exceed were more dangerous, than to be deficient.

Thereon also were engraved all the Virtues, every one with their motto on their targets, and banner, and set in order between their too vicious extremes; at the bottom of all stood valour, who between the extremes of desperation, and cowardice, leaned on a pillar, or support, as a tower, or fortress to defend the rest; at the top of all sat Prudence, who as a queen held a precious crown in her hand, with this inscription, 'For him who knows a mediocrity in wealth.' There were many other Inscriptions, which were definitions of artifice and wit; above all a happy, and serene felicity crowned this curious word, leaning on the wise and famous worthies of past ages, and supported on each side with the two extremes of lamentation, and laughter, whose atlases were Heraclitus, and Democritus, one weeping, and the other laughing. Andrenio took much contentment to see, and consider the epitome of life so fully described, in this miraculous oracle; but by this time were crowded together a multitude of people, who without consulting any other deity than their own will, ran headlong through the extremes, blinded with false spectacles, and delight. And first enters on who without informing himself of any thing, with inconsiderate folly passed through those extremes which the general esteemed the worst, who being the presumptuous, was the soonest lost: after him followed a vain blusterer, who with some few courtesies, and handsome air, and behaviour, without asking any question took the highest way; but being hollow, and empty, was by a sudden puff of wind, blown down, and being high, and so in view of all, was in his fall entertained with the common scorn and derision of the world. There was one way much over-grown with briars, and thorns, which whilst Andrenio persuaded himself none would take, he saw some passionately bent to follow it, striving one with other who should go foremost. The path or track of beasts seemed the most smooth and beaten, and when one was asked why he went that way? he answered him, because he would not go alone. Next to this, was another path, but short, and all that past it made great provision for their bellies, but they journeyed not far, for more died with surfeits, and intemperance, than with want and hunger. Some pretended to fly through the air, but their heads growing giddy, fell down, and these for the most part neither remained in heaven, nor on the Earth. There were others who hurried through a pleasant, and delicious plain, entertaining and sporting themselves with meadows and gardens, till their extravagant motion overheating their blood, cast them into fevers, so that their fair complexions became discoloured, and swarthy, and their faces bad, for having made them good. Not far off some complained of a dangerous passage, infested with thieves and robbers, who notwithstanding ventured on, and at the end turned all to the same profession, one destroying and pillaging the other. But Andrenio observed with much admiration, and Critilo with pleasure, that some were diligently inquisitive to find out those who could inform them which was the way of infallible ruin; one would think it had been to avoid it; but it happened out contrary, for as if there had been a necessity of their destruction, they took the very highway that lead them to it. Andrenio seeing some of them to be of great condition and quality, asked them why they went that way? who answered, they did not go, but were carried by force; nor was less ridiculous that circle that others moved in, who winding in a continual compass, rounding like a wheel, never passed forward, but reeling in a circumference, could not arrive to the point, and centre of virtue. There were others who never found the way, but as soon as they began to set forward, stopped, and gave over their farther progress. These with their hands in their bosoms, sluggishly moved their unnimble legs, which weary of doing nothing, being sick with the scurvy of sloth, fainted before they accomplished their intents. Another said out of love to curiosity he would tread those paths which none had done before him; but being ruled by none but his capricious humour, was soon ruined and lost.

"Do you not observe, Critilo, that all follow in most preposterous ways, and run upon those extremes, which naturally they disaffect and refuse. The fool becomes presumptuous of his parts and knowledge, and the wise, out of a distrustful confidence, is reserved and silent: the coward affects valour, and only talks of arms and war, whilst the valiant disdains them: the comely affect a decent negligence in their dress, and the ill-favoured set out their defects, with helps and advantages, and think they exceed the very Sun in glory and splendour: the prince affects a courteous humility, and the common and ignoble sort vaunt themselves as if they were of more than mortal race: the eloquent are silent; and the ignorant take on them the whole discourse: the dexterous is dissident of his art, and the unskilful fills the world with the unpolished pieces of his rude hand. In fine, you will see all run through extremities, which is the course of error, and which strays from the way of life. But let us pass through the most secure way, the most plausible and happy mediocrity, happy in that it can contain itself in a prudent mean."

There were few whom they could persuade to follow them; yet as soon as they saw them enter on that path, they felt a more than ordinary sense of comfort, and satisfaction of conscience which transported their affections; they observed, that besides those precious jewels which adorned them, they were no less glorious with the rich endowments and abilities of reason, which began to shine, in that degree, that every one seemed a glistering star, forming tongues in his rays, crying out, this is the way of truth, and the truth of life. On the contrary all those that followed the prospects, and glasses of their own brain, soon lost their eyes, and sight, that they blindly wandered, and were eclipsed both in their judgment and journey. Andrenio always observing that they went upward, "this," said he, "seems rather a way to bring us to heaven than to the Earth."

"So it is," said Critilo, "for this is the path that leads us to eternity; for though we trample on the Earth, yet our thoughts are raised above it, and soar to that height, that they become neighbours and citizens with the stars; for these are they which we now eye, and steer by, being engulfed between the Scylla, and Charybdis of the world; for such is the entrance we are now upon into this great city, the Babylon of Spain, the treasury of riches, the theatre of learning, the sphere of nobility, and the large compass of a human life."

Andrenio was more astonished to see the strange accidents of the world, which before he knew not, than when first he proceeded from his cause to the unknown light: for than he beheld them only at a distance, and in a long view and perspective, when to see only and contemplate on them was not so much as by experience to try them; so that all seemed strangely disfigured, and the face of things of a different complexion; but that which was most strange, was that in a populous city, and at midday no man appeared, though they with great diligence and affection sought them.

"Where are the men," said Andrenio, "is not this their country, their beloved world, their desired centre, where than are they gone, or in what part, or place, do they lie concealed?"

They diligently searched in one place, but discovered none, until - but how and where they found them is related in the following Crisis.

The Sixth Crisis

Whosoever hears this word, world, presently conceives an orderly composure of this universe, fitted in the most perfect, and best manner. For the word mundus, signifying as much as clean, or neat. We ought to consider it as some stately palace contrived for the divine and infinite wisdom, erected by omnipotence, and by his provident bounty fitted for man's convenience, that he as king thereof may rule, and maintain the original agreement, and harmony, which the divine creator has settled and ordained. So that it is nothing but a house made, and fitted for God and man; nor is there any other definition, by which its perfection may be more plainly declared; for the very word mundus does sufficiently denote its perfection, and both the beginning and ending are testimonies thereof, but how man's ill management has disappointed this order, and disgraced the honour of this title, was the consideration of Critilo, who, together with Andrenio, were placed in the world, but not in the society and conversation of those, to whose words, and actions they could not confide or trust. They were now busied, and inquisitive in search of men, for having trod many steps, and weariedly travelled over much ground, they met no man, unless it were one, half a man, and half a beast, an encounter welcome to Critilo, but strange and unexpected to Andrenio, who starting, demanded the nature and condition of this deformed monster.

"Do not fear," said Critilo, "for it is more man than man himself; this is the master and ruler of kings, and the king of rulers, this is that wise Quiron, whose presence is as welcome, as the occasion; for his prudence and direction must guide us into this entrance to the world, and hand us in the way, through the journey of our life; with that they went towards him, and saluting him, had their salutes returned with the like civility; they acquainted him that they had been in search of men, and after a hundred turns and walks, either through ill fortune, or scarcity of them, they had met none.

"Wonder not at it," replied the centaur, "for this is not an age for men; such I mean whose noble acts have famed the years of former times. Do you think to find now a don Alonso the Valiant in Italy, a Great captain in Spain, a Henry the Fourth, in France, whose sword has maintained his sceptre, and the Flower-de-Luces made up the hilt and guard of it? There are now no such heroes in this world, nor memory of their past acts."

"And shall there be none hereafter?" replied Andrenio.

"There is no appearance of them at present," said he, "and shortly it will be too late for them to remedy the evils past."

"But why are they not now," demanded Critilo, "and the offspring of this generation?"

"There is much to be said in this," answered Quiron, "for there are some affect to be all, and in truth they are less than nothing, and better that they never had been; some say also that envy cuts off many with the scissors of Tomeras; but I say, that neither this nor that is the cause, but that whilst vice prevails, virtue cannot flourish, by whose assistance heroic greatness receives its being: believe me, Venus benumbs and stupefies minerva in every joint, and member, and in regard her chief habitation is in the smoke of the forge, and in conversation of mean mechanics, is not to be esteemed a fit companion for noble Belona. In fine, let us not weary ourselves in so vain a search, for this is not an age for eminent persons, either renowned for arms, or learning; but tell me, where have you sought them?"

"Where should we," said Critilo, "but on the Earth; in this country, and element of their life."

"You are much mistaken," said the centaur, "and in this time of scarcity you will have good fortune to find them there, since their inconstant humour desiring change, has with a nauseous stomach, and glut of this ordinary enjoyment altered their natural habitation."

"If we find them not on the Earth," said Andrenio; "we shall have less hopes to find them in heaven, and if we find them in neither of these; where can we expect them, in the air? for there they have built castles and towers of wind, in which they have fortified themselves, not being willing to depart from their own chimera's."

"But these feeble bulwarks," said Critilo, "will soon dissolve in confusion; for they not being like a Janus of prudence, looking on all sides, become a common derision, and the mark of the scorning finger, whose disgrace is pointed out, and are denied as bastard sons the title of their more noble ancestors, that what some have opprobriously derided behind their backs, others with the same contempt, like dirt will spatter in their faces."

"There are some," proceeded Quiron, "who have raised, and exalted themselves to the very clouds, and in their fond fancies, though buried in the dust, have imagined their heads advanced to the stars; there are some who walk in imaginary paths, and climb up into the highest rooms of their own presumption, and would yet get higher than the moon, did not more noble bodies possess the place."

"It is true," said Andrenio, "there they are, for I have seen them wrapped up in the clouds, some stumbling, and others falling, all changing according to the inconstancy of the planet, which sometimes shows one countenance, and than another; nor do they cease to jostle and shoulder one another, and tripping up each others heels they fall with more hurt to themselves than they are sensible of."

"Was there ever such folly," said Critilo, "is not the Earth the proper and natural centre of man, his beginning and his end? Were it not more prudence to preserve himself in a moderate mean, than by too high aspiring, incur an imminent danger? Never was there such folly."

"If the folly be great," said Quiron, "there is place for pity and for laughter; to behold him who yesterday slept in a tottering cottage, to day is lodged in a palace, esteeming it too mean a dwelling for his greatness; and speaks over that shoulder, which yesterday boar the weight and burden on it: He that was born under the thatched roof, now contrives his fretted ceilings, and cedar rafters, he condemns the society of those, who in his poverty despised his, and to the highest point stands on the punctilios of his base family; he who yesterday had not to buy bread, his stomach is now curious, that the greatest delicacy becomes nauseous, and runs the line of his unknown pedigree: Thus all pretend to rise, and to mount above the horns of the moon, which are more dangerous than the bulls; for being removed from their own centre, must naturally decline, and return to their own place with exemplary infamy."

Whilst he was thus discoursing, he had led them into the High-Street, where they encountered multitudes of beasts, free, and unbound, dangerous to unwary passengers; some whereof were lions, others tigers, leopards, wolves, bulls, panthers, foxes, intermixed with serpents, dragons, and basilisks. Andrenio at this sight, was much troubled, and starting backwards, demanded whether this were a habitation of human society, or a wood of beasts.

"Do not fear," said the centaur, "only be cautious."

"Doubtless men," said Critilo, "the ancient inhabitants out of a distaste to the miscarriages of this world, are retired into the solitary mountains, and left these palaces desolate, and to be inhabited by beasts, who only imitate and counterfeit citizens."

"It's true," replied Quiron, "for in the tower of the potent, with whom there is no contending. resides the lion; to the murderer, succeeds the tiger, in the wealthy coffers of the covetous lies the wolf, the fox hides himself under the deceitful covering, and vizard of the fraudulent, and the viper within the bed and curtains of the harlot: So that all is filled with beasts, and brutes, who walk the streets, inhabit the dwellings, whilst the true men are banished thance; and live retired within the limits of their own wisdom and moderation."

"Let us sit," said Andrenio, on the rising of the hill, that so we may with more ease, and security over-see these passages."

"No," replied Quiron, "for this is not a place nor world to take a stand, or sit in."

"Let us than," said Critilo, "repose us against some of these Pillars."

"No," said he, "for these will soon deceive us, being false, weak, and unstable; it is better to be still in motion, walking and passing from one to another."

The ground was here very unlevel, and unequal, for at the doors of the Powerful and Rich, were high heaps and mountains, which shone with much lustre and splendour.

"How much gold is here," said Andrenio?"

"Observe," said Quiron, "that all is not gold that glistens;" and coming nearer, they perceived that it was nothing but counterfeited wares, and ordure gilded over; but on the contrary at the doors of the poor, and feeble, was such a deep, and horrid abyss, that struck a terror to all that beheld it, so that all shunned it, and beholding it at a distance, would not come within a thousand leagues of it; whilst certain beasts unweariedly travelled all the day long, still casting a continual mass of mud and dirt, on those large heaps, and hills of the rich, adding as it were mountain unto mountain."

"What disparity is this," said Andrenio, "were it not better to cast these superfluities of earth to fill up those cavities and deep abysses of the poor, so as to level and make smooth these rude and uneven ways?"

"It's true, it were better," said Quiron, "but what is there in this world which tends unto the best; we may here disprove that conclusion of the schools, that impossibility in natural philosophy, that there is no vacuum, or emptiness; for alas! in our moral Ewxperiments we daily find the contrary; the world gives not to them, who have not, but to those who already plentifully enjoy; and there are many who loose the small bounty of fortune which they have, for no other reason than because it is adjudged and condemned to more crowded and over-slowing coffers. Gifts are not the companions of poverty, nor do presents follow the foot- steps of departed friends. It is gold that guilds the plate, and one calls and invites the other; the rich are those that inherit, and boast of their lineage, whilst they scarce give license to the poor to acknowledge his parent. The hungry shall scarce obtain bread to support Nature, and the over-burdened stomach be a continual guest to a luxurious table: So that he that is once poor, shall be always poor, the general rule of the world's inequality."

"Whither shall we go now?" demanded Andrenio.

"Let us go," said they, "through the middle, where we shall pass with less throng, and more security."

"I think," said Critilo, "I see some men, or at least those who esteem themselves such. These are less than any," said Quiron, for looking toward the corner of the street, they perceived some walk with much gravity, hanging their heads downward to the ground, and their noses grabling in the dirt, and kicking up their legs, and feet in the air, made no progress nor way forward, but at every step stumbled and fell, and notwithstanding this, they still obstinately persist in this course of walking which was as dangerous as ridiculous. At this sight Andrenio much admired, and Critilo laughed.

"Suppose now," said Quiron, "that you dream waking: Oh! How excellent well did Bosio paint these things; for now I understand his fancy. Do but observe, and you shall see incredible follies. Those who ought to be the chief heads and commanders for their prudence, are despised, and forgotten, drooping, and hanging their heads toward the earth; on the contrary those who for want of knowledge and experience in affairs, ought to be the feet are the commanding heads, and the first movers of that wheel which turns the world, you shall find no thing in its right order and rule, and because the world wants itself both head and feet, does in conformity thereunto commit its government to the weakest understanding."

These were scarce out of sight, before another, as preposterous a spectacle as the former offered itself, and these were men who still went backwards, and according to this motion all their actions tended and looked behind them.

"What other absurdity is this?" said Andrenio, "if the world abounds with such fancies and capriccios as these, we may take it for a college of fools, or associated changelings."

"Has not Nature," considered Critilo, "placed both our eyes, and feet, with a natural aptness to tend forwards, that so we may see where we go, and go where we see, with the most security, and the least danger. How than do these blindly walk, and with small advertency mind either their way or motion?" "Observe," said Quiron, "these are men, who instead of making progress in honour, wisdom, and prudence, relapse, or return backwards again, before they arrive to any perfection of being men; such I mean as our count of Pegmoranda. Consider the folly of yonder woman, man, observe what she drives at; she would by no means pass twenty years, and the other will never count above thirty; for arriving at a certain period, they fix there, as at the full stop or stage of years; for women would never grow old, though they would as unwillingly recall the time of their first childhood. See how lame age has rivelled and furrowed the foreheads of some, and dragging them by their unbound hair, has plucked off the best ornaments of Nature: See what a blow he has given, and another that her teeth drop out before, and eyebrows rot with years? How has he altered their complexions and faces, and transformed their beauty to an uncomely vizard."

"Hold," said Andrenio, "do you speak of women? where are they? for I have but small skill as yet in the distinction of sexes, did not you tell me Critilo, that women were of a weak nature, and men strong and courageous; that man spoke strongly and loud, and women with a low shrillness; that the habits of men are a cloak and breeches, and women are covered with loose garments, and veils: but I find all this contrary, for either men are degenerated, and become women, or all women are become men, or both sexes are confused: men with their tongues between their teeth, stand quiet, and mute, and women with their shrill voice speak so loud, that they open the Ears, and work a miracle on the deaf hearer, these rule the world, and men are only ciphers and actors of their commands. Thou hast deceived me Critilo.

"It is true," said Critilo, sighing, "for men are now more feeble, and less than women; one tear or drop from a woman's eyes, avails more than all those streams of blood which valour has let forth: the least smile and favour from a woman persuades more, than the sweetest tongue, and rhetoric of the eloquent. In fine, we can neither live with them, nor without them; never were they more esteemed than now, and their power so far enlarged, that they are able to do all, and undo all. In vain has Nature denied them the ornament of a beard for distinction; and that their blushes and modesty might be more apparent in their cheeks; for neither of these is available against the impetuous violence of their spirits."

"According to this," said Andrenio, "man is not the king of the world, but the slave and vassal of the woman."

"Know," said Quiron, "that naturally man is king and sovereign, and was so until he had made woman his companion: but that you may be better acquainted with this sort of creatures, you must know that when they have most need of discretion, and courage, it than fails them most; but yet there are some exceptions from this general rule, which are verified in that incomparable princess of Rosana, and that most excellent lady the marquess of Valdueza, and others."

But that which caused most admiration, was one who instead of a horse rode on a fox, which always went backwards, making continual turnings and windings at every step, his whole train also which followed him, and those not few, imitated him in the like motion, together with an old dog, his usual companion.

"Do you see this," said Quiron, "I will assure you, it is to some purpose and intent, he makes these twistings and labyrinths in his way."

"I believe it," said Critilo, "for all the world seems to pass through extremes: but who is this, pray tell us, for he is one who looks more like a knave, than a fool?"

"Did you never hear the name of the famous Caco, that engine of policy, the confused chaos of reason of state; for in this manner all politicians work backwards, that so they may not make discovery of their intentions by their actings: for they would by no means be traced by their footsteps; for though their eyes point one way, the path they walk leads to another; they publish not what they intend, and in saying 'yes,' they mean 'no:' so that they act always by contraries, and their ciphers are most legible when they are read backwards, one had need of another Hercules, who with force, and a sledge of iron, might level and make plain these paths, and cut in sunder their intrigues and knots of deceit."

Andrenio observed that the chiefest part of those that spake, whispered their words not into the ears but into mouth of the hearers, who were not displeased with the gross absurdity, but with the like indecency kindly received, and gaping with an open mouth, and forming their lips into ears, ravenously sucked in the distillation of their words.

"Was there ever such absurdities," said he, "words were made for the ears, not for the mouth; but these people eat them, and drink them, suck them in like sugared comfits"

"'Tis true that they proceed from the lips, but they die in the ears, and their tomb, and grave is formed in the Heart."

"But these seem to lick and chew them in their mouths, and with this aerious nourishment sustain their vanity."

"It is a sign," said Critilo, "they carry but little truth in them, since their taste is sweet, and have no relish of bitterness in the stomach."

"Do you not know," said Quiron, "that the chiefest art is to speak those words which are savoury to the palate. Observe Andrenio how yonder lord sucks in the syrup of flattery; see what draughts he makes of the sweet liquor of adulation; believe me though he seems attentively to hearken, yet his ears receive not the sound, for the words vanish into air. Consider yonder prince how he gluts himself with lies, though never so incredible; 'tis a most strange thing to consider that this man never disbelieved a lie, though he heard never so many, and yet never believed truths, though few were told him, and those seldom. What do ye think of t'other vain fool? what do you think he is filled with? it is nothing of substance but air and vanity."

"This must be the cause," considered Critilo, "that those whom truths most nearly concern, can yet seldom hear them, for they are bitter, and give a bad relish to the palate, so that either as unpleasing they refuse them; or else endeavouring to swallow them, the squeamish tenderness of their stomachs is not able to digest them."

But that which scandalized them most, was the sight of some vile and servile slaves to themselves, dragging their own bolts and chains, wherewith their arms were manacled, that they might not be able to extend them in acts of liberality; or in the pious works of honour, and virtue, their necks wore a slavish collar, the note and sign of their voluntary servitude; their feet chained and manacled, suffered them not to make one step in the way of fame, or of a good reputation, and thus laden with irons, and locked in their bolts, and in a condition more of shame, than glory, yet with an impudent boldness stood enthroned, and applauded, commanding men of better blood, and nobility, enslaving the free-born state and condition of those who willingly submitted to their rod, and bowed their shoulders to receive the weight of their vile burden.

At this sight Andrenio, as being not able to hold longer, cried out, "who will dare to approach near these, and contest with the abuse of fortune? How I could kick down these misemployed seats, and change the condition of the others, into what their own virtue and merits have deserved."

"Do not speak so loud," said Quiron, for you undo us. It is no matter if this be permitted, though all run to ruin and destruction. Do you not see that these are the powerful rulers; those who, &c. ---- are these? If these slaves of their own appetites, servants to delight; these *Tiberius's, Nero's, Caligula's, Heltogabulus's, and Sardanapalus's* are such as are idolized and adored, and the true commanders, and lords of themselves, free, and in subjection to none, are slaves and vassals of servitude. Why than let the sound health, and uncorrupted body, be stretched, and laid out for its grave, and the sick and dead corps walk the streets: let the fresh, and lively colour faint and droop, let those whose sick and ill consciences have made their looks pale, recover courage and strength, let the sound entrails be insufficient to maintain life, and the corrupted lungs breath the strongest blast: let those whose weak stomachs the smell of nourishment offends, grow fat; and let the dropsical and the lame be supported with sound feet and active hands."

"For thus," said Andrenio, "all things walk contrary in this world, the good creep and crawl humbly on the earth, and the base vileness of the bad is exalted."

But that which was pleasing and new, caused much laughter, was to see a blind man, with eyes more dim and dark than his own vileness, more thick and misty than an April cloud; with as much presumption as blindness undertook to conduct, and guide those of more quick eyes and sight than himself, leading the van whilst they silently followed, without any doubt, or fear of the way.

"This is a brave daring blindness," said Andrenio.

"But dishonest and base,| said Critilo, "that the blind should lead the blind, though there be folly enough in the thing, yet it has been seen and known with the fall of both into the same pit of ruin, and destruction; but that the blind should guide those that see, is an unheard of folly, and a preposterous madness."

"I, said Critilo, "do not wonder that the blind should pretend to direct others that see, because he may believe that all are as blind as himself, but that those who see, and observe the danger before their eyes, into which their blind guides would precipitate them, should accept of their service, and tumble with them, and yet go forward till they fall into the same deep pit, and abyss of infelicities, is a most incredible folly, and a monstrosity of madness."

"Know," said Quiron, "that though this be a most transcendent piece of rashness, yet it is a folly that each day represents us with, and more often is it acted in our preposterous times than formerly; for those who know least, pretend as great doctors to instruct others; the intemperate and luxurious undertake to read lectures of sobriety, and to sit in the chair to expound, and comment on lessons of morality. Our own experience can testify how one blind with affections of a woman, as ill favoured as infamous, has seduced infinite to follow him, and thrown them down the precipice of eternal misery: This is not the eighth miracle, but the eighth prodigy. For the first step of ignorance, is a presumption of knowledge, and many would know more, did they not already think they knew too much."

They had no sooner let pass these sights, but they heard a confused noise and combustion, amidst a crowd, and throng, in a corner of the marketplace, as if a quarrel or contest had arisen amongst the people: for it happened that a woman, the usual cause and author of disturbance, ill-favoured and deformed, but set out, and adorned to the best advantage; for the whole world had bestowed the best ornaments she could find to dress, and deck her with; but she scolded and raved, and railed at another woman, which was of much better temper, and wholly contrary to her disposition; for she was a woman amiable and fair, her clothing course, but clean, and becoming, yet scarce sufficient to cover her nakedness, which some attributed to the poverty of her condition, others said, she did it to show her comely stature, and the due proportion of her parts. At these revilings and scorns which were cast upon her, she was silent, for the prevailing force of her enemies, who were the chiefest and most numerous of the world, overawed her in her speech, so that she durst not reply to those many affronts, but received all with silence. In fine, all sided against her, passing from jest to earnest, from words to blows, and as it were stifled in the crowd of adversaries, none durst to oppose so strong an enemy, or like the champion take up the buckler in defence of the oppressed; but Andrenio, naturally compassionate, was inclinable to take her part, had not Quiron prevented him, by saying, "do you know whose cause you patronize, and against whom you declare, know you not that it is against plausible falsity, which is as much as to take part against the whole world. However the simplicity of children would have taken the part of truth, and have risen in her defence; but alas! their childish strength, and policy was unable to prevail against inveterate and old malice, so they were content only to praise truth, and speak it. Thus was beautiful truth stripped, and forsaken, and by degrees so pushed and shouldered, that at length she was jostled into those remote parts, from whence we can have no news or tidings of her abode or residence."

"It is well," said Andrenio, "I see now there is no justice in this world, and yet it is true, that there are ministers of it."

"There is justice," said Quiron, "and that not far off, since falsity stands so near."

With this there appeared a man, as severe, as Cato, his aspect and countenance rigid, accompanied with others of the same profession; at his first appearance falsity went towards him, and with many of those few reasons which she had in store, she informed him the condition of her present state; he answered, that he would presently give sentence in her favour, and that by his authority she should be licensed to wear feathers; with that she instantly clapped in his hand winged-feet, with which swiftly flying, he firmed the banishment of liberty his mortal enemy.

"Who is that?" demanded Andrenio, who trusts the stay of his body to the feeble support of a weak rod?"

"That is," answered Quiron, "a justice, who is so called, because he sells it, he is one, who feels first, that he may hear the better afterwards."

"What means that sword," said he, "they carry drawn before him, and to what purpose is it?"

"This," said Quiron, "is the ensign and badge of his dignity, and the instrument of punishment, and justice; and that which lops and cuts the over-grown branches, and weeds of vice."

"It were more available," replied Critilo, "to tear them from the root, than only to pare the luxuriant branches, by which they gather more strength daily."

"So it ought to be," answered Quiron, "but these men prune the roots of vice, that they may yield more fruit, and a constant harvest, whereby the sins of the people may be their livelihood and maintenance."

This judge suddenly, and without more appeal condemned to death a poor fly, for no other reason than because it was entangled within the web and net of the law: but an elephant who had trampled, and trod down all, without sparing or respecting, either human or divine justice, was so far from being chastised for it, that with much reverence the Judge treated him in his passage, and let him pass undisturbed, though loaded with prohibited weapons, as grenades, daggers, pick-locks, and wild-fire, and in complement demanded of him if he would permit him leave to crowd in amongst the rest of his attendants, and to accompany him to the entrance of his den. Nor did his injustice stop here, but catching another poor fellow by the shoulder, who durst not cry out, without farther matter condemned him to be whipped, and some asking the reason of his punishment, it was answered again, that he had no back to support a burden, which if he had had, he should like others have been charged with load upon load. This judge was no sooner out of sight, but appeared another, who as some valiant general was introduced with the applauses, and acclamations of the people, and might be compared to don Paula de Parada, he was armed with back and breast, and fitted for all numbers, times, and persons: his arms were two pistols, but dormant in their holsters; he was mounted on a cropped horse, but had not lost his ears for his own faults; he had a thing gilded for a sword, which for many good respects was never drawn; he was more than a man in his words, but less than a woman in his fears; he had a cap of feathers, a very pye of gallantry, but a hen in valour. "Who is this," demanded Andrenio, "a man, or a monster?"

"The question is very apt," said Quiron, "for some nations unused to this sight, have at first view, imagined the horse, and man both one. This is a soldier, who were he such in his manners, he would not be so ragged in his conscience."

"Of what use are these in the world?" said Andrenio.

"These are," replied he," the chastisers of our enemies, but a worse scourge and plague to our friends; these are those who defend us, but may divine providence defend us from them. These fight, destroy, and kill, and are the terror and devourers of our adversaries."

"How can this be?" said Andrenio, "for they say that these very men make, and raise enemies themselves."

"Hold," said Quiron, "I speak what their office does enjoin and oblige them unto; but now is the world so corrupted, that the remedies of evils, are the causes of them, and the medicine to cure our sickness is the destruction of our health. These that ought to end war, and close the breaches, are those that husband, and prolong them; for they knowing that their own fortunes are small, and their income not sufficient to sustain their lives, piece out their fortunes with the employment of war: for were it ended, they would remain without office, and without benefit: wherefore than should they kill the sentinels of the marquis of Peseara, since they live by the enemy? This is a policy which to the very drummer and meanest officers is known so well, that the breach which prudence and sincere conscience might make up in one year's space, is continued seven, nay double, and would remain for ages, or to eternity, had not valour and success been now united in the marquis of mortara. The same censure did they pass on another, who being likewise on horseback, as bold and confident as a mountebank, pretended knight errant like to ease the afflicted, and with his art to cure languishing Nature: but he was but a charlatan, for all his drugs operated so ill, that the sound were impaired by them in health, and the sick by his means were given over by the physician. He was one who declared war against life and death, the open enemy of them both, neither a friend to the dead, nor to those who were perfectly living, but ran in a medium (the only bad one) between both. That himself might eat, he brings his patients to short allowance, and beguiling them of their meat grows fat himself: whilst they lie under the mercy of his hands, his care forbids them meat, and if their health admits them to quit his cure, which seldom happens, the patient will soon perceive the policy the physician used to restrain the danger of his future excess; so that these live, and feed on the spoil, with more cruelty than the executioner: for as he studies with the nimblest art, to end the pain of the malefactor, these are the tormentors of life, esteeming it the best part of their skill, to linger out life to the last gasp; and to sustain a continued course of sickness, a better art than to recover health, these are as an infected air of sickness, and where are most physicians, are most diseases; This is the common calumny that the vulgar has cast upon them; but for my own part, I think none can either speak good, or bad of the physician; for he on whom his art has not been exercised, rails at his cruelty, would be censured as passionate without Reason: and he who has already fallen into his hands, has neither tongue, nor breath to make his complaint; but mistake me not, for here I speak not of the natural physician, but the moral, into whose hands is committed the distempered condition of the republic, who instead of easing, and remedying indisposed affairs, foment and distract them, and where is required a sudden recovery, the unskilfulness of these physicians reduce the fever to a lingering consumption."

"How comes it to pass," said Andrenio, "that we can meet no man of honesty passing this way?" "These," said Quiron, "are not in motion, but are permanent pillars, and durable, whose immortal fame never dies, and their number so small, that they are enrolled and listed in letters of gold: who are named in the same scarcity, as the unicorn in Arabia, or the phoenix in the East; however if you will feign see one, look for Cardinal Sandoval in Toledo, the Count de Lemos, Governor in Aragon, the arch-duke Leopold in Flanders; and if you will find integrity, justice, truth, and all virtue concerned in one, behold d. Luis d' Haro in that centre, which he enjoys and deserves."

They being now wearied with these prodigious spectacles, desired to retire some time for repose; but Andrenio stretched out his arms, lifting his eyes to heaven, fetched most deep sighs, as if he would make the stars take notice of his complaints.

"How is this," said he, "have I myself lost my reason, or with the society of the frantic, has my own brain been made giddy? methinks all is blasted with the world's contagion, nay the heaven seems confused, and time to have changed his course, and as recalled to move backward: Is it day, demanded he, or night? but let us have a care that we fall not into guesses, or conjectures, for that will serve more to perplex, and confound us than we were before."

"Hold," said Quiron, "for the world's misrule is not to be attributed to the influence of heaven, but to the Earth's own disorderly motion; for things have not moved contrary to their natural course only as to place, but are confused also as to times, and seasons, for some make the day night, and the night day. One rises hot from his bed, when another as weary with his labour, inclines to repose: some go than from home with the light only of Venus star, and return to their rest, with the beams and dawning of the morning; and these who are thus singular in their lives, are those of the most famous families, the illustrious nobility, who yet deserve that sentence, which one passed on them, *'That he who by night lives and wanders like a beast, by day must live more like a brute than a man.'*"

"This is the course of the world," said Critilo, "but let us retire to our beds, least we incur the same censure; nor am I willing to desist now, since it is night, and little to be seen."

"Why," said Andrenio, "do they call the world *mundus*, the very name seems to belie it, being not worthy of so honourable a title, its nature being better expressed by something that denotes uncleanness, and corruption of it?"

"There was a day," replied Quiron, "when this word was but a true description of its nature, when first this uncomely fabric proceeded from the unpolluted hands of the divine creator,

"But whence comes this disorder than?" demanded Andrenio, "or who has subverted, and overthrown its foundation, or with an unskilful pencil defaced the lines of this equal proportion?"

"There is much to be said in this," replied Quiron, "this subject have the learned already treated on, and these defects are sufficiently bewailed in the philosophers' meditations. Some attribute this disorder to the blindness, and Folly of Fortune, who each day changes her motion, and neither leaves place, nor seasons unaltered. Others say that when Lucifer of the morning fell, he gave so hard a blow on the Earth, that he struck the world from off the hinges, turning it from one side unto the other. Others lay the fault on the woman, styling her the universal disturber, and the sole cause of all confusions: But I say we need not seek any other subject, on whom more justly to cast the guilt, and accusation hereof, than on man himself, the unquietness of whose spirit is sufficient to distract a thousand worlds, and that there are not more worlds for him to disturb, is the sorrow, and complaint of the principal inquieter if the divine providence had not fixed the *primum mobile*, or first mover into that sphere, to which his malice, and fury has not possibility to climb, the Sun had before now changed his course, and made the West the place of his arise, and terminated his stage in the confines of the East: so had Spain become one of the extreme poles of the world, and so made inhabitable by any. It is a thing worth observation, that man, who is a creature endued with reason, should in the first act and operation of it, commit it to the subjection and obedience of his appetite, from whence, as from the fountain and original of all are derived those contradictions which succeed; nor can it be otherwise since they are but consequences of the first capital disorder. Hence it is that virtue is persecuted, and vice applauded, truth silenced, and falsity endued with a three-fold tongue to vent its deceits, the knowing are robbed of their libraries, and the ignorant confounded in the multitude of their leaves, the doctor is without his books, and the books without the doctor; the discretion of the poor is esteemed folly, and the extravagant discourse of the rich a treasury of knowledge, those who undertake to recover life, destroy it, youth withers and decays, and the decrepit years of the aged grow green, and flourish; In fine, man is arrived to that pitch, and height of madness, that he has forgot almost to know his right hand, so mistaking it, he placeth the way to happiness on the left. Thus does he cast the greatest matter of importance behind his back, treads virtue underfoot, and instead of going forward, turns again."

"If things go thus," said Andrenio, "why than didst thou Critilo draw, and seduce me from my own world, wherein I was free in my own solitariness? Let me return again to that cave of my nothing, to that high precipice of my rock, and retire from this sink, and confusion of the world."

"It is now too late," replied Critilo, "O how many would return now back again if they could; but this has Nature denied, being that policy whereby the world is preserved and peopled. Observe how we still move us this ladder of life, and how we leave the steps of our days behind us, which we no sooner pass, but they vanish, leaving us no means, and remedy of descent."

"How is it possible," said Andrenio, still contesting, and tormenting himself, "that we should live and suffer this preposterous humour of the world; must I be mute, and see the enormities of the world in silence, can my patience bear this, and yet not burst with choler?"

"Alas!" said Quiron, "if you were left to your own humour but for four days only, you would accommodate yourself to the age you live in, nor would you be so severe in your censures of other men." "Who," said he, "am I, one of those distempered brains, or one of those vulgar and mean spirits?"

"Do you hear," said Critilo, thou art not able to pass, and imitate the wise Sages of past times, though it were only in swallowing your own spittle. The world is the same now as than, the same which they found it, the same they left it. The wise Count of Castrillo lives now, and yet he is not outrageous as you are. Likewise the marquis of Caretto passes with patience."

"What course than," replied Andrenio, "did they take being so prudent?"

"Why," said Critilo, "they did only see, hear, and were silent. But is there none that endeavours now to correct things? Yes, Fools. Why Fools? Because 'tis as impossible, as to unite the two Castiles, or to discompose Aragon; for who can hinder that cardinals should not adopt nephews, and others entertain private favourites, that the French should not be tyrants, that the English should not be as deformed in their souls, as they are comely in their bodies, that the Spaniards should not be proud, and the Genoese, &c."

"Well than," said Andrenio, "I will return to my ancient grave, to my former society of beasts, since I see no remedy to ease these miseries."

"Hold," said Quiron, "I will give you as easy, as true a lesson, if you will hearken to me in this following Crisis."

The Seventh Crisis

The whole army of passions banded themselves against man, as their common enemy, and declared the quarrel on no other grounds, than his favouring reason. The battle being now ranged, and both sides ready to give the assault, discord entered the field, coming neither from Hell, nor as some report, from the tents of war, but from the house and habitation of hypocritical ambition. Her business was to move a competition amongst them, who should lead the front and van of the battle, each vice pretending to it, with such boastings of its strength, and valour, as made the question more hardly to be decided. Riot pretended the principal places, because she was the first passion that encountered man, and had gained on him the first victory in his cradle. Lasciviousness alleged the success of her valour, and that her merits might deserve a greater command, since her victorious successes had so often gained the laurel, and made such spoils on youth the strength of man. Covetousness pleaded to be the root of evils, pride vaunted its noble descents, and family, as a seed and branch of Heaven, and was the only vice peculiar to man, and the rest in a lower degree common to beasts. Anger took these boastings much in disgust, and in a furious rage began the fight, the success as yet being doubtful, the end concluded in a general confusion. malice desirous to make up the difference in a grave oration, represented the danger of this civil war, and that their strength united would be more available, where the power of one would be assistant to the other; and as to the present dispute, told them, that this command from whence the present discord arose, was always adjudged due to her eldest daughter falsity: for she is the author of evil, the fountain and source of vice, the mother of sin, the infectious harpy, the many-headed hydra, the various shaped proteus, the centimanus of war, the Caco of policy, and the fruitful womb always pregnant with errors, and deceits. It was fraud that assaulting credulity, and malice taking advantage on ignorance, which entrapped the world, and delivered it into the immense grasp of the world's monarch; It is falsity and deceit which invest the easy nature of man, and take advantage on his childhood, and youth, whereby he is disabled to resist their stratagems, treasons, frauds, delusions, fallacies, and the whole train and method of Italian devices, to that either sooner or later he yields his judgment a trophy to deceit.

The truth of this philosophy has been confirmed by the success of Critilo and Andrenio, who having but lately quitted the society of cautious Quiron, who by his industry, and council, had exempted them from the confusion of Babel, the world's register; and having placed them in the direct road, returned again as guide to direct others. Andrenio was now well armed against these dangers, with the various lectures he had received from him, but especially by the assistance of a glass, which changed the common prospect of the world, and made all things appear with their natural defects, though disguised with the mask which fraud had put on them: for so ought every one to behold this world with an eye different from the vulgar view, and to understand things in the same notion, that the wise Count d'Oniate apprehended them. When you see a presumptuous opiniator, believe him a fool, the rich suppose poor, in respect of those true riches of felicity: He who commands all, is the common slave; the man that is biggest, is in bulk not much a man, the gross and fat have but little of substance; he that would seem to be deaf, hears more than he would, and the acute-sighted is blind, or will be so. He that smells out much, leaves a bad savour of himself in the nostrils of all; the talkative speaks nothing; he who laughs, raves with fury; who excuses, condemns himself; who eats most, eats least; who discommends the merchandize, desires it most; who acts the fools part, is the wittiest comedian; who wants nothing, wants himself; the covetous enjoys equally that which he has not, as what he has; the greatest clerk is seldom the wisest man; who desires a good life, desires a good death; and he who loves life most, most abhors it; who invites his friend to a plentiful table, is he that causes him to fast; folly is often seen in good conjectures; the most straight, is crooked; he that goes the nearest way home, goes the farthest about; who would not lose one mouthful, loses a hundred; the best which cost most, is best cheap; he who makes thee weep, is thy best friend. In fine, that which one affects most, and esteems the greatest, is the most unworthy, and of the smallest value. With this discourse they eased their tedious steps, which insensibly passed away, till the encounter of another monster interrupted them, which now did not, as formerly, astonish nor distract their thoughts, for they had learned that they must in this world expect to meet diversities of prodigies one after another. For now came towards them a coach, which was not usual in so bad a road; but being made so artificially, and with such nimble joints, it passed through all rubs, straights, and difficulties; the beasts that drew it were two flea-bitten jades, like serpents, and the coach-man a fox; Critilo asked if it were not a Venetian chariot; to which the coach-man replied in a manner far from the purpose, as if he understood not, what he demanded; within rode a monster, or rather many, for so often changed he his colour, and shape, sometimes black, anon white, than young, anon old, sometimes great, sometimes little, than a man, a woman, a beast, that Critilo soon discovered him to be the famous Proteus. As soon as he came near them, he alighted from his seat, and with more bows and cringes than a young French monsieur, which are the prologues to deceit, and than with more complements than an Aragonesa, welcomed them in behalf of his great master, offering them the convenience of his palace, where they might ease, and refresh their bodies already wearied with so long a journey. They both having returned their thanks, for so unexpected a favour, demanded who was his lord, who in so small knowledge of them, and their deserts, had so courteously obliged them.

"He is," says he, "a mighty prince, whose territories, though they extend over the compass of the world, yet keeps the famous metropolis of his court, in this first entrance of the Earth and life. He is a monarch more great than any, in that kings are his feudatories and vassals, and few there are who unsubdued by his power pay him not tribute; for besides the flourishing estate of his kingdom in peace, and plenty, it is the academy of arms, and learning, and rewards the most forward proficient's herein; let him who would understand the root of policy, artifice, and cunning, apply himself to this court, where he shall learn to thrive, and pass in the world, to insinuate into the affections and favours of advantageous acquaintance, and both win friends, and preserve them, and especially to cloak and disguise things with fictitious colours, which is the masterpiece, and most useful lesson of art, and knowledge."

This report was persuasion enough for Andrenio, to visit his greatness, and to be educated in a court, or school rather of so much policy; and being overcome with his civilities, stepped into the coach, reaching out his hand to draw in Critilo; but he being more cautious and experienced than the other, turned again to demand the titles and name of this mighty prince, who being so great as fame had reported, could not but be adorned with titles and honours equivalent to his dominions.

"His titles," answered this Officer, "are many, summing up a catalogue of names, and surnames, run over multitudes of appellations, and told him that every part of his territories, and successes of his noble achievements, had inserted new titles into the list of his honours: but his most natural, and original name is not vulgarly received, being his majesty and Greatness admits few to see him, much less to know him: he is a king of much authority, not to be reckoned amongst the petty number of provincial princes, but one of great state, whose retirement and difficulty of access renders his person more awful and reverenced. At the end of lustrums, or some period of years, his courtesy admits the longing curiosity of some to his presence, which is a blessing of their Fortune, and excess of his favour,"

With this discourse he had insensibly drawn them out of the way, into another path more intricate and crooked, which when Critilo observed, he was desirous to return from whence he had erred, before it was too late; but what with the windings and turnings of the road, and with the persuasion of the guide, who confidently assured them of his knowledge of the way, and the multitude of the passengers that they saw travelling therein, he had much ado to retreat back. Howsoever Critilo made a stop here, and coming to a way with three paths, was doubtful which way to take, and therefore warned Andrenio to be now careful of himself, and more watchful and cautious than ever before. For being now come to the fountain of thirst, so named from the longing thirst of those travellers, that were enamoured with its fame; for its curious invention exceeded the works of Juanelo, and the continual current of its waters was the celebrated theme by heroic poesy. Though the head arose and bubbled in the greenness of an open plain, yet such was the concourse, and crowd that pressed to obtain a draught of this stream, that the wide and large champion round about seemed too narrow to receive the multitude of visitants; for such was the number that encircled this fountain, and swelled with the excess of the sweet waters, that one would think the whole world were in this confluence met together, and indeed few there wanted who sucked not at the spouts of this renowned fountain. The water sprang from seven pipes, though not of gold but iron, a circumstance well observed by Critilo, and also that the spouts were not formed in the fashion of lions, and griffins, but of serpents, and dogs; and though the water flowed in much abundance, yet with such thirst did every one receive it, that there was not one drop spilt, nor was there need of a pond or a cistern to receive the over-flowing waters; for all praised the sweetness to their taste, and being weary, and heated with their journey, sucked them in excessively, until they had filled their bodies with hydropical humours. The nobles, and those of higher quality, as more esteemed, were served with cups of gold, which a pretty nymph, the vintners of this Babylon, filled with much courtesy, and compliments, and to entertain her guests danced like a courtesan before the streams. Here Andrenio both moved with thirst, and with the present entertainment, unadvisedly approached to the head of the waters.

But the cautious Critilo drew him back. "Hold," said he, "consider well first, see if this be water."

"What can it be else?" replied he.

"It may be poison, and if not, yet it is always good, especially on the terms we now stand to suspect, and fear all things."

"If my eyes deceive me not," said Andrenio, "it is water clear and crystalline."

"This," replied Critilo, "is a sign which I like the worst, the clearness makes me suspect it most; for as with a pleasant colour it often smiles, so adulterated liquors, and beauteous outsides, serve commonly for a gloss to set forth an inward corruption. See but how the deceitful water sometimes smiles, and anon murmurs, and acts the part of flattering courtship."

"Let me alone," replied Andrenio, "let me satiate myself with this water, and refresh my parching heat, for if I die with thirst, may I not (if it be dangerous to drink) wash away this dust, bathe my eyes, and limbs, and refresh my body favoured with our travels?"

"Nor this neither," replied Critilo, "for believe me, remit it to experience, behold others, and read my lesson in their destruction. Observe the effect, and operation it has on these, who now come; consider what their humour was before they went, and how different they are now at their return."

With that passed by a great crowd of passengers, more lead with a thirsty desire, than reason, plunged themselves into the waters, and began to bathe and dabble, and to wash their eyes, that they might see clearer: but it is well worth our observation, that these who at first, were clear, and their skins fair, and of a natural pale, were with the first touch of the waters, dyed like a glass into several colours. Some were blue, that whatsoever they saw, appeared like a sky, and their raptures so transporting as if they had been caught into a heaven, and there enthroned. These were fools who contented themselves in their own senseless paradise; some turned white like milk, that whatsoever they saw appeared good, and acceptable, without suspicion of evil, thus all deceived them, especially if recommended by the flatteries of their friends, with less caution than a Polander they were ready to receive them. On the contrary others there were, who turned as yellow, as choler, their eyes malicious, always made a pause, as fearing treason, they interpreted the best kindness amiss, abhorred society, unless with circumspection, and these were men who had more of malice, than of judgment; some turned green, fancying all of the same colour, which being a badge, and signification of hope, gave encouragement to their humorous ambition: some turning gray, and of waterish eyes, grew stark blind: but it is strange, that these waters did perfectly clear some men's eyes, and yet though they saw well, they beheld ill, and these were envious; some had the natural force of sight, so impaired, not so much in the quality, as the quantity of the object; that mole-hills, as in a magnifying-glass, appeared as mountains, and ordinary toys, applauded by a Castilian, for but being his own, with praises as might befit the ultimate of all perfection, and others on the contrary became of a murmuring querulous spirit, never contented with the present government, repining at the greatest caresses, and embraces of fortune. There was one whose eyes read best at distance, he beheld all in a large prospect, especially the dangers of death, and this was an unwary person. Another was of a humour, that he thought he had all ready at hand, and with that confidence assured himself to conquer difficulties, that impossibilities were esteemed easy, and the prey sure before it was taken; there were many of a merry humour, that every object they saw seemed to smile upon them, that every one caressed, and made much of them, and these were in a condition of childish folly. There was one observed to be extremely contented, as in a fool's paradise, he supposed to see always a vision of angels, and there was nothing, that he saw, but he picked out some beauty whereof to be enamoured; and this they say was a Portuguese, or the nephew of macias. There was another who spoke of nothing but himself; this was the theme both to begin, and conclude his discourse; one had his eyes so dazzled, that he supposed to see that which he never beheld; this was a man of a perverse will, and crooked intention; he had eyes for his friends, and eyes for his enemies much different; there were some maternal, and tender eyes that looked on a dunghill worm, like an oriental pearl; and some eyes cruel, like a stepmother's, which frowned with an evil aspect on all: In fine, some eyes were of a Spanish black, and others of a French azure. Such were the monstrous effects of this venomous liquor, on the bodies of those who bathed in it; that some who only washed their mouth and throat, became a more strange metamorphosis than the rest; for their tongues, which were of solid, and substantial flesh, turned into a fire, that the whole world was in danger of its flames; others into wind, which seemed to breathe a spirit of falsity, and like bellows puffed men's brains full of the air of lies, and flattery.

Some that had tongues of silk, were turned into baize, those of velvet into satin, others were transformed into tongues of burlesque, consisting of scum and froth, without substance; but the most of these had an impediment in their speech, and were tongue-tied in modest and decent discourse; some women had their tongues eradicated, but in anger talked the more, for having no tongue to rule, spoke at random. One began to speak earnestly loud.

"This," said Andrenio, is a Spaniard;" but Critilo, said not, but some presumptuous or confident boaster, for he who speaks most deliberately, and soberly, is most commonly best heard, and understood. Indeed, so it is, said another, which he whistled out with an effeminate Voice, like a French man; but he was not so, but one affected, and foolishly nice. To meet him went forth another, who spoke as if he had a plum in his mouth, that all supposed him a German; but he answered he was not, but one who to speak fine and elegantly did not regard whether his matter were to the purpose or not. Another spoke through the teeth with such a lisping pronunciation, that all believed him an Andalusian, but others, who could better distinguish languages, judged him of a malevolent tongue, who serpent-like hissed out his malice. Another in a bustle disturbed all, and with an unquiet spirit, without knowing the reason why, endeavoured to discompose the whole world, having no other excuse, but that it was his natural infirmity, so that he was supposed to be an islander of Majorca; but he was not of that country, but a barbarous hot- brained Furioso; another spoke, and none understood him, that they took him to be a Biscayner, but was not such, but one who was always making petitions and requests; another spoke not at all, but endeavoured to be understood by signs, whom all derided and scorned.

"This certainly is one," said Critilo, "who desires to speak the truth, but either cannot, or dare not;" others spoke hoarse and low, "these," said he, "must certainly be parliament-men;" but they were not so, but men who were counsellors to none but themselves; others snuffed words in their nose, which some understood, and stammering answered them in the same dialect, but neither appositely, nor to the purpose, and some biting their tongues, spoke inwardly, and answered them as if the questions propounded to them were troublesome; some pronounced words hollow, as from an inward sound and cavity in their breasts, which was both as unpleasing to the auditors, as troublesome to themselves. And so it was that none remained with his own voice either good or true, no man spoke clear, equal, or without artifice. So all lost the natural accent of their tongues, but feigned, deceived, lied, blasphemed, and injured; whence it seems, that the French especially, as good fellows in this meeting, drinking in the freest plenty to pledge the Italians, neither speak as they write, nor perform as they say, that a man had need of good ears and good learning to understand their words, and letters, but to apprehend them rightly, you may interpret all to a contrary sense. But the most pestilential effect of this liquor, was shown in those that drank it, that like a vomit it moved the stomach, as soon as taken in, to spew it forth again with all the true substance, and sound nourishment they had before, leaving room for wind and air; for lies and deceits, with which they swelled as with a tympani. Their hearts turned to cork void both of valour and courtesy, their entrails were metamorphosed into stone, their brains to cotton, dry and without judgment, their blood hydropical and waterish, without colour or heat; their breasts, which should be of steel, were turned into wax, their nerves grew flaccid, as if the spring of their motion, were composed of wool, their feet as clogged with lead, moved with a slow pace toward good, but like a mercury winged to pursue the flight of evil; their hands turned to pitch, which grasped, and retained all they touched; their tongues blurrers of fame, their eyes paper; in fine, here was the original of the worlds metamorphosis, the cheat of vanity, and the best masterpiece of the worlds deceiver. The operation it had on poor Andrenio, was, that the strength of one drop, he but supped in, did so intoxicate his brain, that ever after he grew giddy, and reeled in the way of virtue.

"What do you think now," said Critilo, "of this constant spring and stream of fraud of this tottering mansion of the worlds falsities? If you had drunk with the same liberty that others have done, how had your joints been dissolved with its strength? how had your reason abated, and your feet tripped at every rub? Can you possibly esteem so little an eye clear of blood, or beams, a tongue clean and true, a man of verity and substance, such as a duke of Ossuna, or a Prince of Conde? believe me he that is so, is as strange and unusual as a phoenix."

"Would one think," said Andrenio, "there should be so much evil in so smooth a water?"

"The more dangerous is it," replied Critilo, "for those smiles and gentleness are symptoms of its danger."

"How is this fountain called?" demanded Andrenio, which he asked of one and the other, but none could inform him. At last Proteus answered him, that it had no name, for in being unknown, consisted the efficacy, and success of its operation.

"Why than," said Critilo, "it may be called the fountain of deceits, of which who once drinks is by the virtue, and strength thereof metamorphosed into another shape."

Critilo was now desirous to turn back, but Andrenio could not, nor would consent, and Proteus pressing them forward, would needs persuade them that it was better to be a fool for company, than singular and wise alone. Thus he led them astray, rather than guided them, in by and cross ways, through delightful fields and meadows, where youth stood sporting in the pleasant greens, under the fresh shades of leafy boughs; but the trees wanting heart, and sap, were barren, and unfruitful. By this time being come in view of the city, they observed it to be covered with a cloud of smoke, a certain sign, that it was inhabited by mankind. The prospect was composed of a pleasing variety, and seemed best at the farthest distance; such was the general concourse of all provinces to this common place of resort, that the road was crowded with travellers, which raised such a cloud of dust, that nothing in the way thither could be seen or observed; but in their nearer approach, they easily perceived that that which at a farther distance appeared beauteous, and comely, was within a confused mass and heap, no street, direct, or strait, but like a labyrinth or den of miniatures. Andrenio was about rashly to enter in, but Critilo pulling him by the sleeve, said, "Hold open first your eyes, those inward faculties, I say of the soul." Whereupon he bended down to the Earth, and looking narrowly, he espied traps and slips covered in the dust, made with golden threads, and fair hair, to catch, and ensnare silly and unwary innocents.

"Observe well," said he, "where and how you enter, let not your feet tread without an assay first, and certainty of a secure, and firm foundation; do not move one foot from my side, unless you will wilfully precipitate yourself to an evident destruction; believe nothing, though urged with oaths, and protestations; grant nothing, though petitioned with the most submissive humility; do nothing what they command, and so armed with the virtue of this lesson, which is to see, and hear, and be silent; let us venture up this street." All the atreet was rowed with the shops of handicrafts-men, no foreign labourer appeared there, whose simplicity was unpractised in the art of fraudulent dealings; through these streets crossed flocks of crows, which bred under the eves of the houses, and maintained a sociable familiarity with their landlords, which Andrenio judged for an ill omen, that presaged some future disaster. But Proteus informed him, and bid him not to wonder at this, for that these had not been the ancient inhabitants, of the city, which Pythagoras in honour of his foolish opinion, supposed to be the souls of evil livers, whom God for a just punishment, had transmigrated into the bodies of these irrational creatures making their being now the same with theirs, since their death, whose actions they so fully imitated in their life; the scarlet souls of cruel tyrants he transfused into tigers, the proud into the lion's skin, and the souls of the dishonest to animate the boar; but souls of artisans, especially those that make our clothes, were covered with crows feathers, for they having always used to say to their customers, tomorrow it shall be done, tomorrow without fail, has aptly in punishment thereof, put the same term into their mouths, that continual *cras, cras,* a time which eternity itself shall never overtake.

But having passed the suburbs into the heart, and middle of the city they saw most stately palaces, magnificent buildings, the first of which, they said, was Solomon's Seraglio, (before any asked the question) for there he lay slumbering amidst of his three hundred concubines, making Hell, with these sports, and pastimes equivocate a paradise; in one house, which seemed a fortress, but was no other than a tottering cottage, founded on an unstabled sand, sat Hercules, made effeminate, spinning with his omphale, the shirt or winding-sheet of his dying fame; at the same window peeped out Sardanapalus, dressed in woman's habit, and attire; and marc Anthony not far from him, unhappy man, whose fortune was both told and made by a gypsy. In another ruinous castle, did not live, but died the Goth Roderigo, since whose time the nobles have been fatal to Spain. Another palace there was half gold, half dirt, cemented with human blood, this was the house of extravagant Nero, whose reign began with the mild calm of a prodigious clemency, but ended with a storm of bloody cruelty; within the next room sate Pedro the Cruel, mad and enraged, grating his teeth, and crackling bones with anger. There were other edifices erecting in all haste, but none could tell as yet for whom they were, though diversely reported by the world, certain it is, not for the enjoyment of those whose pains and cost raised the structure, but for the possession of others, who perhaps as yet unborn, will reap the fruits of another's labour; but one in a green coat standing by, told them, that in this part of the world live the deceived, and in the other the deceivers; these laugh at the others, and the others at them again, but at the end of the year they balanced accounts, one having no more cause to laugh than the other. Andrenio being weary of the company of the deceived, desired to see all, and to divert his humour, would needs pass to the quarters of the deceivers, so that proceeding forward, they found none but merchants' shops, and those dark, having no other but false, which they called shoplights, to set off their counterfeit ware; others sold false teeth, and periwigs, and all sorts of habits and disguises for comedians. There was one shop full of nothing but foxes' skins, which the cunning citizen swore, that they were more in demand, and in esteem than the best sables, which they easily believed, when they perceived the shop so well customed by the famous Themistocles, and other modern heroes of our time. It was really the only fur in fashion here, for want of the lions skin, which was grown a scarce commodity, because it was not in demand; and it is said that the subtlest and greatest politicians used to line their garments therewith, instead of ermines. In another shop, they sold spectacles by the wholesale to blind men, so as neither to see, nor to be seen, and these were all grandees, who bought them, for to blind their porters, which carried them on their shoulders, that they might be the more tractable and quiet, as they do horses to make them stand still. The married wives bought them up a pace to blind their husbands with, and to make them believe they loved them more than they did; some were like multiplying glasses, which were of all sorts, and sizes for young and old, men and women; and these were the dearest, because most in demand; another shop was full of cork heels to raise men in their stature, and make them seem more personable than they are. But that which most pleased Andrenio was to see gloves, an unknown invention, and a novelty to him.

"What means this," said he, "these seem to be an useful contrivance for all occasions, against the heat, and cold, the sun, and air, nay they are very convenient for those, who have nothing else to do, were it only to put them off and on."

"Above all," said Critilo, "they take most excellently a perfume, and is the cheapest way to conserve rich smells."

"How well you understand it," replied the Glover, "if you had said they serve to mask the fingers, that they should not behold the hands, you had hit the difficulty; for there are those who catch at their prey with gloves on."

"How can that be said Critilo, for that is against the proverb?"

"The proverb," said he, "alas! Sir, all proverbs now either lie, or are belied, for there are gamesters nowadays that hunt in gloves, and though the proverb says, 'the mousing cat preys not with mittens,' it here meets an exception; and let me tell you, that more is given now for gloves than formerly for clothes."

"Reach me one," said Critilo, "that I may try it."

Having thus passed the streets of hypocrisy, ostentation, and artifice, they came at last to the marketplace, on which was erected a famous palace, overtopping all the rest, and situated in the heart and centre of the city, it was spacious, but not uniform, nor of equal proportion, but all angles and confusion, had no prospect nor equality, many gates it had, but all false, and those shut, and more towers and pinnacles than Babylon itself. The windows were green, a grateful colour to the sight, promising fair, and deceiving most. Here lived, or rather lay undiscovered that hidden monarch of the world, who one day appeared in public to honour certain feasts which he had dedicated to the deceived vulgar, to whom it was not permitted to argue, or ask questions. His sacred majesty sat retired under the cautious covert of his jealousy, or lattices, and this day more especially he desired to sit close, intending to entertain the people with the subtleties, and legerdemains of a cunning juggler. The people, for the more common view of all, had made a ring to see these exploits, and swarming like flies, settled themselves on the filth of evil customs, till they swelled with the ordure and filth which they had sucked from moral wounds. At the vulgar applauses mounted an eloquent impostor, on a stage above the people, and with more impudence than good manners, after an affected prologue, began to act such rare subtleties, and frauds, that an innumerable number of people stood astonished at his devices. Amongst the rest of his tricks, he persuaded some to open their mouths, promising to fill them with some rare julep or comfits, which they swallowing down, it gave them immediately such a vomit, that they spewed forth most vile corruption, and beastly ordure, ungrateful to themselves, and ridiculous to the beholders. This prattling charlatan made them believe he had swallowed cotton, and opening his mouth, there issued out a thick smoke, and flame of fire greater than his art could quench. Sometimes he swallowed down paper, anon he drew out ribbons from his throat, but it was all a cheat, and a mere deception of the eye. Andrenio was much pleased to see this entertainment, and began to praise his art.

"It is well," said Critilo, "he has deceived you amongst the rest, who notwithstanding our lectures of morality cannot yet distinguish truth from appearance. Who do you think this confident gypsy is? it is the false politician, the cunning machiavelli, who gives potions of his false aphorisms, to the greedy throat, and vitiated palate of the ignorant, which being plausible, appear true to them; but being well examined, are no other than painted corruption, and the gilded pills of sin, and vice, not so much the plots of state, as devices fit for the stalls of beasts: he seems indeed to carry a mildness in his lips, and suavity in his tongue, and yet breaths infernal flames, consumes good manners and customs, and burns up the flourishing condition of republics; that which seems ribbons, are such politic laws as tie and bind up the hands of virtue, and loose the ravenous claws of vice; the paper he swallowed is the book and pandects of falsity, and that which in the form of truth invites so many fools and knaves to receive pernicious maxims. Believe me all here is deceit, it would be better to disengage ourselves quickly and retreat back."

But Andrenio taken with these pastimes, desired another day's recreation here, having received much satisfaction with that which was past. Scarce was it day (though there, seldom more than a dim twilight appears) before the impatient vulgar weary of their beds, returned again to the same stage desirous of the second day's festival; the representation was a masque of various apparitions, and scenes, acted on the grand theatre of the universe. Andrenio was not backward to be one of the first spectators, induced thither by his own fancy, and Critilo assented thereunto that he might advance his knowledge, and increase his experience. Here now, instead of music, which is the ravishment of our senses, and usual prologue to a comedy, were the harsh and untunable clatterings of tongs, and kettles, and instead of tuned instruments, and the ravishing quavers of a voice, the doleful sobs of deceived wretches grated their ears, and in the conclusion, or last act, entered a man, or one rather newly stripped out of his childish years, known by his habit and fashion to be a stranger, though ragged and naked, had no sooner (being one whose laments kept consort with the music) wiped off the tears from his eyes, but instantly stepped out one to meet him as complemental as a courtier, giving him the welcome, and desiring his commands wherein to serve him: He made large proffers to him, in what his abilities could reach, or he desire in a strange country, and all with such an affluency of complement, that the credulous stranger turned that to deeds, which he only promised in words. At first he invited him to his house, a place as full of inventions, as void of realities, where he freely presented him with gifts, and stripping off his rags seemed as if he would perform the act of charity in clothing the naked; but yet with so slight an art, that what his right hand seemed compassionately to bestow, his left hand with as much cunning juggled away: upon his head he put a hat with a band of diamonds, but that on a sudden it was hooked away, without knowing how, nor where, which he excused with a multitude of complements; than he gave him a rich jewel, which with as much dexterity as the former, went the same way, placing in the room a counterfeit stone, anon he attired him with a costly robe, which in the twinkling of an eye, was converted to a winding-sheet, a sad spectacle, and at length being left *in cuerpo*, was laughed at by all there present, who took no small delight to see the simplicity of the foreigner so wittily deceived. But whilst they were attentive on him, they observed not how the art was operating on themselves, who insensibly had their pockets picked, lost their cloaks, and looking one on the other, it was some comfort to them to have companions in the same misfortune; at length every one slunk away, more troubled for their loss than ashamed of the cheat. This was no sooner gone, but entered another wheedler, who promised more civility than the former, and like an epicure, treated of nothing but sensualities, and to satisfy the enormous lusts of his own appetite, in order to which he prepared a plentiful table, with all varieties of sallets, and quelquechoses, and set out chairs for the guests, one whereof without farther ceremony taking the chief seat, had it slipped from under him, and so fell with the common shout of the whole theatre; but suddenly a compassionate woman applied her assistance to recover him, and giving him her hand helped him up to be partaker in the remaining banquet, but the meat was all imaginary and fantastic, the pie was empty, and hollow, the gammon was dried to nothing, and the birds, had only the names of partridges crude and without substance, and the salt falling with him was a token of ill luck, and the occasion that the meat was without taste or savour; the bread which seemed of the purest flour, was gritty and full of sand, neither bean, nor any coarseness sifted from it; the third course was of the fruit of Sodom, dry, and choky, and the cup they drank out of, full of leaks, and holes, that they sucked more of air, than wine; their music was but drunken acclamations; at the midst of the banquet, one already satisfied glutted after his eager greediness, and sleepy with a full stomach, reposed his body on a false support, which wanting force for the weight he laid on it, gave way, and so falling, counted every step backwards, till at last he came to the Earth, where he was stifled in the ill air of mire and filthiness. Of all the present spectators of his fall there was not one so much as to assist him, until looking on all sides to see if any would compassionate his case, he spied an old man, whose age he thought was past the wagery of youth, to him he reached his hand, and desired his help, which he readily gave, and not only assisted him with his hand, but lifted him on his shoulders, but he being lame with age, and no less false than the rest, in a few paces, stumbled on his crutches, and fell into a secret snare of flowers, and greenness of effeminacy, where he slited him off, catching at his flying coat, let his body drop where it was no more seen, nor heard of; at which the mechanic theatre shouted with acclamations, and thereby performed the obsequies of his dying memory. Every one, even Andrenio himself, clapped their hands applauding the jest, and trick of the one, and the ridiculous folly of the other. Andrenio turning himself to Critilo perceived he did not only laugh as the rest, but sighed to see the madness of this age.

"What is the matter," said he, "is it possible that you with so much affected singularity should go in opposition to the common humour, when some laugh, you weep, and in their rejoicings you lament?"

"It is true," said Critilo, "for this has been rather a torment, and spectacle to exercise my patience, than a pastime for my pleasure; and if your experience and judgment knew how to interpret these passages, you would side with me, and be partaker in the same resentment."

"Why, who is this," replied Andrenio," but a credulous foreigner, whose folly is his destruction, and his ears being open to all stories, is subject to all frauds, and is paid with that gullery, which his indiscreet facility has deserved; such an one I would rather deride, than pity, and in this case be rather a Democritus, than an Heraclitus."

"Tell me," replied Critilo, "if you were in his condition, whom you thus despise, what would you say?"

"Who I," said he, "in his condition, how is it possible, that I who am alive, healthful, and perhaps more in my wits than he, should so far outrun them as to arrive at this pitch of madness?"

"This is the error," replied Critilo, "know than that this unfortunate stranger, is a man as we all are, who enters weeping on this tragic theatre, is encountered with the songs, and enchantments of falsity, as a remedy of his melancholy: naked he comes in, and as empty goes out; which is all the treatment he receives from ruinous masters; his entrance is encountered by the first deceiver, which is the world, who proffers and complies in nothing, gives and enriches him with the spoils of another, which he suddenly returns to challenge again, and to draw away with one hand, what the other offered, that all those gifts, and caresses of fortune, at last like smoke vanished in nothing. The other, which invited his appetite to the feasts of sensualities, was a deceiver, who importunately vexed this guest, till he was fallen into the sins of lust, and after as much tormented him, with the pangs of conscience; the meat was without substance and nourishment, the drink a poisonous potion, or at the best but a falsified liquor, which fumed and intoxicated the brain, that cast him down, and his fall received with the songs of sorrow, and the acclamations of misery, the vile rabble of fortune. Lastly, that old hypocrite the worst of all, inveterate with malice, was time, which tripped up his heels, and cast him into the grave, where he left him dead, solitary, naked, and forgotten: So that if we observe well, all take advantage on miserable man. The world deceives him, life flatters him, fortune derides him, health forsakes him, his youth passes, felicity withdraws, years fly away, and contented ones come not, time runs, his life ends, death catches him, the grave devours him, the Earth covers him, putrefaction dissolves him, oblivion swallows him, and he who yesterday was a man, to day is dust, and to morrow nothing. But how long shall we loose precious time, let us return to our former road, our straight and direct way; for here is nothing that we can expect more, unless to entangle ourselves in a labyrinth of errors."

But Andrenio, bewitched with this vanity, and having found gracious reception in the palace, became an idolater of this king's greatness, which was fantastic, without reality or substance: The many favours he had received there, and the good eye with which he was looked on by the greatest ministers, made him promise himself no small preferment; he made often means and friends to be admitted to the presence of his majesty, and to kiss his feet, though he wanted those parts, being an imperfect piece of Nature. Critilo returned again to him, desiring and persuading with what arguments he could, his departure; and being at length wearied with his importunity, and requests, at last consented to his demands: But being come to the gates of the city, with an intention to leave it. O unhappy Fortune! they were stopped by the guards, who suffered all to come in, and none to go forth, so that they were forced to return again, and to lament the misery of this snare, into which they were fallen. Andrenio returned again to the former folly of his ancient pretensions, who was yet entertained with large promises, but no performance. Which Critilo objected as an argument to wean his affections. But which way their escape was effected is related in the following Crisis, together with the acts of the famed Artemia.

The Eighth Crisis

A resolute courage is a good remedy against an inconstant fortune, an humble nature will bear patiently the severity of laws; art, and science overcomes the unpolished rudeness of Nature, and a discreet judgment is a secure protection in all difficulties. For art perfects Nature, is a second being, endeavours to adorn the first, and pretends to exceed the rude lines of her work with a better air, and neater curiosity. Well may she glory to have created another world, and reformed its rudeness, that what blots and errors Nature has committed and blurred, art has expunged, and been an assistant to her feeble operations. This without doubt was the employment of man in paradise, when God invested him with a power of predominancy over the world, to rule and make up the discomposed breaches, which was but to polish Nature, and to teach rude clownery a more artificial behaviour. So that art is a trimming of Nature, the mount of this level simplicity, and miraculous in her works; so that if a desert by the gardener's hand may be turned to a paradise; Why should it not take the same effect in the soul, and cultivate the over-grown soil of man's reason. Let than our Roman youth try these mysteries, view the effects on Andrenio, who now though clouded, and captivated in the confusions of this court, is yet ransomed with felicity, and by Critilo's importunities obtained his liberty.

There was a queen, whose prodigious miracles and actions had celebrated her praises in the farthest world; her territories bordered on the confines of this king, so that such potent neighbours, differently disposed, must necessarily contract hatreds and distastes, which breaking out into wars, often ended in a bloody conclusion. This lady was called (for never did she belie her name, or actions) the wise, and discreet Artemia, famed in all ages, and her actions chronicled to all posterity. Every one spoke honourably of her, and with that variety of adoration worshipped her, as the distinction of religions, directed their devotions, and though the wise, and prudent were only those (and amongst them the Duke del Infantado) who had procured a true and right notion of her worth; yet the vulgar report spoke her to be a famous medea, an enchantress whose art worked not like the charms of Circe, which metamorphosed men into beasts, but rather disenchanted, and regenerated the bewitched estate of man into original reason. Some say they have seen enter into her house, something without shape, a brute, or beast, which in a few days, she turned to so different a Nature, that he became a polite work, and piece of rationality; she made the blind mole more acute in sight than the spotted lynx; crows she has turned into the mild innocence of candid doves, the timorous hare has received a lion's courage, and the ignoble kite become as long winged, and generous as the eagle: a horse committed to her charge, proceeded as an effect of her school, eloquent in speech, so that they generally reported, she taught beasts to speak, but of greater honour it was, that in convenient occasions she taught them silence. She inspired life into statues, and gave breath to appearing shadows. Out of lumps of clay she produced flesh; into giddy fancies she infused gravity; the dwarf she has raised to a giants stature, and turned apish postures to a composed countenance; of a scoffing jester she has made a severe Cato, and by the strength of nourishment, she has nurtured a Pygmy infant to a lofty Tipheus, such as were men only in title, and name; she has really and substantially made them so; to the blind she has given sight, and fixed the lights of reason like Argus's eyes; she has quitted the prejudice of the blind interested, and against their own advantage obliged them to profess verity. men but of straw and clouts, she has turned into true and unfeigned figures; from the viper she has plucked his sting, and not only cleansed its venom, but made it an antidote against other poisons; her art has been most extolled, in the greatest difficulties, and her skill than most renowned, when it worked on the bad materials of incapable subjects; for into dull wits, she has instilled wisdom; she has not only endued the prosperous with memory, but the unhappy with judgment and discretion; a mere fool she has made a Seneca; an ignorant citizen a high politician, and an unskilful soldier she advanced to a knowing commander. Of some deformed monsters she has made angels, a miracle that the feminine sex ought to esteem and gratefully to acknowledge. Of a ruinous desert she had oft composed a delicious garden, and gave so much virtue to the soil, that trees began there to eradicate where but lately a shrub wanted moisture. A court, and city she had formed, and rendered as polite and neat as Florence itself; nor was it impossible that her exploits should erect a triumphant Rome. In this manner did everyone discourse of her actions, not as if she had produced them by miracle, but as plausible and honest effects of her own power.

Critilo had soon intelligence of this Lady, for his troubles obliging him to seek a remedy, he was the more inquisitive to receive an exact information concerning Artemia; and in regard that all the arguments and persuasions which friendship suggested were little available to the deaf ears of Andrenio, he resolved to depart, and to force his way against all difficulties, which he found not so environed with obstacles, but that he, who was resolute to escape, might find a door; from whence I say resolving to depart, he found an easier passage than was expected, and remained as happy as contented, and being freed from any detentions, followed the road that directed to the desired court of Artemia, to consult about a remedy which might uncaptivate his beloved friend, whom so much the more he entertained in his thoughts, by how much the farther the distance of the way had separated him from his society. many passengers he encountered in the way, who journeyed thither, some for curiosity, others for their advantage and profit; the wisest and most observing, passed their journey with stories of her actions, how she had made lions to couch at her feet, and transformed them into human souls, and with muttering some few words disenchanted serpents, and raised their crawling bowels from the dust, and erected their heads towards heaven: how she had sucked out the venom from the basilisk's eyes, that an infant might behold them without danger of emissions, or infections, which dart into youthful tenderness; all which were things as rare as profitable. All this is nothing, said another, her power can charm the Sirens' songs, transform their lascivious tongues into chaste matrons, make the ravenous wolf become a mild turtle, and the highest that possibly can be imagined a sensual Venus, take the vow of a Vestal virgin. All agreed that this was very admirable and rare. The artificial palace of this queen, was situated on an eminent rising, where she commanded the waters to ascend in streams in token of their obedience to her powerful art, in imitation of which that famous artist invented those crystal fountains, that arise like dews from the running Tagus; her garden was crowned with flowers, surrounded with beds of pinks, prodigies of fragrance and odours; for the brambles produced roses, which faded not like other flowers, but continued their lively blush, and sweet smells, as rarities in all seasons of the year, the very elms produced pears, and the thorns grapes, the choky Aragon pear changed its nature, and turned mellow, and became more delicious than the bergamot, and the dry cork-tree sweated forth drops of nectar; in the pools were heard the continual harmony of melodious swans, which was an unknown note to Critilo; for though the vulgar speech report them to sing their own funeral obsequies, yet so rare is one song from them, that none can say he has been an auditor of their sadness; for they being of a candid, and undeceiving Nature, if they sing, it must be in the satiric meteor of unsavoury truth, which so grates the cars of the generality, that they think it more convenient to be silent, till either their agony, and pangs of conscience force them to breathe out truth, or that than in their last farewell they fear not to pronounce boldly their own sense, fearing neither punishment, nor loss of estate; hence it is said, that such a preacher, or that minister spoke clearly, that such a secretary of state confessed and published secrets, and that this councillor disclosed the most inward thoughts of his breast, and breathed out truth together with his life. At the gate stood a lion, a gentle porter, whose fierceness had been lately turned to the mansitude of a lamb, and a tiger to a sheep's innocence; at the balconies appeared prattling birds, who yet worked, and discoursed together with the prating parrot, who held the distaff? The cats and domestic animals of that house, were not ravenous, nor given to prey, but loyally acknowledged their mighty empress, and each day prostrating at her feet, renewed professions of obedience. At her door attended multitudes of modest virgins, well fashioned, and comely, though mechanics, and of mean degree. The more noble and ingenuous ladies, all attendants of the discreet Artemia, were advanced to such forms, as some vertuous heroes thought fit to advance them, reparting unto every one their peculiar lessons and places of preferment; in judging of which, and of every ones particular abilities, the chief arbiter employed was don Vincentio de Lastanosa. Her mouth was little and modest, her eyes full, and piercing, her speech though grave yet pleasing, and above all, her hands were of sovereign quality, that they gave life to those on whom she laid them, and worked a miracle on benumbed souls; her behaviour was with a good air, and fashion, her body handsomely proportioned; In fine, all she did, became her, and all her actions were full of art and virtue. Critilo being arrived, had audience of her, with the greatest civilities and courtesy, that could be expressed, for she quickly discovered his constancy and inclinations to virtue, and judged of his good nature and affability from the ingenuity of his countenance, which is the index and character of the soul. Whilst Critilo approached near to kiss her hands, she retired with some wonder backward, to see one such a master in virtue, to enter the school, and one so wise to walk unaccompanied, in regard that society is affected by the wise, and carries with it much of the comeliness of the graces, which are at least three in number.

But he pressing forward, let fall a flood of tears, and answering, said, "I was not wont to walk thus solitarily alone, for I had once another companion, whom I now give over for lost, by means of an ill conductor, and a traitorous guide, who in this country sometimes directed us, and at last destroyed us; in his behalf, I apply myself to you, thou sole remedy of misfortunes, petitioning your favour to rescue my otherself, who remains a distressed captive, and the more unfortunate, because I know not where, nor how, nor with whom, I lost him. If you know not, replied she, where you left him, or with whom, how shall we know where to find him? This I commit to the skill of your mysterious art, said he, for he remains in the court of a famous king (whence I durst swear, he could never be recovered) an emperor universally powerful, and only singular in being unknown."

"Hold," said she, "I understand you now, without doubt he remains in the great Babylon (but no court) of my great enemy Falismund, in whose territories the whole world runs to confusion, and all hasten their end there, because they know not, nor consider it. However take good courage in a bad fortune, and our policy shall not be wanting to countermine his deceit," and so calling one of her chiefest ministers, and greatest confidents, who attended with great readiness, and being a person of much resolution, and illustrious for his integrity, and clear dealing, she committed to him the charge of this business. Critilo having informed him concerning the particulars of all passages, Artemia gave him directions, and therewith a glass of pure crystal, the famous workmanship of one of the seven Greeks, and having acquainted him of the efficacy and virtue of it, and how to make use of it, she referred the rest to his own management. Before he departed he clothed himself after the fashion of that country, in the livery of Falismund, which was made up of many folds, linings, furs, counter-furs, covered with coats, and cassocks, and over all a cloak to hide frauds; and in this manner he departed to comply with his commands and confidence reposed in him.

Critilo was as much contented as favoured in the court of Artemia, entertaining himself with improving his knowledge, and every day observing miraculous operations; for there he saw (what seemed impossible) a rugged clown transformed to a refined courtier, a mountaineer to become a gentleman, and principal in his art; nor was it less wonderful, that a Biscayner should be made an eloquent secretary. There were cloaks of baize, transformed into velvet, the scholars rags of poverty to eminent purple, and the novitiate's bonnet to an episcopal mitre. Those who commanded in one part, she has given commission for another: the poor shepherd of a thin flock, she has made an universal pastor: Besides, her power knows no limits, but works most intense at the farthest distance, for some have seen a post-boy promoted to Bethlem Gabor, and a lacquey, to a lord of Tenza; and there are witnesses how in former times the goad has grown into a sceptre, and a scrivener become a Caesar; the shadows of one night over-past she has so changed and altered the faces of some, that their intimate friends have scarce taken acquaintance of their altered countenances; their judgments, opinions, and wills, have been changed, and their affections reformed. men of wild, and inconstant brains have been made grave and severe; and others of vain and empty carriage have been confirmed in solidity, and substance. In like manner she has supplied all the defects and infirmities of the body, for on some she has bestowed shoulders, feet, hands; to others she has given eyes, teeth, and hair; but above all she has cured the rotten ulcers, and gangrenes in the heart; all which are not less than miracles of her admired art. But what Critilo most admired was to see her shave, and hew an unfashioned log, a trunk, an unformed lump, till she brought it both to the form and rationality of a man, which could speak, discourse and reason in a manner as was worth the attention; but let us leave him here a while entertained, and follow the discourse of this prudent minister, who is now on his journey, and pursuit of Andrenio, remaining as yet in the court of the famous Falismund.

Still did the drunken surfeit of the Bacchanalian feasts go forward, the streets were filled with sports and masquerades, walked with more licentiousness than in Barcelona itself, both men and women sported in disguised habits, fashioned not only in the mode and cloak of sin, but in the white attire of sanctity and virtue, whereby the credulous simplicity of some was deluded, though the wise clear-sighted men, knowing them well, advised them to unmask themselves. It is a thing very observable, how desirous all were to clothe themselves in foreign habits, and some contrary or different to their natures; for the fox put on the skin of the lamb, the serpent the feathers of the dove, the usurer desired to paint his avarice with the twins of charity, the adulterer to be styled the familiar friend of the husband, the wolf ambitious to be esteemed abstemious, the lion to be accounted as gentle and mild as the sheep, the cat affected with a Roman beard, would hear of nothing but Rome's customs, the ass would imitate the lion, whilst he is silent, and the angry dog that snarls, affected to show his teeth in smiles and laughter. This faithful officer travelled in quest of Andrenio, through cross-ways, and by-paths, and though he was skilful, and wary enough to avoid errors, yet so was he changed, that he knew not Critilo himself, for his eyes were now clouded with a mist, not fully open, as formerly, but dimmed, and a little obscured; for the officers of Falismund do chiefly design at first to vitiate or debilitate the sight of strangers; for that besides his voice began here to fail him and to change both pronunciation, and accent, his ears grew deaf, and the rest of his senses disturbed and distempered, that if man each hour has his changes, and in the evening is altered from his mornings strength; what can we expect but a change in those who descend from virtues more different climate, to the centre of error and falsity. But yet breaking through all difficulties, with much industry and diligent enquiry he came at last to hear of Andrenio, and one day found him employed in what he usually lost his hours, in beholding others sport away their wealth, and make an end both of their estate and conscience: for there he stood gazing at a match at tennis, the most natural and fashionable entertainment of the world, which was performed in the high street by parties of different natures and conditions: the one side was black, and the other white, one tall, the other low, these rich, and the other poor, and all dexterous gamesters, and accustomed to the sport, in which they eternally consumed their time, and thoughts. The balls were puffed with wind, in fashion like men's heads, which the ball-maker had filled with blasts, at the eyes, and ears, making them as hollow as empty; thus one giving the word warned them to play with attention.

"All," said he, "is but sport and madness," and with that, gave the ball so hard a stroke, that it flew through the air, by the virtue of that violence which the blow had impressed on it, which another taking at the rebound, returned it again without suffering it to rest from its motion. Thus all endeavoured to kick, and foot away this common ball, for in that consisted their dexterity and victory. Sometimes it was tossed so high, that it was out of sight, anon so low, that it bounded and trilled on the ground, so as to bemire itself with the filth and ordure of the Earth; some kicked it with their feet, others stroke with their hands, but the most with Rackets in the form of tongues, that sometimes it mounted through the air, and again descending quarrelled with the ground, suffering great varieties and changes of fortune; one cried out he won fifteen, and so he did, for at those years men gain vice, and loose the treasures of virtue; another said he had won thirty, and gave the game for his own; but these years do conclude the set. In this manner they sported with the ball, till at last it fell down and burst, and than every one trampled on it. Thus concluded the game, some winning at their own cost, whilst others were entertained with the view of this pastime.

"These," said Andrenio, "turning himself toward him, that sought for him, "seem to be the heads of men."

"And so they are," said he, "and one of them is yours. men I mean who have lost their brains, and filled their sculls with air, and wind, with dregs, and cobwebs, and fantastic apparitions. The world throws up her balls of vanity, which the elevated and happy souls, catch and hurl down again to their contrary opposites trouble and calamity: whilst miserable man standing in the middle way, sometimes depressed, than exalted, and subject to the strokes of both, till at last he tumbles burst into the mire, and filth of his sepulchre."

"What art thou," said Andrenio, "that seest so much?"

"And, what art thou," replied he, "that seest so little?"

Thus in discourse he began to insinuate himself into his favour, and first to gain the fort of his will, the better to command and over-awe his understanding; so that Andrenio discovered unto him his breast, declaring his hopes, and those great promises were made of obtaining his pretensions. But this cunning artist seeing his time and season, informed him, that the course he took was vain, and would never gain him admittance to see this king, much less introduce him to a private audience; "for to see him is to be effected by your own will, and the sole being of this prince is to be unknown: the way his ministers take to give a view, and prospect of him, is to blind you first. Consider but awhile how blind you are: What will you give me if this night, I show him to you?"

"You do but jest," said Andrenio.

"No, for I am most usually serious. All I shall desire is, that when I discover him, you would view him well, observe, and eye his humour."

"This," said Andrenio, "is to desire me what I have so earnestly entreated."

So having appointed the hour, both punctually complied with their promise, one as desirous of this novelty, and the other as zealous of the others deliverance. But whilst Andrenio believed he should be first introduced into the favour of some intimate ministers, he on the contrary perceived himself lead another way, and carried always to a distance from the court, which made him give a stop; willing to return backward, suspecting a greater fraud, and abuse in this than in those former snares to which his errors had betrayed him. But this discreet officer still detained him,

"Observe," said he, "and view through this glass, what is denied us at a nearer prospect; for ascending up this hill, a little raised from the ordinary level of the Earth, we shall I know discover most hidden secrets."

With that he persuaded him to ascend a little up, and place himself just opposite to the windows of Falismund.

"I think," said Andrenio, "I see more than I did before," which much encouraged his instructor, who knew that to see, and understand, was the only remedy, and cure for his sickness. Andrenio turned his eyes, and looked toward the palace, to see if he could espy any glimpse or appearance of that hidden majesty; but he perceived that it was all in vain, for the windows were shut, the lattices obstructed, and the glass so thick as no sight could penetrate it.

"This is not the way," said this grave instructor, "to behold, and take a prospect on the world;" but turning his back upon it, advised him to consider all in a different nature, from what they appear, the inward and most natural affections having another force, than the outward visions."

With that he drew out his looking glass, and uncasing it of its silken-cover, put it before his eyes, in that manner, that the reflections of the palace, whose view deceived the eyes of common beholders, gave here a perfect description of all its infirmities.

"Look now," said he, "contemplate on it, and glut your longing desire with a full enjoyment."

With which Andrenio was so astonished, and amazed, that every joint began to tremble.

"What is the matter now," quoth the old man? What is it affrights, and dismays you?"

"I see," said he, "what I never desired, nor ever believed; I see a monster, the most horrible my life has seen, one that has neither feet nor head, a most disproportionate piece of Nature, one part not corresponding with the other, a prodigious shape of monstrosity; his hands cruel and brutish, a counterfeit composition of all kinds, and yet of none in reality; his mouth like a wolf, where never truth has had a habitation, and is so prodigious in all respects, that a chimera is an ass in comparison hereof; take me, take me away, lest I faint with these affrighting apparitions."

But his prudent companion told him, and bid him observe well his mouth, which at the first glance represented the lively features of a man, but in reality was a fox's snout, his middle a serpent, his body was so crooked, and his bowels so twisted, that he seemed as if he would vomit them up. His back was rising like a camel's bunch, his nostrils stuffed with knobs, his upper parts like the sirens' countenance, and his lower supporters of no nobler substance than the rest of his composure. Do you not see with what pain, and trouble he walks forward, how he turns his neck, how a bunch on his back, depresses his steps, how ill inclined he bends, his hands lame, his feet splayed, his sight a-squint, his speech stammering, and scarce intelligible. In fine, all is bad, to consummate the full catalogue of all imperfections.

"It is sufficient," said Andrenio, "that these deformities are so contrary to my Nature, that I start in beholding them."

"And it is sufficient," said his instructor, that it is with you, as it is with others, who having once seen these things, they have enough, and never desire to see them more."

"But who is this crowned monster?" demanded Andrenio. "Who is this horrid spectacle of a king?" "This is one," replied he, "as famous, as unknown, this is one to whom the whole world yields obedience, the general discourse and speech of all, whom all would rather visit in their neighbour's house, than entertain in their own. This is that grand hunter, who entraps the whole world in his universal toil. This is that lord who commands the half of the first year, and afterwards possesses himself of the other half. This is the powerful commander of weaker heads, the judge who condemns all those who make their appeal to his sentence. This is that universal prince of all, not only of men, but of birds, of fish, of brutes. In fine, this is that famous, that renowned, and that common deceit."

"Let us not than stay longer here," said Andrenio, "for methinks my affections are more estranged from him at this distance, than when I was nearer to him."

"Hold," said his tutor, "this is not enough, but I would have you know and view his whole kindred, and family," and so having laid aside the glass, on a sudden appeared a fiend more mad, and furious than Orlando, an old hag more fraudulent and crafty than the wife of Sempronio.

"Who is this meguera?" demanded Andrenio.

"This is the princes' mother," said he, "who commands, and governs all, which is lie, and falsity, old, and decrepit, and almost as ancient as the world, being not long produced after its creation.

"It seems," said Andrenio, "than that she is very ancient. O! the monstrous deformity of this creature; when she discovers herself, she halts so, that the slowest pace of those that follow, may overtake her. What great attendance is that which accompanies her."

"These are," said he, "the whole world, her two dwarfs are Yea, and No, which waited on her in her promises, offers, excuses, compliments, favours, and flatteries."

With that turning the glass on the other side, they perceived an honourable train, if antiquity, and ancient blood may more ennoble a family than honesty; for there was ignorance the grand-mother, malice the spouse, folly the sister, calamities, troubles, discontents, shame, repentance, perdition, confusion, contempt, and the rest of the brood, and spurious offspring of so vile a parentage. Those who stand attendants at her side, are the brethren, and kindred of her nearest blood, and cheats, wheedles, and intrigues, are her grand-children, born in this present age.

"Art thou now content Andrenio?" demanded his Instructor.

"Content, no, but yet I am glad, I am thus undeceived: Let us depart therefore from hence, for every minute seems to me an age, and everything produces to me a double torment. First by an importunate desire to enjoy it, and after enjoyment to hate and abhor it."

So they went forth by the gate of light, from that Babel of fraud. Howsoever Andrenio was not yet fully satisfied, nor could he say that he was perfectly recovered, complaining, that though he had found half of himself, yet the other half was lost, that is, his friend, or rather brother, or his own self, for such is a friend, whose real sincerity knows no falsehood.

"If you have lost a friend," said his instructor, "you have reason to lament your loss: But tell me, was he discreet?"

"Yes."

"Why than, fear not to recover him."

"He told me," said Andrenio, "he went to the court of a wise queen, called Artemia."

"If he were wise," replied he, "he must needs reside there, and let this banish all farther care from your thoughts, for whether can he go, who has drawn you from the confines of deceit, but by the path of wisdom to the court of that discerning queen?"

"Who is this famous woman, this lady so renowned in all parts of the world?" demanded Andrenio? "With reason you style her queen," said his Instructor; "for there is no power without discretion, and who has that, has a sufficient ability to command the world. But those who deduce her pedigree from the first original of her long descended ancestors, account her rise from Heaven itself, as being a ray and glimpse of that glory which descends from the immense wisdom of the eternal creator. Some call her daughter of time, and observation, the sister of experience, though others maintain her to be the only child of necessity, bastardising her nobility with base blood, whom I know to be the legitimate product of the understanding. She is one who lived in ancient days, no child, nor infant in age, but one who has found the greatest favour in the courts of the mightiest monarchs, her original was in Assyria, from thance she travelled into Egypt, and Chaldea, much respected; she has been in Athans, that great theatre of Greece, in Corinth, and Lacedemonia; and after she was crowned in Rome, where in a competition with valour, she had the laurel judged, as due to her deserts. The Goths, a barbarous and uncultivated people, were condemnors of her sacred name, banishing not only her, but her devoted worshippers from the extent of their dominions, with which barbarous moorism, not yet fully satisfied, pretended to give a full period to her being, had she not retired to the protection, and sanctuary of the famous tetrarchy of Charles the Great, where she sat installed in as much glory, and lustre, as ever she had shined in the most potent empires. But now at the fame of this powerful and dilated empire of Spain, which possesses both the worlds, she has changed her seat to this ample centre of her estimation."

"But why," said Andrenio, "does she not rather choose the famous court, for her habitation, to whose altar the various nations of her universal dominions might resort, and the polite courtiers adore her in the nearest devotion; than to fix her tent here amidst the converse of rustic clownery, to enjoy only the scrapes of the clouted shoe, and the homely respect of country behaviour?"

"It is," replied his Instructor, "because she would have experience of all, having found of late, but bad entertainment in courts, caused by the countenance which is there given to vice, which has often times attempted to throw her from her seat; nor is it long since she lived amongst courtiers, where she found to her own damage, persecutions, misfortunes, and malice, much want of truth, and excess of fraud, for there is most folly, where there is most presumption; and I myself have heard her say, that if there be most courtship there, here is most reality, if there most pastimes, here is most leisure; there things pass away, here we enjoy them, and this is to live, and that to die."

"Notwithstanding," replied Andrenio, "I would rather live with knaves, than fools, for though both be bad, yet folly is an intolerable plague (I mean) to understanding men, this I speak with reverence, and submission to wise Artemia."

Her palace began by this time to appear, and shine with such a splendour, that it represented Heaven, engraven with inscriptions, and crowned with laurels of her conquests, where being now arrived, they were both received with many welcomes, but Andrenio especially with embraces; only security was required for his constant perseverance in that profession, which is so severe, that it indulges no permissions contrary to that duty it imposes. Here to honour her two guests, Artemia worked many famous miracles not only on others, but on them, themselves, and more on Andrenio, being one who most wanted her art: In a short time he became a person well armed against other encounters, that if one lesson of her council, is able to make our life happy, what than must the effect be in him, of so many repeated instructions, both of his life and fortune, wherein she sprinkled some lessons of a superior and spiritual knowledge. many times she questioned Andrenio of his life, and made him repeat the story of his strange condition, when he first entered into the world; what effects the novelty of this universal theatre produced in him; but one thing she told Andrenio, that she was most desirous to know, in what manner he first beheld this admirable creation, and how he admired these strange prodigies, and who was he, who gave the greatest satisfaction to his reason. But what Andrenio answered is related in the following Crisis.

The Ninth Crisis

The ancient ministers of Delphos had engraved on the temple walls, in letters of gold, and the wise philosophers had imprinted in larger characters in their hearts, that recorded sentence of *bias, cognosce teipsum*, know thyself. For none of all created natures, errs in that way he should run, or misses that mark the race of his life should tend to, but man only whose distemper is chiefly caused by that noble faculty of free-will, nor can the knowledge of other things avail, whilst ignorance dwells at home, and misapprehends the operations of itself. So often does he degenerate to the vile servitude of a slave as often as he renders himself a captive unto vice. There is no robber pillages so much, nor oppresses the unwary traveller, as the ignorance of a man's self betrays him to be preyed on by others, which in many is such a height of stupidity, that they are neither sensible, how insensible they are, nor do they observe how little they observe or consider. Yet Andrenio seems worthy to be exempted from this common folly, when he thus satisfied the curiosity of Artemia.

"Of all these wonders I saw, and varieties of satisfaction I that day enjoyed, there was none which more affected my thoughts, (I speak it with some astonishment, but yet with truth) than myself, which the more I revolved, and considered in my understanding, the more I found it a subject to admire."

"This is that," said Artemia, "which I have longed to hear you relate, and was a theme, that the greatest wit of our times has so much applauded, calling man, above all other created wonders, the greatest prodigy, and effect of omnipotence. The same conclusion we may make from the general maxim of the principal philosopher, *Propter quod unumquodque est tale, illud est magis tale,* that always is more, for whose sake another is such. So that if for the sake of man, stones were created with so much virtue, flowers with so much beauty, and the stars twinkling with so illustrious a glory, in what sphere of beauty must man shine above all these, to whose use and service they were designed, and destined, he is the creature of all most noble, the monarch of this great palace of the world, invested in possession of the Earth, having a commission delivered to him as governor, and deputy to rule for the best advantage both of himself and his maker."

"At first," proceeded Andrenio, "I had only some rude notions and conceptions of myself, till light of the day illuminated my thoughts, and the crystals of a fountain was the only glass wherein to contemplate and view the delineation of my parts, whereby I perceived my proportion different from what my imagination fancied, which caused in me so much admiration and delight, that I cannot express, with how much content, and pleasure I was deceived. I reflected again on myself, and methought I was not yet so foolishly ignorant as I was contemplative. The first thing I observed was this composition of my whole body, which is straight, and direct, not inclining to one side, nor to the other."

"Man," said Artemia, "was created as a servant of Heaven, and so he ought to have his mind and body incline thither; for the material rectitude of the body often sympathizes and corresponds with the soul, that where accidents and mishaps have made a deformity in the members, the mind has often been misshapen with them, and both have become crooked and humoursome in their actions."

"It is true," said Critilo, "for in a crooked composition does seldom dwell a plain, and direct intention, in the nooks and bendings of a body, we may fear some folds and doublings in the soul. The eyes which are dull and misty, are accustomed to grow dim with passion, whom we do not compassionate as we do blind-men, but rather fear them, as those who may kill with the squints of an indirect glance; the lame often stumble in the road of virtue, and their will halting between their affections, makes these maimed cripples, incapable to walk with equal steps; but reason and understanding in better judgments, has prevented the prognostics of such sinister infirmities."

"The head," said Andrenio, "I know not whether I speak improperly, I call the castle, and fortress of the soul, the court of her powers and faculties."

"You have reason," said Artemia; "for as God is assistant, and present in all parts, yet the glory of his court, is most apparent in the celestial Jerusalem; so the soul manifests itself most in her superior stations, which is a lively resemblance of the heavenly orbs. Who believes not this, let him look into the soul through the windows of the eyes, hear its voice through the mouth, and speak to it through the crevices of the ears, the upper, and most eminent place does best become the authority of the head, that its office may be best executed in its command and rule over other parts."

"And here I have observed," said Critilo, "with much attention, that though the parts of this republic are so numerous, that to every day of the year may be allotted a bone, yet this variety is with so much harmony, that there is no number that may not be applied to it; for the senses are five, the humours four, the powers three, and the eyes two, all which come to reduce themselves, and terminate in one common unity, and centre of the head, resembling the first and divine mover, in whom the whole series and degrees of creatures come to end by an universal dependence."

"The understanding," said Artemia, "possesses the most sublime and purest spirituality of the soul, and has no small interest in the government of the material faculties, but as king, and lord of the actions of life, soars aloft, penetrates, subtilises, discourses, understands, and has fixt its throne in a candid and flexible disposition, the true essence of the soul, banishing all obscurity and darkness from conceptions, all prejudice from affections, and as a good natured creature, encourages the gifts of docility, with moderation, and prudence. The memory looks on what is passed, and eyes that behind, as the understanding does that before; so that what we pass, we still see, and because we cast that commonly behind which most concerns us, every wise man becomes a Janus, and sees as well behind as before."

"The hair seems to me," said Andrenio, "a gift bestowed on man, more for his adornment, than necessity."

"They are roots," replied Artemia, of this human tree, which radicate him in Heaven, and by one hair he is drawn thither, there ought his cares to be, and there he ought to receive his substantial nourishment. They are the index and almanac of our age, and change their colour, as we our affections; the forehead is the heaven and sky of the mind, which is sometimes clouded, anon serene, and clear, the seat of the senses, where a shame of our crimes discovers itself, and is the place where passions sport, and delight; anger in the stretched forehead, sadness in the fallen countenance, fear in the pase, modesty in the sanguine, deceit in the wrinkled brow, good nature in the smooth, immodesty in the bald, and a good capacity in the spacious forehead."

"But that which I most admired," said Andrenio, "in this artificial fabric of man was his eyes."

"Do you know," said Critilo, "with what name that great restorer of health styles them, Galen that retainer of flying life, and searcher into Nature, he calls them divine parts, who in this spake well; for if we observe, they are invested with a kind of divinity; which infuses veneration: they work with a certain universality, that they resemble omnipotence, producing the images, and species of external objects in the intimate and inward rooms of the soul: they seem to be endued with a kind of infinity, being present and assistant in all places, and commanding at one instant the whole space, and circumference of the hemisphere."

"At one thing," said Andrenio, "I have been much amused, that though the eyes see all, yet they see not themselves, nor those beams that usually obstruct them, a condition and paradise of fools, who are acute spies of disorders in their neighbor's house, and bats of blindness in their own: it were no small conveniency if man could retort his own eyes upon himself that he might start at his own deformity, moderate his passions, and compose himself again into the beauty of that form, he has destroyed with the loss of his original perfection."

"It were of much advantage," said Artemia, "if the choleric could come to see the lowering frowns of his own brow, and his own fury affright himself; if the finical and amorous lover could come to the sight of his effeminate gestures, and the rest of vain fools to see their own follies. But wary Nature has omitted these small advantages, to prevent more dangerous inconveniencies; for could the vain reflect and retort his eyes, he would be enamoured of himself, court and adore his own shadow, which how deformed and monstrous soever, yet his fond affection would still limit, and confine, to the sole prospect of himself, it is sufficient he can behold his own hands before another, or view his life, and attend to his actions, which may be as many, as perfect, that he can see his own feet, and know where to direct them, that he knows where to fix his footsteps, on a secure, and firm foundation, this is the chiefest use to employ our eyes."

"It is true," replied Andrenio, "but yet two eyes seem to me too small a light for so spacious a prospect, and this animate and lively palace could not have been better adorned than with ranks of this precious furniture, which since they are but two, their order might have been better disposed, one fixed before, to see that which comes, and the other behind, to consider what we have past."

"Some," said Critilo, "have reproached Nature, and accused her of this absurd oversight, and feigning a man more agreeable to their sense, fixed his eyes both behind and before, which served only to make him a man of a double countenance, and more double in his actions, than in his sight. Were I to correct the faults of Nature, I would place these lights of the soul on each side, and over the port-holes of his ears, which should neither by day, nor night close their lids to the softness of sleep, that so they might see with whom they associate and link their sides in a friendly familiarity, so would not many be easily subject to the deadly pleurisy, a disease, as epidemical, as mortal: so might man, see with whom he speaks, know with whom he sides, rules most important for the government of life, it being better to be deserted, and left to our own heads, than to be subjected to the whispers of bad advice; but know, that two eyes well employed are sufficient for our necessities, which looking forward, spy the coming of bolder dangers, and with a retorted glance see the timorous assault of backward treasons. One wink in an attentive beholder is sufficient to make discovery in the most hidden secrets; and therefore the eyes were made in the form of spheres, the most proper figure, and fittest for sight, they being of a square have no corners to dim any part or virtue of their light; their situation is proper also, both to look upwards, and before them, for if besides our proper eyes others were set in the hinder parts of the head, whilst some looked upwards towards Heaven, others might look to the Earth and breed a schism, and dissention in our affections."

"But another wonder I have observed of them," said Andrenio, "that in a foolish tenderness, and good nature they dissolve in tears, for what remedy is it to weep, or can the showers of our eyes prevent, and drown our misfortunes? Let us not sigh, but laugh at the world, and where our policy cannot avail us, let our contempt, and scorn despise its malice."

"Alas!" said Artemia, "the eyes are the first messengers of our bad news, who having the first notice, are the first lamenters; who is not sensible of troubles, is dead in a stoic stupidity, and who heaps up wisdom, heaps up sorrow; common laughter is most proper for the foolish mouth, and that which offends most often. The eyes are the faithful doors to let in verity, in disposing of which nature was so scrupulous and cautious, that she has not only fixed them in the same order, but united them in exercise of the same act, she suffers not one to see alone, but makes one a witness for the other, that they may consent in the same operation; one cannot see white, and the other black, but are such twins both in colour, and bigness, that one equivocates the other, and their agreement dissembles an unity."

"In fine," said Critilo, "the eyes are in the body, as those grand luminaries are in Heaven, and the understanding in the soul, they supply the defects of other senses, but all are not able to make up the infirmities and imperfections of them. They do not only see, but hear, speak, demand, answer, contend, affright, embrace, attract, consider, and perform the acts and offices of all, and what is most considerable, their vigour never abates by seeing, as neither do the indefatigable pains of state ministers, who are the eyes, and sight of the public welfare."

"Methodically has provident Nature, proceeded," said Andrenio, "in reparting to every sense, their rank and order, as befits the dignity and honour of their several excellencies. Some it has disposed in the most honourable seats, and fixed the sublime operations of life in the public view, and eye of the world, and contrarily seated the homely and mean works of necessity in more occult places, the better with modesty to conceal their uncomeliness."

"In this," said Critilo, "she has reconciled honesty with decency, and particularly in that convenient disposure of the mother's breasts, by which with much decency she tenders nourishment to the unweaned infant."

"In the next place to the eyes," said Andrenio, "the ears challenge their degree, which are well disposed in a rank so high, but their being placed on each side, seems, I must confess inconvenient to me, it being a means to lay them open, and facilitate an entrance to introduce deceit: for as truth always meets us face to face, so fraud, traitor-like, crowds to one side, and insinuates entertainment in to unwary ears. Would not, the ears, be better and more securely seated under the eyes? by which means they might first examine treacherous spies, and call them to a parley, before they admit them into the bowels of the city?" "How well you understand it," said Artemia, "were the eyes in that place you speak of, that small remainder of truth would be banished out of the world, together with the rest; let them rather be separated ten fingers breadths from the sight, or placed in the hinder parts, for that's not truth is flattered to our faces, but what proceeds from sincerity, and is without passion, spoken behind our backs. How well do you think justice would proceed, should she see that decency, which excuses her, the riches that defend her, the nobility which pleads her cause, the authority which intercedes, and the abilities of other ministers whose rhetoric charms her adversaries? it is better, that she is blind, and most convenient for her own, and others advantage: our ears stand well in this mean, not before, lest they should hear too soon, nor behind, lest they should hear too late."

"Another thing," replied Andrenio, "has busied and troubled my thoughts to resolve, which is, that being the eyes have the conveniency of those fringed curtains, to bar out the importunate entrance of unwelcome spectacles, and to close themselves against the view of displeasing objects: Why should not also the ears have the same privilege, and shut a door against the ribaldry of vain discourse, become serpents, and deaf to charms, and so excuse impertinent follies, and intercept at the entrance relations of bad news, and sorrow, the chief destroyer and ruin of our lives. I cannot, I must confess, but condemn Nature's error in this, especially when I see the tongues rashness curbed within the wall of reason, and as an unruly beast imprisoned within the grates of teeth, and doors of the lips. Why than should the eyes and mouth have this advantage, above the hearing, which seems more needful of it, as being most subject to the danger of errors?"

"Upon no terms," said Artemia, "will Nature consent to shut the free and open passage of the ears, which should always be ready to admit an entertainment to the welcome access and entrance of instruction. So that wise nature is not only content to unhinge these doors, and unlock the bars which interrupt the passage, but has made them the only immoveable parts of man, as esteeming the least diversion from their proper office, but time misspent, and leisure prejudicial to man's condition. These watch, and every hour give audience, that when the other senses weariedly retire to their repose, and rest, these careful sentinels of the soul, attend their guards, and give alarum at the approach of danger; the soul might sleep in an eternal lethargy, were not this watchful sense an early waker at the mornings approach. There is this difference between sight, and hearing, that the eyes seek the species of distinct objects, how and when they will, but sounds and voices move first, and are received without choice into the organs of the ears. The objects of sight are permanent, and durable, and though at present we see them not, yet they vanish not away, and may be visible at a second review; but sound flies like time, and who meets not the fore-lock in its approaching steps, shall like bald occasion, too late seek detention in his past progress; its proper the tongue should have a double fence, and lined walls to enclose it, and the ears two passages of free entrance; for we ought in prudence to hear twice more than our tongues should utter. I am not ignorant, that the half of what our ears are auditors is impertinent, and fruitless, for which wise men have a singular remedy, and that is by making themselves deaf, or composing wise men's ears, which is a rare invention and of great advantage; for there are some shrill sounds of unprofitable reasoning without reason, that so thin a covering as an eye-lid would not be sufficient proof against its penetrating violence, and than we have need to stop our hearing with both our hands, whose actions as they often express our minds, and open the ears of others, so also are they helpful to stop our own: let the serpent teach us subtlety in this, who stops one ear by laying it close to the other, and the other with his fall denying entrance to bewitching charms."

"You cannot deny," urged Andrenio, "that were there a guard or stoppage in the ear, there would not be so free a passage for dangerous enemies, for the hissings of venomous serpents, for songs of deceitful sirens, for flattering schisms, discords, and dissentions, and other monsters, who crowd to get admission at this entrance."

"You have reason," said Artemia, "and therefore has Nature formed the ears like a colander, or strainer of words, making them almost rational and able to judge of verity; and if you observe, she has before hand prevented this inconvenience, and formed the organ of this sense with so many turns, and twines of labyrinth, that they seem the portcullis and trenches of a fortress, in which words are so drained and examined, that there is time and opportunity sufficient to bring them to the touchstone and test of reason. There is also within a bell, which beaten on by the hammer of words, gives a certain sound of their truth, or falsity: hast thou never observed the bitterness of that choleric humour which purges forth at these parts; and can you agree with the vulgar errors, that it only sweats forth as birdlime to dam up an entrance from flies, and blinder animals? Know that Nature had thoughts of higher preventions than these, and intentions by this to detain the gentle words of Circes, and the smiling breath of the deceiving flatterer, whose palates being displeased with this wholesome bitterness, which is tempered with the unsavoury relish of discretion, are here stopped, and retained."

"And therefore," considered Critilo, "that surfeit which many take with a glut of sugared words, is only curable by this antidote of bitterness. in fine, there are two ears, that so a wise man may keep one unviolated, though the other be affected with falsity; for there is a first and a second information, that if one ear be prepossessed by a too forward and rain reception, the other may be yet conserved for truth, which is commonly manifested by the latter relation."

"The smell," said Andrenio, "seems to me a sense more delightful than profitable, and more requisite to feast and indulge our genius, than to serve our necessities, and therefore it should not advance its self to the third degree, and displace others of more importance."

"O yes!" replied Artemia, "for this is a sense of greatest acuteness, and is the reason why the nostrils our whole life long are in continual growth, and that through the same organ of our nostrils are breathed the respirations of life, which makes our smell as necessary as to live. This distinguishes perfumed odours, from the displeasing stenches of corruption, and comforts the soul with the cheerful fragrancy of a good fame, which is the nourishment of it; a corrupted air infuses a pestilentious noisomeness, and infection to the bowels, which a sagacious and acute nose discerns, and knows the comfortable refreshments of a sweet savour, and the danger of poisonous scents, and camerines of customs, which use to envenom, and infect the soul; it is the guide of the blind, and tells him what meat is tainted, and what is wholesome, and is our taster before we eat; it is that sense which only enjoys the fragrant respirations of flowers, and refreshes the brain with the odoriferous smells of those perfumes, which virtues, glory, and fame fend out from their natural sweetness. We may know the principal worthies of our time, in whom the blood of true nobility resides, not by their perfumed skins, and amber ointments, but by their parts and excellency of their abilities, which cast out a fragrancy of odours from them, unlike the clownish blasts of garlic, which the Plebeian breathes."

"With much reason," said Andrenio, "has provident Nature endued each faculty with a double power, bestowing several offices on one, not to multiply agents: so that not only the nostrils serve for their principal use, but in a more servile condition, are the channel to convey away the brains superfluities."

"This is true," said Critilo, "in children, but in men of riper years, they rather serve for a channel to convey the passions, and the swelling ventosities of vanity, which belch through them, and that impostume of the head, which usually causes a giddiness, and meagrum, vents and discharges itself by this way. through these also are eased the oppressions of the heart, and steams evaporate from the stomach. The nose is a feature that much adorns the proportion of the face, and is the pin of the souls dial, which points at the temperature of its nature; a lions nose denotes valour, an eagles beak generosity, a long one gentleness, the sharp ingenuity, and the thick folly."

"Having already treated of sight, hearing, and smelling, the next," considered Andrenio, "is speech. The mouth seems to me the principal gate, and door of the soul; for as through the passage of the senses, objects enter, so this is reserved only with respect, for the mind to go forth, and to manifest herself by the help of her expressions."

"It is true," said Artemia, "for in this artificial composure of man's countenance, the mouth is the gate of its royal person, and the teeth the guards, all set and composed in a decent rank, and order; in this resides the best and worst part of man, which is his tongue, having its root radicated in the heart."

"There is one thing, said Andrenio, I have beaten my brains to understand, What was the intent of wise Nature in making our speech and eating to have one and the same instrument for both operations; that our words, which are most peculiar and proper to man, should dwell in the same office, wherein is acted and framed the vile occupation, and exercise of brutes; were it only those inconveniences that proceed from hence, it were enough to persuade us of Nature's oversight; were it only that change of the tongues accent, which sometimes speaks smooth, and gentle, and anon with bitterness, and choler breathes out rage, and varies with the relish of material food; this makes the tongue trip and stammer, equivocate and talk at large, that it were better this nobler member were set apart, and consecrated as a temple of the soul's oracle."

"Hold," said Critilo, "the argument you urge well, and a little more difficulty would puzzle my reason to resolve; but howsoever, I appeal to the providence of Heaven, which governs, and directs the function of Nature; and therefore I may boldly affirm the conveniency which speech enjoys, by joining houses, and mansions, with their taste, that so the relish may examine and tell us the nature of our words, before we pronounce them, inform us how sweet or bitter they are, chew and prove them, whether they be substantial, and accordingly sweeten those which may embitter, and dress, and confect them for the stomach of the receivers; besides the tongue is employed in the taste and eating; for speech well moderated, ought not to be so long, but that the instrument of it may afford time for other duties."

Actions ought to follow, or accompany our words, and our hands readily to execute that which our mouth promises.

"Is it," said Andrenio, that the hands are called *manus*, from *maneo*, denoting by an antiphrasis their duty of continual employment."

"They are called so," replied Critilo, "not from their continual employment, and unwearied motion, but from that constant permanency they ought to retain in their travels, or because they are the fountain from whence spring our works of piety, and they like branches from the hearts roots, which are laden with fruit of famous, and immortal actions: by their palms are obtained victorious laurels, and they are the source from whence distil the precious sweat of heroic labours, and the ink which memorizes their actions to all posterity. Does thou not consider, and admire their artificial, and commodious composure, which are as slaves and servants to the other members, and are fitted to serve all our necessities? they help us to hear, assist our tongue, and give a life, and vigour to our actions; they administer meat to our mouths, flowers to our smell; they are prospectives to strengthan our sight in a large view, and help some so to discourse and reason, as if their genius and wit were more lodged in their hands, than in their brain. So that they are the officious ministers to all our necessities, they defend us, clean us, clothe us, cure, and protect us, and sometimes rub, and ease our itching."

"All which offices," said Artemia, "because they agree with reason, Nature has ordained them in number, weight, and measure; in the ten fingers of the hand consists the beginning and principals on which numbers are founded; so that all nations count till they arrive to ten, afterwards proceed in multiplication. weight itself is judged by waving with the hand, and guessing at its quantity. This punctuality is necessary for information of man who operates in number, weight, and measure; and to raise our thoughts yet higher, the tables of the law were included in ten precepts, that men might not only carry them in their heart, but that so small a bulk might be likewise portable in the hand. These put in execution, the intent of the soul, which are not imprinted on those common lines which divide the palms, but signified and made manifest by their own works. These are they which form our letters, and with silence speak in writings, the three principal fingers concurring with an admirable dexterity in the several offices, the first fortifies the motion, the thumb teaches, and the middle as corresponding with the heart, rules and directs; that our writing may record the testimonies of valour, subtlety and truth; since than that the hands put the seal and stamp on virtue, it is no wonder if other members of the body should in courtesy, and estimation, seal them to their lips, and give them a *besolas manos*, in gratitude for their works of virtue. And because we now anatomatize man, and contemplate from head to foot his mysterious being; it would not be from our purpose to cast our eyes on his feet, and consider his steps and progress as he moves; the feet are the pillars and foundation on which the body is established, they tread the Earth, and trample on it in contempt; they make it serviceable to the bodies burden, and measure out the paces of their stage, that they may tread on a plain, and secure foundation."

"I observe," said Andrenio, "and admire too the firmness with which Nature has planted the body, for lest it should fall forward, it has placed the feet before, nor stagger on either side, it has underpropped it with equal supports, but yet you cannot deny, but she has negligently overseen the dangerous precipice of a backward relapse, where the hands cannot with their usual diligence apply themselves to their help; which inconveniency might be easily remedied by enlarging the same proportion of the feet as much behind, as before."

"This is but a fond conceit," replied Artemia, "for this would give men occasion to retreat backward from the path of virtue, whose inconstant humour being apt to retire, would give a fuller turn, had they found in Nature encouragements for this motion. Such is the outward proportion of man, and visible anatomy, whose harmony of powers, proportion of virtues, agreement of affections, and passions, is a more interior inspection, and must be referred to philosophical conclusions. Yet above all, I would have you know, and admire that principal part of man, the original of all the rest, the fountain and spring of life, which is the heart."

"The heart," replied Andrenio, "what is that? and where is it placed?"

"It is," answered Artemia, "the king of other members, and therefore is placed in the centre of his dominions, greatly and inwardly conserved, and is sometimes in Latin called *cura*, or care; for that which rules and governs, is always placed in the centre. it has also offices, the one is to be the fountain of life, infusing strength and courage, by its spirit, into other parts, and the other, which is the principal, to be the cause of affection, and in which are blown into a flame the smallest sparks, and warmth of love."

"And therefore," considered Critilo, "it is always scorched like the phoenix."

"And its place," proceeded Artemia, "is fixed in the middle, denoting how much our affections ought to be moderated, and not to exceed the bounds of reason. its form is with a point downwards, as if an indivisibility were enough to touch the Earth, but upwards is of a spacious breadth, enlarging itself to receive the bounty of Heaven, and greedy to suck those dews, which can only content, and satisfy the soul; it has the *systole*, and the *diastole*. Wings not only to fan or cool its boiling heat, but also to raise it higher, and make it soar to the upper region; its colour is ruddy and sanguine, the emblem of charity, and from hence springs the best blood, to show that noble persons should be qualified with best hearts. it was never so unworthy as to betray, though so indiscreet as to err, by being more careful to prevent misfortunes, than cautious against the surprise of felicity; but what we ought most to esteem, is its cleanness, not engendering excrements, like the crude digestion of other parts, it having an obligation on it of purity, especially in the formality of life, which makes it breathe and pant after the most sublime perfection."

In this manner let us leave the wise Artemia in philosophical discourses, applauded by the acclamations of her scholars, whilst we consider the inventions, and policy of deceiving Falismund. Who being vexed, for the escape of Andrenio, and some others, as blind as he, from the toils of his labyrinth, both out of sense of scandal to his reputation, and also of that ill consequence it might bring by its example, made him treat of the fullest extremity, and excess of revenge. To which purpose he dealt first with envy, the assassinate and destroyer of the good, a subject sit to be made actor of the most horrid villanies, and to her he communicated the ground of his distastes, and entrusted to her art the sowing of the weeds of malice, and planting this root of anger amongst the rabble and scum of vice. This was not a work very difficult to so skilful an artist, being assisted also by that acquaintance and familiarity which malice had obtained amongst the vulgar, by a long habitation in their homely cottages, ever since which time, bad intention, the mother of the two sisters, flattery and malice, drew out their brood from the nest of their nothing, to advance them with as much ambition as the most aspiring vice: so flattery fled to the court, not the direct way, but yet at last arrived there, where she was introduced with the welcome entertainment of all, that in few hours she became intimate and privy to all consults; but malice had not so good encouragement, or hopes to preferment, being neither well spoken of nor courteously looked on, an affront sufficient to burst with choler her haughty stomach, and her speech and liberty being restrained, and uncivilly treated, she took a resolution of voluntary banishment, and changed her station to inhabit with the rural clowns, where she was received with a dull kindness, and adored with a devotion of fond simplicity. There she might triumph, because speak, discourse at large, and in rude appellations vent the rancour of malice, which she calls the plain dialect of evident truth; with this policy she insinuated so much into the esteem of the people, that they resolved to reserve her, from any that might ravish her from them; and therefore, have buried her within their own bowels, where those are sure to find her, who least desire her. In this opportune conjuncture came envy, who began to sow her seeds, and to affect people with a sense of anger against Artemia. She called her another Circe, or one worse, and that she would appear most deformed, were that cloak of pretensions stripped from her nakedness. That she had destroyed Nature, robbed her of her true solidity, and plain simplicity, and by a fond affectation, defaced her original comeliness; taxed her of ambitious covetousness, in depressing Nature, and usurping the birthright of a legitimate heir. Know that since the government of this feigned queen has been introduced in the world, all is adulterated and corrupted; so that every thing bears another face, her whole proceedings being effects of fraud and falsity: hence it is that men are not what they were wont, nor worthy to be accounted the race of former ages; for antiquity, as it is venerable, so it is best, and men with time grow worse, having lost the candid simplicity of infants, are also stripped of that livery, and badge of innocence. Farewell that noble offspring of ancient worthies, those defenders of truth, and solidity, whose yea, was yea, and no, no: but now contrarily men are become malicious, and revengeful, all is deceit, and policy, which they style with the honourable title of artifice; so that he who is most dextrous in this, has the greatest advantage in all exercises, he is renowned both in arms, and science, and to this pitch and height has sin proceeded, that malice is now more predominant in a child of seven years, than formerly in a man of seventy. Women from top to toe, are a continued tale and blot of falsity, as spruce and pert they are as daws, full of policy and alluring fraud; this feigned queen subverts republics, destroys families, exhausts the most immense treasures, gives encouragement to the vanity of modes, and fashions, and consumes more in the adorning of one woman, than formerly was required to cover and clothe a nation, with the honest and simple garments of necessity. In our diet she has taught us to vitiate our palates with luxurious dishes, of which formerly our simplicity was ignorant, and knew no more than to satisfy Nature, and not by adulterated meats to provoke appetite to be overcharged in gluttony: she boasts that men are not men but by her polishment, who only makes them vicious and dissolute, blinding their eyes with false apparitions, giving no occasion for their judgement to interpose itself, as a sun to scatter these clouds of falsity. With these scandalous reproaches, she so incited the revenge of her vile multitude, that all with an unanimous consent conspired to ruinate her palace, exclaiming, and crying, "let the witch die." And scarce could moderation prevail to keep off these flames, which threatened its ashes. With this the wise queen perceived the vulgar to be her enemies, and though the presence of daring champions were than wanting, her own policy supplied the defect. But the manner of her conquest, and the stratagems by which she triumphed, and was delivered from the dangers of the base and rude rabble, is delivered in the following Crisis.

The Tenth Crisis

It is the vulgar error of preposterous man to make ends of the means, and means of the end; for that country which should only serve for a passage to him, he takes up for his habitation, and makes that his inn, which should only be the way of his pilgrimage: men often begin where they should end, and end where they should begin. Wise and provident Nature introduced delights for diversion, whereby the operations of life might be eased, and alleviated, and we enabled to run the sedious course of this world without faintness, or discouragement; but here it is, where man does most confound, and dishonour himself, becomes more brute than the beasts, degenerates from himself, in making an epicurial pleasure the ultimate term, and his life subservient to a bestial appetite: he eats not now that he may live, but he lives that he may eat; he rests not to recover new strength for next days labour, but labours not that he may be insensibly surprised with drowsiness; his lust provokes him not to an intention of propagating his own species, but of indulging his luxury; he studies not to know, but to forget, and be acquainted with himself; he makes not use of his tongue for necessity, but to please himself with the vanity of his own talk, so that he makes not recreations a means to continue life, but his life a means to continue pleasure; hence it is, that all vices have made delight their general; this is the defender of the appetite, the captain of the passions, which violently drags men to accompany sin, and lays a force on their yielding affections; let than the wise reader observe, and learn to reform this common absurdity, and that he may be admonished by the misfortunes of another, let him observe those accidents which happened to the discreet Critilo, and unwary Andrenio.

"How long," said angry Artemia, (than most constant, when most disturbed) shall the neglect of this insult vulgar, despise, and condemn my lectures? How long shall inhumane barbarity reproach and scorn my wisdom? How long will it be before your own ignorant audacity shall confound itself? By Heaven I swear, that since your boldness has proceeded to this uncivil language, as to style me with the name of enchantress, and Circe; this very night in chastisement of your folly, I will raise so powerful a conspiracy, that the very Sun shall revenge my quarrel, who withdrawing the comfort of his bright rays, shall commit you to the punishment of thick darkness, which is the blindness of your own vulgarity."

Thus did she treat them as their folly deserved; for knowing that in base spirits severity prevails more than courtesy, she struck in them a terror of her power, and so amazed them with the persuasion that her fame was obtained only by magic enchantments; that they grew cold and faint in their purposes, and changed the resolution of assaulting her palace. Their courage began than to fail them, when they saw the Sun really to withdraw his light, and by points to eclipse himself in their hemisphere, fearing an earthquake might follow, as usually the elements conspire to perfect the destruction of a falling adversary; thus all discouraged fled, as is ordinary in all commotions of the people, whose sudden insurrections raised with heat, and fury, as soon vanish with a panic terror, so they stumbled in the dark, and not distinguishing their foes, converted their swords one against another, and so ended the war in a miserable slaughter. By this victory Artemia found opportunity with the rest of her instructed family to escape from the midst of these barbarous incendiaries, and to deliver the treasures of curious observation, and jewels enveloped in the eternal and memorable writings of imperishable philosophers, and other esteemed leaves from the rapacious hands of envious ignorance. And so went they forth, assisting with instructions our two travellers Critilo, and Andrenio; the latter of which amazed at so strange a miracle, believed her magic extended so far as to influence the stars, and that the Sun itself was obedient to her charms, which made him the more reverence and adore her, and even to over act his part in the praises he gave her. But Critilo undeceived him, telling him, that this eclipse of the Sun was but an effect of the celestial motion, which Artemia foreseeing by her astronomical knowledge, took advantage of this occasion, calling that the power of her art, which was only the effect and course of Nature.

Artemia consulted much with her learned disciples, in what part of the world to fix her residence, all agreeing in an unanimous resolution no more to enter into country villages, and therefore propounded divers places for their secure and convenient habitation: many times she propounded Lisbon, not only for being the most populous place of Spain, but one also of the three empires of Europe; for if other cities have some appellations from their chiefs excellencies, in this may be united, and meet the glories of all as in a common centre, and bear the name of faithful, rich, healthful, and abundant; for never was a Portuguese a fool, whose first founder was the wise Ulysses; nor was the fantastical humour of the nation so much an obstacle to her entrance, as was the confusion there, which is contrary to the quietness which speculation requires. Again, she cast her thoughts upon the royal Madrid, the centre of monarchy, where perfections concur to the height and chiefest eminencies, but yet she could not fix her choice on that which her stomach nauseated, not so much loathing the filthiness of the streets, as the mire of corrupted hearts; for besides the prejudice she boar to it, for being a village, she was no less displeased with it, for being the Babylon of nations of different interests. Seville was no sooner nominated, but it displeased her, covetousness and lucre being enemies, with whom she admits no treaty, and that indigested stomach of her plate was highly displeasing; her inhabitants are neither black nor white, but as the twilight of Nature stand as neuters little, which is the common disease of Andaluzia. Upon Granada she made her cross, and Cordova she called Caludry. Salamanca reads the pandects of the laws, and makes men rather learned than wise, teaching men to plead at the bar, and in what manner to form a battery against riches. She once resolved to pitch her residence in the plentiful Zaragoza, the metropolis of Aragon, the mother of a famous line of kings, the supporter of the great pillar, and the basis of faith, famous for convents, and endowments of the church, beautiful in magnificent edifices, and populated with the religious inhabitants of undeceiving Aragon; but the haughtiness of their spirits was a fault outweighing her other perfections, and that kind of original folly which mixed with all her actions, were no less displeasing and ungrateful. The cheerful, noble, and flourishing Valentia abounding with all, that is not substance, was the next propounded to her election, but here she feared that with the same easiness wherewith to day they received her, to morrow they would eject her. Barcelona, though rich, and when it shall so please Heaven, the ladder to scale the Italian fortresses, the stop of gold's continual currant and motion, the sanctuary of the judicious amidst barbarity, was not yet esteemed a secure retirement, being a place where we must always walk with our beard turned over our shoulders. Leon and Burgos were situations too near the mountains, having more in them of misery than poverty. Santiago displeased her in nothing, but being in Galicia. Valladolid seemed a place not inconvenient for her dwelling, and therefore determined to journey thither, supposing truth could not but inhabit with plain simplicity; but the prejudice she conceived against the court, diverted her from hence, (having been formerly the court of Spain) and still retaining too fresh a memory and savour of her past condition. Of Pamplona was made little mention, being a place like to Navarre, consisting of nothing but points and punctilio's. In fine, by the election of this Catholic queen, was preferred the imperical Toledo, confessing she was never so passionately affectionate to any seat as to this. For this is the forge where men are fashioned, this is the school of rhetoric, all court, and city, and more since the spunge of Madrid, has sucked out the dregs from thance: corruptions may chance to enter here, but not remain in other parts many have their wits in their hands, but here in their foreheads. And though the censure of some is, that Toledo never produced any of a profound and deep judgment; howsoever Artemia kept still constant to her resolution and choice, extolling its wisdom and learning, saying, That one woman there has spoke more pith and substance in a sentence, than a grave philosopher of Athans, in whole volumes of his writings. Let us, said she, hasten thither to the centre of Spain, not for its situation, but for the real confluence and concourse of all vertues. Thus travelled she on with her discreet attendants, amongst whom were Critilo and Andrenio, who with no small advantage and improvement to their judgments, kept them company until they came to that way which leads to madrid, and there taking their leave with many acknowledgments and expressions of gratitude, acquainted her what important occasions called them to the court in search of Felisinda; she therefore giving them her benediction, armed them against all assaults, with necessary instructions, telling them withal, that since they were resolved to go thither, they would be careful not to mistake their way, because there are many paths which lead thither.

"By this means," replied Andrenio, "we cannot err, since all paths direct the same course."

"This is the great danger," said Artemia, "for amongst so many roads is the most difficult choice of a secure passage; for many have been lost in the royal highway. Go not therefore by the way of curiosity in seeing, for that is the road of fools, nor yet by that of pretension, for that way is long, and tedious, and few there are which obtain the end: nor by the way of suits, or contentions in law, for it is always chargeable and the journey long: the way of ambition is unknown, and those who follow it are disrespected, and that of interest is an unbeaten path, trod by none but ignorant foreigners; that of necessity is dangerous, being environed by multitudes of hawks and birds of prey; that of delight and sensuality is so foul and dirty, that from our knees we step up to the ears, and thus bemired we are plunged and stopped in our progress, the way of living is but short, and you shall soon arrive at the end; that of servitude is death, that of eating has no end, and that of virtue is unknown, and in this ambiguity you have no way but to abide there as little as you can; for believe me, in Madrid a man can neither live well, nor die well. Observe above all, where you enter, for many come in by Santa Barbara, and some by the street of Toledo: some of refined spirits pass the bridge, and others come in by the Puerta del Sol, and stop in Anton Martin, some come in by Laua Pies, but more by Unta Manos, but the most ordinary passage is not by the gates, which are few, and those shut."

With this parted the wise Artemia to the throne of her estimation, and our two travellers to the labyrinth of the court. And so travelled they together, easing their journey with discourses they made of the admirable excellencies of Artemia, whose strange miracles and prodigies made them glory in her power, and in the happiness and advantage they had obtained by her profitable society. To these thoughts they were so intent, that unsensibly they fell into one of the most dangerous snares, and adventures of life; for on a sudden they saw a numerous multitude both of men and women, bound and manacled, whilst thieves robbed and ransacked their coffers.

"We are undone," said Critilo, "for we have now run ourselves unawares into the hands of robbers, who usually swarm in this road: here they are now pillaging and were they satisfied with the spoils alone, it were well, but are so cruel, that they rob and murder, and afterwards deface the countenance of the slain with wounds and scars, that they are not to be known who they are."

Andrenio was so terrified at this, that fear had already deprived him of his courage, and colour, but recovering himself a little; "what shall we do, said he? Shall we fly, or hide ourselves from their sight?" "You Phrygian, or inconsiderate like," replied Critilo, "propound late remedies, their eyes have already discovered us, and their voice commands us under their power; wherefore we must now go forward, and be contented to submit our hands and necks to their chains."

They looked on one side and the other, and saw a multitude of passengers of all conditions, nobility commons, rich, and poor; nor was their kindness more indulgent to the women; for they were all bound and corded to the trees of themselves. At the sight of this horrid spectacle Critilo and Andrenio sighed, and passed through the spoils to see who those cruel assassinates were, but could not come to have a full sight of any; they beheld one and another, all seemed to be involved in the same misfortune, and yet none knew who had ensnared them; at length, espying an ill looked fellow, they all concluded that he was one.

"This,| said Andrenio, "must be he, with that unlucky look, and such also must be his soul."

"You may guess what you will," replied Critilo, "of his equivocating eye; and yet methinks I am more afraid of that squinting fellow, for may we believe Artemia, they never shoot with the aim of reason; take care of a pouting lip for those are always of a surly and morose humour; that other with a flat nose promises cruelty and danger in his disposition; he with a tawny face, looks like a master of Bridewell, and he with a snarling look puts me in mind of the hangman at Tyburne; and that other blustering boy, and angry brow, seems always to threaten a storm and tempest."

Than they heard another speak with low whispers; "this," said they, "must needs be a person, who admonishes us of what we should beware;" but he was one, who sucked up his words with a hum and a hau, and as he drew in his breath, he swallowed down men. They heard another snuffle through the nose, and him they avoided, for that accent through the nose declared him a true champion of Bacchus, and Venus; they met with another worse, who spoke so hoarse, that he could only be understood through a trunk. In this manner they examined all, nor yet among these captives did they espy any one who had committed the spoil.

"What means this," said they, "what are become of those pillaging rogues who have riled these passengers? Since none are here of those who can steal by the snipping of the scissors, or that can leave us naked, whilst they clothe us, or unfeather our nests, whilst they enwrap us in the quilts, who can mistake their yard, when they measure, and bear down their scales without weight, who is it rules here, who borrows, who recovers, who executes, does none detect the faults of the merchandize, does none entice the customers, are there no ministers, nor scriveners, no keepers of books? Why who than robs? Where are these tyrants of so much liberty?"

Scarce had Critilo said thus, but something between a woman and an angel, answered him, "hold, I go:" and having newly bound two confident presumers, she was as I say, a beautiful woman, not rude, and unfashioned, but of a courtly behaviour, affable, and courteous; she showed a fair face, and outsight to all, but evil actions. Her forehead was more smooth, than serene; she looked on none with an ill eye, and yet all were enchanted with her bewitching emissions; i.e: nostrils were white, which was a sign that she was not ill affected with fumes, and vapours; her cheeks were roses without thorns, her teeth when she smiled and laughed at the world showed like so many rows of pearl, or ivory. The knots she tied with such air, and negligence, that her dexterity and art appeared pleasant, and her very sight was enough to captivate; her tongue doubtless was of sugar, for her words distilled nectar, and her two hands made signs of affection, for never did she extend a real hand in friendship, though ordinarily her arms made indissoluble twinings, with counterfeited embraces, the more easily to entrap and entangle in her snares; so that none could probably suspect an aspect so promising to be guilty of theft or robbery: nor was she alone, but assisted by a flying squadron of Amazons, beautiful and active, which continually bound one, or other, executing the commands of their supreme lady. But it is well worth our observation, that the captives they manacled, had the election of their own bonds, and many so willingly submitted to the servitude, that they brought their chains with them; some were fettered with chains of gold, others with lockets of diamonds, an invincible tackling for such feeble captives; many they bound with garlands of flowers, and others as their humour pleased them, with roses, for only to encircle their brows was an enchantment sufficient to enfeeble their hands; another they saw tied with one lock of a fair and golden hair, which though at first he thought to rend with the smallest force, yet at last it proved more strong than a cable, which held him anchored, whilst he tumbled in the storms and tempests of love. Women ordinarily were bound with threads of pearl, with bracelets of coral, and embroidered ribbons, which seemed something, and their value nothing. The courageous, and valientons of the world, after some few bravadoes and blustering words, contentedly submitted with the rest to the loss of liberty: and what is very admirable they enticed many of their comrades with feathers, and plumes, and these were in a prison the most secure of any; persons of greater quality, they pretended to manacle with small twists, from whence hanged shells, keyes, and links, which bound them so fast, that their whole strength could not break them; there were bolts of gold for some, of iron for others, all being equally content, and as safely secured; but what I admired most was that in wanting chains to imprison their numerous captives, they committed some to the bonds of women's embraces, which though, but feeble, were yet the chains of the most robustous champions. Hercules was ensnared in a tender thread, and Sampson with some hairs, they cut from his own head. One they would have bound with a chain of gold, which he himself brought with him; but the extremity of his covetousness would not endure the cost, but desired rather the cheaper courtesy of the rope; another companion of his, they pinioned with the strings of his own purse, one they bound with his own stork's neck, and another with his ostrich's stomach, till they could secure others with links of savoury sallats, who were so much pleased with their fetters, that the very licking of their fingers was a pleasure to them; some grew frantic with joy to see themselves fettered with laurel and ivy wreaths; which is not so much as that others should turn fools at the melody of their own music. In this manner these wanton robbers assailed the innocent and unwary travellers, ensnaring the feet of some, fettering the necks, and hands, of others, binding their eyes, carried them away as spoils, robbing and depriving them of their hearts. But what made a tragedy of these comic scenes, was one who wounded the hands of those she bound, devouring, and gnawing their bowels, making their torments the delight of others, and hell and the wrack, a paradise and glory of their enemies. Another there was so prettily furious, that she strained the cord until the blood started forth, at which they were so much pleased, that they drank it in full bowls to several healths; and what is most pleasant, after they had bound so many, they would persuade these silly persons that they had touched none. But they coming now to execute the same on Critilo and Andrenio, and asking them with what fetters they would choose to be manacled; Andrenio as young and inconsiderate, suddenly resolved them, and told them with flowers, believing that this would rather be a garland, than a fetter, or binding; but Critilo seeing there was no way to resist, desired they would tie Andrenio to him with the strings of some ancient, and oraculous volumes, which though it seemed a new sort of binding, yet in fine they were contented, and so satisfied his desires.

And now this courteous and wanton tyrant commanded they should beat a march, with which she carried her spoils in triumph, and yet with so much gentleness, that though they were dragged with chains, yet being riveted to the socket of their hearts, they so voluntarily followed, and submitted to their contented servitude; that there was no need to enforce obedience on such willing slaves; for some posted on the wings of wind, others slid along with a good air, the most stumbled as they went, and all were involved in inextricable toils. They soon arrived at the gates of a place, which neither was a palace, nor yet a cottage, but those that understood it best, called it an inn; their entertainment was not on free quarter, nor the house lent them longer than for a night's repose. The building was stone, and of so attractive a virtue, that it drew the hands, the feet, the eyes, the tongue, the heart, as if these members had been iron, and those walls the loadstones of pleasure, cemented so close and strong, as if pearls had been a principal ingredient in that mortar. This pleasant inn without doubt was the centre of delight, the paradise of content, and a mass of those delicious enjoyments which sensuality could invent. The golden palace of Nero, in which he turned steel into gold, was but a cottage in respect of this; the resplendence of Eliogahalus his house, was obscured and benighted by the glory and brightness of these beams, and the very castle of Sardanapalus, was in comparison hereof a sty or dunghill of its own beastliness; over the gate was engraved this motto, *The delightful, good is profitable, and honest.*

Critilo ruminating on the inscription; "this." said he, "is to be read backwards."

"How backwards?" replied Andrenio, "I read it forward. But if you read it backward, it goes thus, *The honest good, is profitable and delightful.* But I shall not dispute of this, only give me leave to say it is one of the most delightful places thy eyes have seen. What an excellent fancy had that builder who contrived it!"

In the front there of were seven pillars, and though the odd number might seem to carry some disproportion in it, yet it was in emulation of that which wisdom had erected. These gave an entrance to seven other lodges or habitations of princes, whose agent this pretty robber was; so that all those which she captivated, she lodged and quartered so much to their contentment, that every one had the election of his own prison. Many entered by the chambers of gold, called so, because they were covered with golden shingles, and beams of plate; the walls were of precious stones; it cost much to get up thither, and when they were above, all the pleasure was with stones. The highest and most lofty rooms were the most dangerous, yet notwithstanding the gravest heads were the most forward to mount thither. The lowest quarter was the most convenient and delightful; for the walls being of sugar, were eaten into, or mouldered away, the mortar was tempered with exquisite wines, and the clay kneaded into biscuit; many crowded to get in here, who affected to be esteemed men of the highest gusto and palate, and had reduced eating to a science. On the contrary there was another room furnished with red, and paved with daggers; the walls were of steel, and doors beset with fire- arms, the windows were portholes for cannon, and from the ceiling, instead of mosaic work, hung down dangerous knobs, threatening the death of the careless lodgers, and yet there wanted not guests, though they paid the hire with their own blood. Another chamber there was painted blew, whose excellence consisted in diminishing or shadowing the comeliness and beauty of others. The furniture hereof was of dogs and griffins, and gaping mouths of wild beasts, and the materials were teeth, not of an elephant, but of a viper, and though it boar a fair outside, yet they say the inward parts of the walls were perished by some internal corroding quality. But the room most useful of all, was on a plain floor, which though it had no stairs to go up it, was yet full of seats and benches, and well furnished with chairs and cushions. it seemed a house of China, without upper chambers; its materials were tortoise shells, where all the world took up their habitations; those that entered here went so slow, that the place being long, they could never arrive to the end; but the green lodging was the best of all, being the apartment of the spring, where beauty reigned; it was called the knot of flowers, for all was flourishing within it, till time and age come to crop the blossom; many lilies were there turned into violets; all who entered in, crowned themselves with roses, which soon faded and turned into thorns, and the flowers became dry and withered as the grass, and yet this was generally the most delightful place, which afforded the most general diversion for all humours.

Amongst the rest they forced Critilo and Andrenio to enter into one of those lodgings which their own fancy should like best. Andrenio being rash and in the flower of his age, thrust himself amongst the beds of roses, bidding Critilo go in where he pleased, for at the end they should all meet in the centre. Critilo being much urged to choose his entrance, replied, that he never followed the current of the multitude, but went always contrary, "not that I think by this," I say, "to excuse my entrance, but I desire it may be at the door where none else have passed."

"How is that possible," replied they, "since there is no door here which stands not continually open to the throngs of guests," some laughed at his singularity, and wondered to see a man so differently disposed, and his humour formed of a disagreeing mould and nature to the vulgarity of the world.

"I must confess," said he, "it is only this, which makes me refractory to the general humour, for my entrance is where others go out, and my eyes fix themselves rather on the end and conclusion, than on the principles or beginnings," and with that turning himself about; the house appeared so changed and metamorphosed from the appearance it had at the first view, that he could not say it was the same; for all that mass and pile of stately buildings, seemed an unfashioned and rude heap, the beauty of those gilded beams appeared only the glistering of rotten wood, the pleasure, and delicious sight turned to horror, and the whole fabric stood continually tottering, and threatening its own ruins. The stones had not now only lost their magnetic virtue, but followed behind their backs, inviting the very pebbles of the Earth to rise against them. The delicious gardens were become overgrown fields of thorns and thistles; and as Critilo observed with much admiration, that those who smiling entered in, returned again with tears in their eyes, sighing out their lamentations and complaints of their misfortunes. Some they flung out of the windows of that chamber, which looked into the garden, amidst hedges of thorns, which pierced their bodies with an infinity of wounds, and thus pained in this Hell of torments, breathed out their cries to Heaven for assistance. Those who had ascended up the highest, had the sorest fall, one of whom fell from a lofty pinnacle or turret of the palace, with as much contentment to others, as of misery to himself; for all stood gazing on him as he tumbled, being delighted to see him fall, and he having his wings clipped, could soar no longer, but fell with irreparable ruin; those that beheld him, crying out, that he deserved so much, and worse, for evil ought to be his portion, who never did good. But he which moved pity in some, was one, on whom the moon had more influence than the stars: this was an unfortunate person, who in his fall lighted on a dagger which past his throat, and thereby wrote in characters of his own blood, "*the first attempt, without a second*." Critilo observed, that through those windows which formerly appeared of gold, but now of dirt, were flung out some naked, others so bruised, as if their shoulders had been beaten with bags of golden sand. Others fell down through the windows of the kitchen, and of these their bellies suffered most in their fall, which turned their stomachs; one there was, and but one, that went out at the door, whom Critilo observing, went to salute him, and coming nearer to him, the stranger made a stop, as if he knew him.

"Heavens guide me," said he, "where have I seen this man? I have certainly seen him, though I cannot remember where."

"Is not this Critilo, "demanded he?"

"Yes, and who are you?"

"Do you not remember when we were both companions in the house of the wise Artemia?"

"O! now it comes into my mind," said Critilo, "are not you he of the *omnia mea mecum porte*."

"The same, said he, and that has been the only spell to deliver me from these enchantments. But what means did you use to make this escape?"

"The way," replied he, "is short and easy, and with the same facility do you but only desire it, and I shall unbind you; see but those blind and dumb ignorants, whose assent of their will is the only bond that ties them; for in desiring and wishing only to be freed, they immediately obtain their liberty."

With that Critilo only desired his freedom, and his chains dropped off.

"But tell me Critilo, how it came to pass that thou didst not enter into this common prison and captivity of the world?"

"Because," replied he, "I followed Artemia's council in not setting foot or step on the beginning, till my hand could reach and take hold of the conclusion."

"O happy man! But this is too mean a praise for thee: for thou art not a man, but an intellectual spirit. What is become of your companion, who was younger than yourself, and less wary?"

"I was about to enquire the same of you," said he, "if you had seen him within, for he having without any reason precipitated himself in there, will, I fear, run the common misfortune, and at last be cast out among the vile refuse of this deceived generation."

"Through what gate did he enter?"

"Through that of pleasure."

"This is the worst of all," said he, "for his exit will be the later for it, and perhaps not until vice and time weaken his body, and strengthan his judgment."

"But is there no means left for his remedy?" demanded Critilo.

"There is only one, and that something difficult."

"What is it?"

"Only to will; for let him follow my course, and not stay till necessity drive him forth; for it is better to take his opportunity and advantage to go forth on his own legs, and rather willingly pass out at the door, than to be compelled and thrown headlong from the windows."

"I have one request to you," said Critilo, "which my modesty denies me leave to demand, and savours more of folly than favour."

"What is it?"

"That since you have gained the clue of this winding labyrinth, you would return in again, and with that rhetoric you are used to undeceive others, to persuade, and instruct him, how to wish and desire his own freedom."

"This will be but to small purpose," said he, "for though I find and speak to him, yet his humour will scarce give way to the counsels of an unknown adviser; for oftentimes the examples and entreaties of acquainted friends prevail more with affection, than arguments and persuasions can with reason. It were better you went in yourself, for your friendship must needs be more prevalent than my word."

"I should willingly go in," said Critilo, "but I fear that not knowing the way, I may wander, and loose myself, and in this manner we may both be destroyed."

"Let us resolve on this to go both together, for a double diligence is very requisite in so important an attempt."

"So you shall be his guide, and I his friend."

The proposition was so well accepted, that they suddenly went about to execute it; but the guard gave them a stop at the entrance, upon suspicion that men of such grave looks, and countenances were not come to be disciples, but enemies to their kingdom: "But yet," pointing to Critilo, for him, said they, "I have order to admit." This made them both to retire back, and have recourse to a second consult. And now considering well of the entrances and goings out, the many twinings and turnings of the labyrinth which was all palace, and being absolutely resolved to enter, they made a full stop in the middle way.

"Hold," said Critilo, "let me make you this other proposal, which is, that we change clothes, that you take mine, which are well known to Andrenio, together with a sufficient commission to procure you credit; and thus being disguised, you may deceive the guard, and take off all jealousy of our design."

The device did not dislike him, and so clothing himself like Critilo, he was with freedom admitted entrance. In the mean time Critilo entertained himself without, in viewing the continual falls, and destructions of those, whom they violently hurried from the windows of their own perdition. A prodigal he observed thrown down by women from the beds of roses, upon a bush of thorns, where being naked, the prickles tormented him in every part; his nose being battered in the fall, caused him to snore ever after, and this imperfection remained for his whole life, every one laughing made his nose the common subject of their wit, and derision. Such was the loathsomeness and detestation which this man and his consorts had of this sin, that they continually spit upon their delight, and in revenge cast forth a perpetual flux on the bestiality of their sin. Those who rounded in byways of repose, lingered something in their fall, but being down, were more sluggish to arise; for mere idleness had deprived them of all active motions of life; and these being a people of an unprofitable weight to the Earth only served to fill up the number of mankind, and to suck the fat of the Earth; and having never done any thing with dexterity, being once down had neither courage nor strength to recover themselves. But in the lodgings of arms and weapons, there was heard so great a noise, and confusion, that it seemed a hell or bedlam, from whence proceeded men so hacked and torn by those blows they had received, that they spit blood from their valiant breasts, and vomited also that of their enemies, which they had drank in plentiful bowls, so usually does revenge, extort our victories from our hands. Only those of the lodgings of poison, remained secure, whilst they beheld the miseries of others, delighted themselves whilst others lamented, and one there was, who that another should break an arm, or pluck out one eye, would loose both; they laughed whilst others wept, and lamented at what was the common joy, their pleasure being to rejoice at the miseries of others. Critilo stood all this while looking on this unhappy end, and at the evening of a day of some years, he perceived Andrenio appear at the window, amidst the thorns of those flowers he had elected; at which he was affrighted, fearing his total destruction; but he durst not call to him, lest he should discover himself, but made signs that he should remember and meditate on his deceived condition; but how and which way he got down, is related in the following Crisis.

The Eleventh Crisis

When we have seen a lion or lamb, in them we discover the full nature and disposition of the species; but in seeing a man, we see but one, and his humour and condition too, almost unknown. All tigers are naturally cruel; the dove innocent, but every man is variously disposed and tempered. The generous eagle engenders a brood like himself; but noble worthies are not sure to propagate their elevated spirits in their posterity; nor is the vicious father certain to make his son heir of his depraved works, as well as of his fortunes. For every one has his several pleasure, his different behaviour, and fashion, and opinions in all ages have found heads, and brains like those that first invented them. Wise Nature has bestowed on every man a countenance and complexion peculiar to himself, a voice and gestures different from others to serve for characters, and marks to know him by, that so the good may not be confounded among the number of the bad; that women may be distinguished from men, and that none may pretend to conceal his own faults under the guise of another. There are many who spend much time and study in knowing the nature and quality of herbs: but how much more would it import, and advantage them to know the nature, and operations of men with whom they are to live, and die; for all are not men who appear so outwardly, but horrible monsters and acroceraunian rocks in the gulfs of great populations. There are wise men without works, aged men without experience, youths without subjection, women without modesty, rich without compassion, Poor without humility, lords without nobility, commonwealths without government, deserts without reward, and men without humanity: These were the reflections of this wise person, in sight of the court, after he had rescued Andrenio with so exemplary prudence.

Whilst Critilo stayed for Andrenio at the free-gate, he observed him at the window involved in the common danger; howsoever he comforted himself with this, that there was none now could tempt him farther, before he might take the garland from his head, the which having done himself, he untwisted it, and having tied some other bows to it, made a rope, and thereby let himself down, and without any danger, or hurt, had the happiness to come safe to ground. At the same time also appeared his wise instructor at the door, a double joy to Critilo, who now thought it not time to use complements, or embraces, but hasted away as fast as they could. Only Andrenio turning his head to the window, said, "hang there thou cord, the ladder of this my liberty, and trophy of eternal memory to be dedicated to my undeceived condition." Their way was the direct road to the court, which this wise philosopher called a falling upon Scylla to avoid Carybdis. Howsoever he accompanied them to the gate, being much taken with their society and converse, which was the best pastime of this tedious journey, and travel of our life.

"Let me know," said Critilo, "what house this is, and inform me of what passages, and accidents have happened to you."

The wise philosopher by the courtesy of Andrenio, taking the upper hand, "know," said he, "this is the deceitful house, the inn of the world; the gate at which men enter, is delight, and through which they go out, is charge and expense. That famous robber is Colusa, whom we call delight, and the Latin Voluptas; she is the gracious protectress of vice, and draws mortals to their execution on the slid or delight. This is she who enslaves and captivates men, imprisons them where they please, some she lodges in upper rooms of pride, others in the dungeon and cellars of sloth, but none inhabit the middle, all situations being extremities in vice. All enter in, as you see with songs and music, but go out with no other melody than their own sobs, except the envious, who do all things in a contrary humour. The remedy not to miss of the end, or be destroyed in the conclusion, is to cast an eye first upon the beginning, which was the counsel and advice of the wise Artemia, and the only means for me to escape secure.

"And for me," said Critilo, "not to enter in, for I usually go with more content to the house of sorrow, than of mirth, for the holy days of rejoicing, are always the vigils of repentance; believe me Andrenio, he that founds his beginnings in his pleasure, shall end in his sorrow."

"It is sufficient," said he, "that this way we tread is full of snares, for thereby we become more wary; nor without reason has fraud set a guard at the beginning to intercept our entrance. O house of fools! what little respect hast thou deserved? O false enchantment of bewitched loadstones, which at first attract and entice, and than betray; God deliver us," said their philosopher, "from what begins with the smiles of content. Never flatter yourselves with prosperous and easy success of the first beginnings, but attend always to the difficulties of the conclusion. The experience of this I have tried in the inn of Volusia, and in that dream which ought to awake and revive you."

"It is reported that fortune had two sons, both of a most different nature, and disposition. The eldest was handsome, and of as smiling a countenance, as the other was ill-favoured and frowning; their conditions and natures, as usually it happens, being read in the index of their foreheads. Their mother did accordingly habit them in such garments and dress, as did best denote their humours, and distinguish their conditions, the eldest had his clothes embroidered by the spring with roses, and gillyflowers, and between rose and rose was inserted a G. which served for a hieroglyphic, and was interpreted by some to be gracious, gallant, grateful, great; the lining was of white ermines, which rendered his aspect cheerful and smiling, so as it betokened an inward serenity of mind. The other was clothed in a different manner, in a black, or mourning buckram, worked with thorns, and briars, and between every one an F, characters of his foul, fierce, furious, false disposition; his countenance and look struck terror to all that beheld him. in this garb they went forth from the house of their mother, to the school, or to the market. The eldest was adored by all, invited to receive entertainment, the doors of their hearts were opened to him, and the whole world followed him, esteeming their eyes blest which saw so gracious a youth. How much more happy their arms which could embrace him? The other despised found none so courteous, or charitable as to admit him to any access, but as from a scourge or plague fled at his approach; when necessity, or convenience drove him to enter into their Houses, their gate was shut against him, and his importunity returned with blows, that so banished from the society of all, he found no place to make his residence, whether he should now live or die, was the subject of his melancholy contemplation; his rage not being able to suffer longer these injuries, he chose rather to die, that he might live, than to live that he might die; but as contrivance is the effect of melancholy, his brains began to work, and thought on a plot, which is always more available than open force. For considering how powerful fraud was, and the several wonders she continually performs, he determined one night to search her out, for light, and fraud are inconsistent together. In a wearisome search of fraud he spent much time, but yet arrived not to a sight, or view of her; for in every place they said she was, but he found her in none. He was persuaded she could not be absent from the house of the fraudulent, but first in his way he searched the house of time; who told him, she used not to reside there, for that he was an enemy to falsity, and endeavoured to undeceive the world; but his words were believed too late; from thance he went to the house of the world, which was always deemed for a deceiver; but was answered here, that he never deceived any, though they desired it; but men deceived themselves, and desired to be blind, that they might be cheated. With that he went to falsity, and to his demand, was answered, alas fool! with what tongue, or face, can I tell thee truth? 'In this very answer,' said he, 'thou hast told me truth, but yet where shall I find it? for if it be so difficult to find out fraud in the world, it must be impossible to discover truth.' From thance he went to the house of hypocrisy, believing fraud was never absent from thance, and here, the answer he received was as unsatisfactory as at other places, for she turning her neck like her crooked intention, shrugging up her shoulders, simpering with her lips, contracting her eye-brows, and lifting up her eyes to Heaven with a soft and demure voice, told him she knew no such persons, nor ever kept such company, though at that time they were both in the same league and conspiracy with her. From thance he went to the house of adulation, a palace of no small magnificence, and here it was told him, that he was ill advised in coming thither; 'for though I lie,' said she, 'I deceive none, for my words are such gross hyperboles, and apparent falsities, that the judgments of the most simple and ignorant cannot but perceive how clearly I flatter them, and yet notwithstanding, they are tickled at my vain and exorbitant praises, and remunerate me well for so unprofitable an office.' Having thus such ill success in his search, 'is it possible,' said he, sighing, 'that the world should be so full of deceit and fraud, and yet I should not meet it, that the world should resound with it, and every corner should lament the injuries received by it, and yet myself the only unfortunate in this wished encounter? Perhaps I may find her hid within the curtains of the marriage-bed, for there will I seek her;' he asked the husband, and the wife, both of them confessing there had been so many, and such false caresses between them, that neither could complain their real embraces were returned by the other in a more flattering way, than themselves had given them. Than he inquired also in the merchants shops, under the lined cloaks of the usurers, and amongst the undone creditors; who answered him, that fraud was not there, for indeed it is not there where it is evidently known to inhabit; the same replied all tradesmen, affirming, that such could not be deceived, for he, who knows where fraud lies, and yet ventures on it, cannot complain of receiving injury; with such ill success as this despairing of his intentions, and made desperate, was resolved to try his last hopes, and to find her out, though it were in the house of the devil; so thither he went, which was at Genoa, I mean at Geneva; but fraud fiercely raged, and thundering out curses and execrations, cried out: 'Who I,' said she, 'deceit? I deceit? How well is my innocence, and my pains rewarded, wherewith I desire to unblind the world; I promise them not Heaven, but Hell, I set not a paradise before their eyes, but continually threaten their persevering sins with sulphurous flames, who notwithstanding, as not affrighted, pursue after me, and upon hard conditions are slaves unto my will; how than can this plain-dealing be styled deceit?' At this reply, as fully satisfied, he departed away, and giving another turn, came to the house of the deceived, being men oftentimes good, and credulous, of a candid nature, and disposition, were apt to admit fraud, and to give credit to false appearances; but they assured him it was not there, but in the house of the deceivers; for those are right, and most truly fools, who endeavouring to deceive others, have the whole weight and misfortunes of their bad intentions retorted on themselves. 'How is this,' said he, 'the deceived tell me the deceivers retain it, and they, that the defrauded; for my part I believe both the one and the other entertain her, and are possessed with her, though they are ignorant of it.' In this inquisitive search wisdom met him, not he her, and gave him this true information. 'Unfortunate wretch,' said she, 'whom seekest thou, or why searchest thou any other than thyself? dost thou not know that he who seeks deceit, shall never find it, its nature lies, in being concealed, and in once discovering it, it is no more the same; get thee to the house of some of those who deceive themselves, for from them it is never absent.' And so it proved, for entering into the house of the confident, the presumptuous, the covetous, the envious, at last he found it, but much disguised and painted over with the colour of verity; he communicated to her his misfortunes, his affronts, the disgusts of the world, and expected from her, as an oracle, some remedy and ease of his discontents: deceit looking well upon him, said, 'thou lookest like the picture of ill-luck, thy ill-favoured countenance speaks thee so, and yet thou art worse than what thou seemest; notwithstanding be of good courage, for neither my diligence nor policy shall be wanting in this, in which I am glad to find occasions wherein to manifest to the world my power. O! how well we two are matched. Be courageous, for if the first step in a cure, is to find and discover the root of the disease, I have done the like in your grief, and know the cause and original of its arise. I know and feel the pulse, and temper of men, though they are ignorant of me; I know on which foot the ill arbitrement of their will halts, and goes lame; for believe me, thou art not abhorred because thou art evil, but because thou appearest so; these thorns embroidered on your coat, make men afraid, and so start at them, which changed for flowers, would give a kind invitation to all to follow you; leave but all to my management, and in a short time the world shall adore you, and your brother fall into the common disgrace. I have already thought the way,' and with that taking him by the hand, they went both together into the house of fortune, whom after fraud had saluted with the usual complements, Fortune said, that she had need of a guide as being blind. Whereupon Fortune's son offered this fraud for her service, declaring the conveniencies and advantages she might receive by it; and running into high commendations of the youths towardlyness, and discretion, that he knew more tricks and evasions than the devils scholars; and above all, that he desired no other pay or reward, than his own merits; Fortune accepted the profer, and admitted fraud to her house, which is the whole world. Upon this all things began to forsake their usual course, nothing remained in its proper centre, nay the very course of time itself, was diverted with an unknown motion; for this guide or conductor of Fortune, directed her always contrary to her intentions; if she desired to bless the head of the virtuous with her presence, the unlucky boy wantonly led her to the house of the vicious: when necessity or convenience required her haste, he stopped her progress, when slowly she should move, he fixed her wings to fly, and so shuffled, changed, and confounded her actions, that all went preposterously disordered; the gifts and favours she should bestow on the wise, became the undeserved blessings of ignorance, and the cowards brow was encircled with the laurel of the valiant conqueror, and so changed her hands, that she unjustly bestowed both happiness, and misfortunes, on those who least deserved them. Thus she strikes out of season, when neither time nor subject requires it; she wounds the pious and virtuous, and with a back-blow of poverty, knocks down the wise and industrious; and to the fraudulent and deceitful gives her hand with all promises, and protestations to make them as prosperous as now we see them. How often have she blows erred and unhappily fallen on those whom all bewailed? she destroyed don Balthasar of Lunniga, when he should have begun to live; also the duke of Infantado, the marquis of Aytona, and other worthies, when the unstable condition of that age most required their government, and prudence to support and conduct it; she gave a back blow of poverty to don Luys of Gongora, and to Augustin of Barbosa, and to other eminent men, when she ought both to have crowned their years and actions with reward; and yet this unlucky boy excused himself, that these men like unseasonable fruit came out of time, their age being in the reign of Leo the Tenth, or of Francis king of France, not in the corrupt years of this present age. What affronts has she done to the marquis of Torrecuso, and afterwards triumphed in saying, had he not done something in war, he should quickly have been forgotten. By another shot her bullet erred in hitting don Martin of Aragon, though the crime was so evident, that she could not but confess her fault: again she seemingly consented to honour Azpilgueta Navarro, with a cardinal's hat, for his liberal endowments of a famous college; but sporting with him one day at hotcockles, she gave him such a blow on the hand as struck him to the ground, and whilst a chorister came to help him up, the unlucky boy laughed, saying, that such as these have no need to live, whose memory and fame shall never die; to others we continue life indeed, who humbly receive it, and thankfully repay it. She had great thoughts of favouring the monarchy of Spain with much happiness and success; and in reward of their Catholic Christianity to bestow on them the *Indies*, and other kingdoms, with many victories; but instead hereof both Fortune and her guide leaped on a sudden into France, to the amazement of the whole world; which piece of inconstancy she excused, by saying, that the race and seed of Spain's former worthies was quite extinct; that France was no longer to be accounted rash and inconsiderate, but wise, settled, and firm to her principles; and to conceal the hatred which her malice bears to piety, she consented to the success of the Venetian republic in some conquests against the Ottoman power, obtained by their own valour. A miracle indeed that the world has admired; till the reason she gave cleared the wonder, saying, she was tired in carrying the Ottoman success up so steep an ascent by mere force, whilst they neither contributed thereunto either by wit, or industry; in this manner all things were shuffled together, fortunes and misfortunes were confounded, and rested on the heads of those that least deserved or expected them. The plot being now ripe to be executed, it was observed, that at night when fortune undressed her sons, for none she would trust with this office of disposing their clothes, but with great care ordered it herself, and laid them in several places, that she might not mistake when she clothed her children again. Deceit was very active to take advantage on the present opportunity, and changed the place of their clothes, those of ill fortune into the place of good, and those of good into the place of bad: in the morning fortune, as unwary as blind, clothed virtue in the garment of embroidered thorns, and made vice gallant with his elder brothers flowers; which being set out in the sophistries of deceit, made so glorious a lustre and beauty, that all the world adored his footsteps, and entertained him both in their houses and hearts, believing it was virtue they than received; and though some at the cost of their own experience, told and informed others of the error, yet few believed them; for seeing vice to be so gallant and gentile, they could not be persuaded to judge amiss of that, which they so much affected. Since that day virtue and vice have been confounded, and the world deceived; for those who embrace vice with low thoughts of sensuality, have speedily found themselves deceived, and too late entertained thoughts of repentance. But on the contrary, those who being undeceived have closed with virtue; though the thorns of his garment have pricked and tormented them, at the first embraces, yet at the end they found the fruit of true content, and lived in the serenity of a calm conscience. How flourishing and fair seems their own beauty to some, and how deformed after, and disfigured with a thousand infirmities; how wanton is youth, but how soon does time benumb their joints? How plausible does dignity appear to the ambitious, and the weight of government to be eased by estimation; but afterwards how burdensome do they find it, and how to their shoulders faint under so heavy a pressure? How pleasing do the cruel imagine revenge, and bathe themselves in the blood of their enemies; but afterwards their whole life is pangs and pricks of conscience to him whose stomach cannot disgorge the draughts and surfeits he has made in blood. Even stolen water is sweet, and the rich is pleased to trample on; and make a prey on the poorer. Yet afterwards with how much violence is he compelled to make restitution. Let the glutton surfeit himself in his curious diet, and please his palate with delicious wines; but what satisfaction can these make for his plethora of body, from whence proceed dropsies, and gouts which twinges his joints, and enfeebles the nerves of his whole body. The lascivious will not loose his sensual copulation, though he buys his delight with the price of his own body. The covetous embraces thorns in his riches, which torment and disturb his sleep, and looses his heart in them, without enjoying of them. All these design to bless their families with the pleasing appearance of delight, which indeed is but a concealed evil, and not a contentment, but a torment, and a deserved reward for their fond mistake. But contrarily how difficult, and steep is the ascent to virtue at first, yet afterwards what satisfaction is there in a good conscience? With how much trouble do we undergo an abstemious temperance, and yet in that consists the health both of soul and body? How intolerable appears continence, and yet in that we enjoy life, health, and liberty? He who contents himself with mediocrity, lives; the humble possess the Earth, and makes his enemies to be at peace with him; but above all, what peace accompanies him, and how savoury is the odour of his good fame? What sweet fruit has sprang from the bitter root of mortification? Though silence seems an effect of melancholy, yet the wise never repented he had held his tongue: so that virtue since that time went always clothed outwardly with thorns, but inwardly with flowers different to vice, which therefore let us distinguish under that character, and embrace in despite of common, and vulgar deceit."

They were now come in sight of the court, when Andrenio looking on Madrid with a great deal of pleasure and attention. The wise philosopher asked him, what he saw?

"I see," said he, "the royal mother of so many nations, the crown of the two worlds, the centre of so many kingdoms, the jewel of both the *Indies*, the nest of the phoenix itself, the sphere of the Catholic sun, crowned and encircled with perfections as rays, and with noble arms as lights."

"But I see," said Critilo, a Babylon of confusions, a Paris of dirt and filth, a Rome of changes, a Palermo of Ætna's smokes, a Constantinople of mists, a London of pestilence, an Algier of captives. I see, said the philosopher, Madrid the mother of all perfections on one side, and a step-mother on the other; for as the chiefest rarities address themselves to the court, so in like manner do vices swarm there, being introduced by those which know not how to bring other than the vicious habits of their own countries. For my own part, I will not go in, as I have already told you, but bringing them to the bridge *Milvio*.

He there left them. But Critilo and Andrenio adventured in by the street of Toledo, and presently they happened into a shop where wisdom was to be sold; Critilo asked the bookseller if he had a clue of golden thread to sell them: but he did not presently apprehend his question, for those who only read the titles of books, are seldom learned by them; but another standing by, a graduated courtier both in years and experience, said, "you little understand them, for it is a compass they desire to sail by in this ocean and Gulf of *Circe*."

"I understand you less," said the bookseller, "for here is neither gold nor silver sold, but only books, a more precious commodity than either."

"It is this," replied Critilo, "we look after, and one especially which may give us some councils, and instructions how to govern ourselves in this twining labyrinth."

"So than," said the bookseller," it seems that you are strangers, and if so, make use of this manual, it is no tome, but rather an atom, and yet it shall serve to guide you to the north of felicity itself: here take this, which I have seen do miracles, it being that which instructs us in the art of being men, and teaches us to keep a society worthy of those who are so."

Critilo took it, and read the title, which was *Galateus of the Court*.

"What is the price?" said he.

"Sir," said the bookseller, "it has no price, it is above account, and is worth more to him who carries it; these books we do not sell, but pawn for two Reals, for the world affords not sufficient riches whereby to make their estimation."

At this speech the courtier gave such a loud laughter, that Critilo admired at it, and the bookseller was put out of countenance, and asked the reason why he so laughed. To which he replied that the absurdity of what he said was worthy of it; for the whole matter which the book treated of was ridiculous.

"I see now," said the bookseller, "that *Galateus* is no more than the elements of morality, the A, B, C. of breeding, nor yet can it be denied; but it is a golden toy, both plausible and important, and though but little, yet it can make men great, and teach them to continue so."

"Nothing less true than this," replied the courtier, "for this book," said he, taking it into his hands, "is heterodox, and might be worth something, did it teach contraries: in those innocent times when men were such, these rules and precepts were fitly calculated for that age, but in these times we now live, they are like fruit out of season, or like almanacs out of date: these were lessons for ancient days when they used cross-bows, but this is an age of more dangerous artillery; believe me they are of no value, and that your own selves may confess the same, hear me these first lines, he says, '*that observing the rules of discreet ceremonies, we ought not to stare him in the face with whom we speak, as if we would espy some mysteries in his eyes.*' Consider how good a rule this is for these times, in which the tongue has lost that tie and string which united it to the heart. Where than should we look, on the breast? It is true, it were good to pierce as far as the heart, had it the transparent glass to cover it, which momus desired; for though our eyes were fixed to observe his postures, and our sight attentive to discover changes in his countenance, yet our greatest attention can scarce guess at the language of his interior thoughts; how far short than must we come of this end, in not beholding him. Let us than look on him, pierce him with the quick darts of our eyes, look nose to nose, and yet pray Heaven the point of our attention may be so subtle and sharp as to read his soul in his face; to observe if he changes his colour, if he knits his brows, or his heart muffles, and plays within him. This rule, as I say, was good and civil in better times: but now wise men will not esteem in unmannerly, unless they could procure the inestimable felicity of such associates, whose words and actions have no need of being tried by the constancy of their countenances. Hear also this other, for it much pleases me as often as I read it, that it is a barbarous slovenry after we have blown our nose, to look on the snot in our handkerchief, as if the filth were pearls or diamonds which proceed from our brain."

"This, sir," said Critilo, "is a fancy as court-like as subtle; but yet in criticisms of this nature, we shall never want words, or arguments for both parts."

"Not so," replied the courtier, "for you understand it not, but in respect of the author, who must pardon me, and teach me better. For I say yes, let every one look on it, see and know his filth, and corruption he casts forth: let the confident sophister know that he is but a snotty charlatan, for though he is unable rationally to discourse, or scarce logic enough to know his right hand, has yet high thoughts of his own abilities: let him who has an elevated opinion of his own fancy know, that those are not sentences, or subtleties which he conceives, but a dull offspring of his brain, which is distilled through the limbic of his circumflexed nose. Let the dainty lady persuade herself, that she is not such an angel as her servant speak her, that it is not amber, through which she breathes, but a kennel and painted pipe to convey corruption. Let Alexander undeceive himself, that he is not son to Jupiter but to putrefaction, and grand-child of nothing. And let every man know that the divinity he conceives in himself is but humane imperfection, a bubble of vanity, and that the wind and smoke of conceit which rises to his head, dissolves into filth and noxious humours. Let us all understand, and know ourselves, that we are but vessels of unclean stenches, when we are children we are snotty, when old phlegmatic, when in our middle age, we are choleric and subject to the superfluity of impostures. Another thing he says is altogether unprofitable, which is, that a well fashioned man ought not to pick the wax out of his ears, and paste it between his fingers. Let me ask you, sirs, who it is that can do so? For in whose ears has the importunate discourses of one or other left it? For this is an age wherein men have but little wax in their ears, it had better he had encharged us, not to suffer the rapacity of the deceitful to pick it out, or the close leach to suck it forth, or to suffer scriveners, or others, whom I will forbear to mention, have so free a passage to the organ of our hearing. But I am most scandalized, that he should call it clownish, for one being in company to take out his scissors, and clip his nails. This I confess I cannot but esteem a most pernicious doctrine, for suppose that men are apt to omit the paring of their nails in secret, how much less should they be in public; it were better to command them this office before the whole world, as the Almiranto of Naples did, for every one must needs be offended to see those long nails some wear, that their scissors may not be said so much to clip as to share them; let them cut off those claws of rapine so close, that they may touch the quick. There are some so charitable as to frequent the hospitals; to cut the nails of the poor, it is true, it is a great charity; nor would it be less commendable to enter into the house of the rich, and shorten those claws of rapine by which they have made themselves as great as rapacious, having stripped the poor, and thrust them from their doors, or at least reduced them to that misery, that they have need of the charitable reception of an hospital."

"As little reason had he to recommend to us the civility of taking off our hats, as a token of kindness and respect; for now they take not only off the hat, but the cloak and coat, and strip men of honesty to the very skin, and flay him alive, and than tell the good man, that it is out of kindness they treat him no worse. There are others who so much observe this rule, that they enter with a cap on wheresoever they go; and thus you see, that this rule is like the others. Another that I read now, is against all morality. I wonder it has not incurred a general censure, and dislike; he said, that a man should negligently move his feet, not observing at every step where he sets them, but set them there, where by chance or occasionally they fall. This I deny, for might I counsel any, I should advise them not to transgress or surpass the bound, and point of that reason, which is in conformity to the law of God; let a man look and see that he does not pass the limits of his estate and fortune, lest he fall into that precipice, in which many have perished. That he treads not on a narrow line without leisure, and due consideration, for this is for a man to measure his own abilities, and to weigh his own burden; that he strain not his hand nor foot to reach farther than he is able; this I advise and counsel: that he consider where he set his foot, see where he enters, and where he goes out, that he makes a firm footing in the middle, and not in the dangerous brims and borders of extremes: for this is to go well, and secure. Another thing he says, that it seems like a fool for a man to go talking with himself; but with whom can a man discourse better, than with himself? What friend, has he more faithful, and sincere? Let him speak, and tell himself the truth, for none else will; let him ask and hear the voice of his own conscience; let him consult, and advise himself, and believe that all others admonish only for their own advantage and interest, that they are ill keepers of secrets, and would even betray the very shirt of the king d. Pedro. The next thing he says, is, that in our discourse we should not use much action, for that is to pump out our soul, as well as our body. He says well in this, if he to whom we speak is attentive; but not if he be deaf, as often men are in those things which concern either them or us most; if he sleeps we have need to awake him, and there are some, though brayed in a mortar, are still inapprehensive, and incapable subjects of the lowest reason; for what can a man do less when he sees his auditors both dull of apprehension, and inattentive to his words? Of necessity we had need with the pestle of our speech to beat it into their brains, for unless it be violently inculcated, they will scarce admit it into their ears. That a loud, and high voice is inconsistent with gravity, is according to those unto whom we speak;

for believe me, words of silk are not agreeable unto cloth ears, and he who actuates not his words with his hands, gives no life to his speech, but stands with that composedness, as if he were angling, or still in expectation the fish should bite, it were a good business if we could by this means distinguish good hands from bad; let me prise those which are good, for than they seem to reach Heaven itself, an grasp it in their hands. Thus, with the authors leave I must be of a contrary opinion to him; for let every man do and say, let him not be all words, but sometimes actions, and executions, let him speak truth, and if his hands are endued with dexterity, let him interpose them on all occasions."

"As this author has some rules superfluous, so he has others idle, and foolish, and this is one; that a man when he speaks to another, should not approach very near to him, least he bespatter him with his spittle; for there are some so indiscreet, that they ought to advise before they speak, and bid them beware of water, that the hearers may retire at some distance, or arm themselves against the torrent, and these are such who ordinarily speak with a continual motion, without parenthesis, comma, or period. For my own part, I think it more dangerous to be subject to those fires some cast from their mouth, than the sprinklings of spittle, and more dreadful are those flames of malice, of murmurings, of flattery, of obscenity, and scandal, which issue from them. Worse also are the foams of rage, and more need had he to advise us of a flood of choler: let him rather reprehend the emissions of poison, which proceed from under their lips, for to discommend spitting, is childishness: small hurt can the shrill noise of a quail do us, God deliver us from the swift bullet of injury, from the shaft of the throat, from the wildfire of treason, from the pikes of sharp tongues, and from the artillery of slanders."

"Another precept he has as ridiculous as the rest, that when we speak with another, we should not lay our hands upon his breast, and twine his buttons till they fall off. I say yes, let us feel the pulse of his breast, touch his heart, examine how it beats, try if he have loops on his waistcoat, for there are some have not: let us pull him by the sleeve who goes astray, and another by his skirt, that he may amend his crooked ways, and so far remember himself as not to be frantic. The next that follows, is what was never so much as mentioned in any commonwealth, no not in Venice itself, nor in any time of former age, which is, that we should not in our eating fill both cheeks at once, as being a great piece of clownery: this you see is a lesson, which the most curious, in their dress and behaviour, least practise, being that which fills up the wrinkles of the face most, and sets off their beauty to best advantage. Another is, that we should not laugh loud: and yet there are such ridiculous mockeries in the world, that a man cannot contain himself by deriding them in his sleeve only; but he must necessarily burst into an excess of laughter. The next is like the former, that we should not chew with our mouth shut; how good a rule is this, for the nature of this age, in which there are so many hungry wolves, that the best security we can take, is scarce sufficient to preserve a morsel within our mouths from rapacious hands. What would become of us than if our mouths were open? for in no occasion it imports us more than in our eating and drinking to keep them shut; which was the rule that the marquis Spinola, observed when he invited the ceremonious Henrico to his table; but that our author may be punctual in all points, he forbids us to belch; for though it be healthful, yet it is clownish; believe me, let all cast out those bad fumes engendered by ill concoction, those windy puffs, that swell them, of which those are most full, who are emptiest of substance: and I wish they may at last work out those fumes from their heads, and therefore when they sneeze may God help them to cast out the wind of their vanity, that we may wish them joy of so fair a riddance: for all may know by the filthiness of the breath, how corrupted the air is when out of its place. Yet there is one precept of Galateus has much pleased me, and seems very sound, that so may be confirmed that common saying, there is no book without something good, and commendable; he therefore premises as a capital precept, and fundamental point of his ceremonious office; that a gallant of his making, should endeavour above all to shine with the endowments of fortune, and upon the basis of gold to erect a scheme of courtesy, discretion, gallantry, and other parts, which commend an accomplished gentleman; for if his fortunes be small, his treasury of knowledge, will be esteemed but poor; nor shall he have the reputation of wise, discreet, courteous, as if his inward perfections were to be set off with an outward foil; this is my opinion of Galateus."

"If this does not content you," said the bookseller, "because he treats of material ceremonies, his doctrine being only of outward carriage: here is than, and it may be better to your liking, the judicious and grave instruction of Juan de Vega, which he gave his son when he sent him to the court: this sublime doctrine is not delivered with the affected gravity of a Portuguese, but is as much as the Count of Portalegre could say when he sent his son upon the like occasion."

"This work," replied the courtier, "is too sublime, and high for me, and fit for those only who move in the supreme sphere of the commonwealth; for he is not to be esteemed a judicious workman who shall think to fit a dwarf with the shoe of a giant; believe me there is no other book which art could form more for the purpose, or accommodated to the humours of Madrid; I know that my heterodox and perhaps stoical tenets may have caused men to censure me as cynical; yet I shall sooner prefer truth, than flatter others in their own sense and fancies. Let me tell you the book, that you should seek, and read, is Homer's *Ulysses*. But hold, and let me declare myself, lest there be a mistake; do you think the dangerous gulf he writes of, is in Sicily, and that the syrens inhabit on those sands with their faces like women, and their tails like fish, or that the Circe performs her enchantments in her isle, and the proud Cyclops in his cave? Know that the dangerous sea, is the court environed with the Scylla of deceit, and Carybdis of falsity: those women you see pass yonder so wantonly modest, and so dissolutely composed, are the true sirens, and false women, whose end is monstrous, and the remembrance of them displeasing It was not sufficient that cautious Ulysses stopped his ears, unless he had bound himself to the main-mast of virtue, and flying from these enchantments, steered his ship to the haven of security: there are Circes, who with the force of magic charms, have bewitched men in that manner, that they have transformed them into brutes. What shall I say of so many cyclopses, as foolish, as arrogant, who having but one eye, have yet fixed that on the objects of their own appetite, and presumption. This very book you turn over, shall, as I say, direct your steps, and teach you like Ulysses to escape this rock, and as I hope, divert you from those monstrous encounters, which threaten your destruction."

Upon this recommendation they took his counsel, and passed forward, much guided by what the courtier had advised, and Ulysses taught. They met with no friend nor kinsman, no acquaintance, because they were poor, and in a mean condition. Nor could Critilo discover his desired Felistuda; and so finding themselves destitute of all relief, and despised because in want, Critilo determined to make use of the virtue of some oriental stones, which the favour of the seas had reserved to him in his shipwreck: but especially to make experience how well the solidity of his diamond could conquer difficulties, and whether the rich emerald (as philosophers write) had the virtue to reconcile wills, and gain affections. With that he brought them to light, which at the same time worked such miraculous effects, that he soon obtained the good will and wishes of all those of the best blood of Spain, the most gallant, discreet, and understanding, were ambitious of his acquaintance. So great was the fame of this diamond, that it betrayed them into the covetous hands of some soldiers, but were freed from them by a multitude of friends, who courted their friendship, and desired to be of their kindred; they gained more cousins than a king, and nephews than a Pope, all which the fame of this diamond had created. But the most pleasant accident was that which happened to Andrenio, for in passing through the great street to the palace, came a page to him, gaudy in his livery, and free in his garb, drew out a fold of a letter, which he kept close up, giving him only leave to look on the firm which was subscribed a cousin and servant of yours; in it she congratulated his safe arrival at the court, much complaining that he who was of so near blood to her, was yet so much a stranger and unknown, with all desiring him not to fail to come and see her, for that page was there to direct him the way, and show him her lodging. Andrenio was much surprised to hear the name of cozen, who believed he had no mother; but being more excited with curiosity to try the event, than with hopes of unknown embraces, together with the page went directly to the house; but what strange successes befell him there, is related in the following Crisis.

The Twelfth Crisis

Though Solomon was the wisest of men, yet he was the most deceived by women, and having been the most amorous person in the world, he was best able to give a character, and a report of their nature, which was this, That an evil woman is a great evil to man, and his worst enemy; she is more strong than wine, more powerful than a king, and being all falsity, is not afraid to bid open defiance unto truth. Less dangerous to us are the rancour's, and malice of an enemy, than the embraces, and caresses of a false woman, said he, who spoke the wisest; for less hurtful is it, to be pursued by the threatening dart of a man, than to have a woman follow our steps with pretensions of love. She is not one enemy alone, but many complicated in one; and in her has malevolence placed its ammunition, and artillery against us, she is composed of flesh to discompose carnal man; the world clothes her, and that she may conquer man, makes a world of her, and the devil over those garments which the world gave her, casts a cloak of deceitful embraces. She is a gerion of enemies, the triple cord, and snare of our liberty, which is hardly broken. Hence doubtless it is, that all the evils of the world have attributes of the feminine gender, as the furies, destinies, sirens, harpies, for all those evils may be united in the wickedness of one bad woman: different passions have their several times, and seasons of age, in which their strength is most vigorous to encounter man, some in youth, others in old age; but a woman without respect of years, is an importunate tormentor in all ages; neither is youth secure from her, nor ripe, nor old age; neither the wise, nor valiant, nor yet a saint can say that he is invulnerable in those temptations: for she as a common enemy always wages war, and yet is so familiar, that she has corrupted all the servants of the soul to assist and favour her; the eyes consent to the entrance of her beauty, the ears are ravished with her voice, the hands attract her, the lips whisper her name; the tongue resounds her praises, the breast sighs after her, and the heart closes with her. if she be beautiful, others seek her, if ill favoured, she seeks others, and had not Heaven provided that beauty should be the ordinary throne of folly, there would not have remained a man with breath, if liberty be esteemed the formality of life, O! how amazed Critilo endeavoured to deliver deceived Andrenio, but with small success and advantage to either. For Andrenio departed blind to seek light at the house of fire and flames, he consulted not first with Critilo, fearing his severe life would prevent him; wherefore guided only by a silly page, he walked sometime through turnings and windings of many streets discoursing in this manner, my lady, said the boy, the honest false Syrena lives retired from the world, estranged from the tumults of the court, which is a life she chooses both as most agreeable to her melancholy humour, and as most healthful and pleasant, whilst she diverts herself in the sweet air of the country, and in her cheerful gardens. At last they came to a house which in outward appearance promised no great commodiousness, much less magnificence, which took much off from the expectation of Andrenio, and at the beginning displeased him: but as soon as he entered in, he seemed to have been enwrapped into the palace of Aurora, for the entrance was first into an open court, a capacious theatre of miraculous appearances, and the house quiet, and still, without noise, or disturbance; instead of firm Atlantes the pillars to support it, the court was encircled with beautiful nymphs most artificially worked, and engraved, bearing on their tender shoulders a Heaven crowned with seraphims, but not with stars; in the centre or middle spouted a pleasant fountain, emitting successively flames and water; it was made in the form of a Cupid, attended on by the graces, and by their hands supplied with darts, which continually shot a scorching shower both of water and fire: these floods past continually through pipes of alabaster as white as snow, and gliding swiftly along, one part of the stream seemed to pursue the other, murmuring afterwards at those whom at their first source their bubbling voice seemed to flatter. At the end of the court stood a green cypress, which appeared beautiful to a curious eye; its boughs were more luxuriant than fruitful, all flower and blossom, but nothing came to maturity, nor proved correspondent to the preceding hopes: it was encircled with delightful flowers, which sent forth odours of a strong fragrance. The birds also seemed to bid him welcome, and a gentle breath of air whistling through the trees, joined in consort with the birds. All which he esteemed as happy omens and courteous salutations to bid him welcome, or indeed rather to bid him farewell. The garden was fitted to nourish pensive thoughts, for whosoever walked in it, fell into melancholy and deep imaginations. Andrenio went still toward the pleasures, and delights of the middle, where the spring stood spinning flax into jasmines, I mean the vain Venus of this cypress, for never was Cyprus without Venus. At his coming Falsirena went forth to meet him, and counterfeiting a sun in her smiles, and forming a half-moon with her arms, enclosed him in the Heaven of her embraces. Sometimes she chid him, anon she spoke kindly, often repeating, "O cousin! O dear Andrenio! thou art as welcome as desired;" and as she spoke she changed her tone at every word, and stringing pearls thread by thread, she twisted and interweaved falsities.

"How is it," said she, "that having a house so solely devoted to your service you should obscure yourself in an inn; perhaps the poor entertainment you may find here would move you nothing, yet the obligations of blood and consanguinity which I have to you might invite you. I look on you, and cannot but call to mind the beauteous features of your mother in your countenance; in truth you very much resemble her, nor can I sufficiently wonder that you should be so strange here, but I consider that you are a novice and a young courtier."

"Madam," said he, "I must confess I am something amazed to hear you say, you are my cousin, who am ignorant of that mother that brought me forth; nor do I think myself ungrateful or stupid in it, in disowning them who neglected me; I have none of my blood, nor kindred, such a product, and child I am nothing; advise yourself, and consider better, if you may not probably mistake me for some of a more happy and fortunate condition."

"Alas," said she, "Andrenio no, I know you well, know who you are, that you were born in an isle encompassed with the waters of the greatest seas: I know very well, that your mother and my aunt, and mistress, O! how beautiful she was, and therefore unfortunate, how modest and discreet a lady, but how like a danae, she escaped from deceit, how like a Helen in her flight, how like a Lucretia from violence, and like an Europa from spoils?"

Felisinda thus arriving here, for so was her name of blessed memory, Andrenio was much moved to hear her named for his mother, who he had heard was the wife of Critilo: which passion and change in him was well observed by the Falsirena. Andrenio urged much to know the reason of this accident; "for I have heard oftentimes," said he, "of this name."

To which she replied, "that you may know I do not lie, take these particulars: Felisinda was married with a gentleman as passionate in her love, as discreet, who was prisoner in Goa, who yet at her departure carried him impressed on her heart, and you in her womb, as a pawn and pledge of her matrimonial bed; but the time being expired, and her travels coming on her, brought forth you in an isle, giving heaven innumerable thanks, which had so providently preserved both her credit, and safety; neither would she trust her maids the enemies of secrecy, but committing herself to the strength of her own valour, and honour, was the only midwife to bring you to light, and casting you on the Earth, more compassionate than our own bowels, committed your helpless body to the mantles of grass, and to the protection of pious Heaven, which was not deaf to her prayers, but provided you a nurse, though a beast, which was not the first time, nor shall be the last, that they as substitutes have and shall supply maternal absence. Oh! how often she has told me this, with more tears than words, by which one may easily perceive with how much passion she related it. How much will she rejoice when she sees you, and in what manner will she now make amends for her unhumane cruelty, to which once she was compelled through the sence of her honour."

Andrenio was much amazed to hear the riddle of his life thus expounded, and comparing these particular circumstances with his former knowledge; his tender disposition caused him to burst into tears, and to dissolve his heart into drops through the conduct of his eyes.

"Let us leave off," said she, "leave off the thoughts of past sorrows, and let not ancient griefs recover a new force to oppress your heart; let us go up, see my poor, but now only happy cottage: bring us a banquet, and collation, for in this house never can want a kind entertainment."

Thus we may now fancy them going up the stairs of porphyry, or of the perfidious; but we shall soon find them coming down with eyes like cats, grown dim at the rays of the Sun in his brightest sphere, and winking at the moon in her several changes: every room was observed to be square, and well-ordered, the roof of admiral artifice, which resembled a Heaven, at the sight of which many contemned the real glory of the coelestial stars. There were mansions and habitations for all times, and seasons, even for those that are passed, and all rarely worked, and adorned.

She continually told Andrenio, "all this is yours, as it is mine."

During this delicious collation, the graces entertained him with songs and music, and the Circes enchanted him.

"There is no way now," said she, "cousin, but you must stay here, and you shall need to be at no farther charge, than at the cost of your own pleasure: order that your portmantles be brought hither, and though this house shall furnish you with all conveniences, yet I would not have you loose any thing of your own; yourself shall not need to go forth for any thing, for my servants shall readily perform your commands in bringing hither your baggage, and satisfying the reckoning which is due in your inn."

"It is necessary," replied Andrenio, "that I should go myself, for know that I am not alone, but the favour you do must be double, and be bestowed on another besides myself, for I must give an account of this to Critilo my father."

"How, to your father, who is he," said Falsirena?"

"I call him father, who has performed the office of it, in being my tutor; and if your relation be true, he is my natural father, for he is the husband of Felisinda, the gentleman who was prisoner in Goa."

"Go," said the Falsirena, "go instantly, and stay not one minute before you return, and bring Critilo with you, for I will neither eat nor sleep till I am blessed again with your return."

Thus parted Andrenio, accompanied with the same page, one of her own creatures, and her most faithful spy: when they were come to their lodging, they found Critilo much troubled, and in a thousand thoughts; but so soon as Andrenio saw him, he cast himself down at his feet, kissing his hands, and saying: "O father! O tutor! for my very heart and mind tells me the same."

"What novelty is this," demanded Critilo?"

"You know," answered he, "it is not strange for me to style yon so; for besides those ancient obligations I have to you, my blood cries now in my veins, and acknowledge you to be him, who begot me; for know, sir, that you have not only given me my being, but by your instructions have produced in me, those qualities which become a man, and my mother is your wife Felisinda: this relation I received from a cousin, the daughter of my mother's sister, and at this instant I am returned from her, to inform you so much."

"What means this of cousin?" demanded Critilo, "this name sounds not well to me."

"Why not?" said Andrenio, "for she is a woman well-fashioned, and seems discreet, let us return to her, where we shall hear again related this never unwelcome history."

At this Critilo stood something in suspense, and though he heard these particular circumstances, yet he feared the many inventions and artifices of the court. Howsoever, as we all are, being credulous of what he desired, under pretence of informing himself better, they both went to the house of Falsirena. It seemed not now the same, but something better adorned, with a state and gracefulness that made the resemblance of Heaven.

"You are welcome," said she, "Critilo to this your house, whose want of being acquainted with it can only be an excuse for not honouring it before. My cousin, I believe has already informed you of those mutual ties and obligations we have of blood, and kindred, and that his mother and your wife the beautiful Felisinda, was my aunt, and mistress, to whom I owe more for her courteous offices of friendship, than on the score and natural tie of blood: I have sufficiently felt the want of her, and already bewailed it."

At this Critilo started, and said, "is she dead than?"

"No," replied she, "not so bad, for her absence is sufficient; her parents are dead, principally caused by a discontent they took, to see, that amongst so many rivals, which stood in competition for her beauty, her constancy to you, would give her leave to make choice of none. She afterwards, under the charge and protection of that great prince Ambassador now in Germany for this our Catholic monarch, went to accompany her kinswoman the marquess, with whom she now lives happy, and contented, and may God in his good time return her again to us in safety: but I remained with my mother, her sister, and though alone and thus deserted, yet with sufficient support to maintain our necessities both of life, and honour; but as misfortunes come not alone, so I having first lost her, soon after, my grief having a little pause, I lost my mother too, whose death I partly believe was occasioned by her absence: my kindred now remaining are my only comfort, to all I owe duties of kindness, virtue being my study, and my endeavour to inherit the honour of my parents, as being one of those who owe most to the piety, and good example of their ancestors: this is my house, but hereafter no more to be named mine, but yours for ever, as long as your life shall last, and may it be as durable as Nestor's. Let me now conduct you into some of my rooms, and chiefest galleries." The which they found full of roses and perfumes; all of them were hung with admirable pieces and pictures limbed by the most artificial pencils; in some of which they saw described the success and tragedies of their own lives, which they with astonishment beheld, admiring as well the art, as the plain description of this unknown history. Now not only Andrenio, but also Critilo, was persuaded of her affection, and of the reality of that information she gave them; so that making their excuses with thankfulness, they began to contrive the sending for their baggage, and amongst that, some precious stones, which were left of the ruins of Critilo's perished house; which being brought, and they had over-viewed them, he judged them a due present for ladies of pleasure, with whom he now drank in a full cup to the health of Falsirena; which jewels after she had much commended for the lustre, and perfections of them, she commanded some of her own to be brought, which she cheerfully desired him to enjoy; but Critilo rather beseeched her to keep his for him, and she as gracefully accepted the proffer. Critilo still sighed for his lost Felisinda, and one day at table proposed to make a journey into Germany; but Andrenio already enamoured and captivated with affection of his cousin, diverted the discourse, much displeased to hear of his departure, and she cunningly praised his resolution, but yet propounded difficulties, and advised him to prolong it, until a time of better convenience. But there offering now an opportunity, that he might be entered into the service of the great phoenix of Spain, which went to crown herself with the eagle of the empire. Andrenio had no farther excuse, yet whilst he prepared for the journey, Falsirena made a motion of seeing the two miracles of the world, the Escorial for Art, and Aranjuez for Nature, the parallel lines of the Sun of Austria in his several times, and seasons. But Andrenio was so blind in his passion, and his eyes so wholly darkened, that he had no light remaining to see other curiosities of art, or Nature: for the Falsirena having bewitched him, Critilo in vain used persuasions and reasons for his departure, but at last his sight not only left him, but his hearing, and from blind he became deaf also. In fine Critilo resolved, though unaccompanied to pay that just debt to his curiosity, lest afterwards he should be troubled he had not seen the high admiration of all, or his fancy, and imagination check him for contemning the sight of the greatest wonder in the world. So that thither he went alone, though to admire for many. He received in this great temple of the Catholic Solomon, the only fabric excelling the Hebrews glory; not only a satisfaction equal to his former thoughts, but an amazement in excess: for there he saw the ostentation of royal power, the triumph of Catholic piety, the perfection of architecture restored; the pomp both of ancient and modern curiosity, the last essay of growing art, and where greatness, riches, and magnificence concurred in one centre. From hence he went to Aranjuez, the constant habitation of the spring, the country of Flora, her arbour of delight in all months of the year, the preservative for flowers; the centre of delights and content: by both which wonders, he remained with such admiration imprinted in him, as well sufficient for his whole life to administer matter of contemplation. From thance he returned again to Madrid, much pleased to have satisfied his curiosity, intending to lodge again in the house of Falsirena: but now he found it shut more close than a treasury, and more silent than a desert: his impatient servant knocked often at the door, and the sound of every stroke made an echo in the heart of Critilo. The neighbours being disturbed with the continued noise, bid them not trouble themselves any more, for there lived none, they all were dead.

Critilo startling at that, replied, "did there not live a principal lady here, whom not many days ago I left well, and in good health?"

One hearing him say 'good,' laughed. "Pardon me," said he, "I do not believe it."

"Nor is she a person of good quality," added another, "who consumes her time in youthful pleasures."

"Nor yet a woman," said a third, "but a harpy, and the worst woman of this worst and present age."

Critilo could scarce persuade himself what he desired not to hear, but turned back again to demand if Falsirena dwelt not there: But in the mean time one came to him, and told him, that he should not trouble himself; for it was true that not many days ago, there was one dwelt there; a Circes, and a siren, for her enchantments, and one that could raise tempests, and vexatious storms; for besides that, she was wicked, and dissolute; she was a famous witch, a renowned enchantress having the power to metamorphose men out of their own shapes into that of brutes, and particularly into asses, not of gold, but of their own folly and poverty.

"In the streets of this court walk thousands converted into shapes, not human, because abused with all kind of beastly affections. That which I can assure you for truth is, that in those few days I have been an inhabitant here, I have seen many enter in, but none go out, and in as much as this siren is half a fish, she fishes away their wealth and livelihood from all that know her; their jewels, clothes, liberty, honour, and that her frauds may not be discovered, she changes every day. I do not mean her conditions, nor customs, but her place and residence, leaping from one end of the town unto another; that it is impossible to have the least hopes to find her: another trick she has, being the compass by which she steers the course of her policies; and that is, that when a foreigner comes rich and wealthy, she presently informs herself, who he is, and from whence and to what purpose he came, endeavouring to know the particulars of his name, and family, and so accordingly calls herself by the name of cousin, or sister, and gives herself some appellations of their house, and family; she changes as often names, as places, sometimes she is Cicilia, anon Sirena, Ines, Teresa, Tomasa, Quiteria: and with these arts she destroys and ruins others, but triumphs herself, and grows rich with the spoils."

But Critilo could not satisfy himself, with the belief of these stories, and therefore desirous to enter in, demanded if the key were at hand.

"Yes," answered one, "I have it committed to me in courtesy to admit those in, who comes to see it." With that he opened it, which when they had entered: "this," said Critilo, "is not the house, or I am blind; the other was a palace."

"It is true," replied he, "whilst it was enchanted, and the most of this nature are so, here are no gardens, but heaps of moral filth, the fountains are become gutters, and sinks to convey ordure and corruption; and the stateliest rooms are but sties, and nests of uncleanness. Has this siren fished any thing from you? tell us the truth."

"I must confess yes, some jewels, pearls, diamonds; but what I am most sensible of, is the loss of a friend, I know not whether most by her fault, or his wilful obstinacy, or whether in the form of a beast, sold to his own lusts, he wanders through this city. O my Andrenio!" said he, sighing, "where art thou?"

He sought him in every house, which gave occasion of mirth to some, but to himself of sorrow, and so taking his leave of them, he retired to his former lodgings. He gave a thousand turns through the court, and none could give any account or advice concerning him; for of a good, and happy success, there are but few informers, he having with diligence broken his brains, and drained his wits to discover him, at last he resolved to return again, and consult with Artemia, and so he departed from Madrid, according to custom, poor, deceived, repenting, and melancholy. He had not gone far, before he met with a man of a far different disposition than those that he had hitherto seen, he seemed to be a strange prodigy of Nature, for he had six senses, one more than ordinarily men are endued with. This was a novelty to Critilo, for many with less than five he had seen, but none with more. Some there are without eyes that see not clearly, but grope in the dark, stumble against blocks, and yet never slacken their pace, not knowing where they go. There are some that are deaf to words, and capable of nothing but the sound of air, of noise, of flattery, vanity, and falsity; there are some who have no smell, and least of any, smell out the savour of their own houses at home, whilst all the world besides receives it hot in their nostrils, and those whom it least concerns, have the strongest sent of it; these senseless animals are stuffed in their heads against the smells of a good repute, either of their own, or that of their enemies, and having noses only to wind the sent of small punctilio's of honour, are not touched with the fragrance which proceeds from the perfume of true virtue: there are some also without any kind of taste, disrelishing all things of substance and wholesome nutriment, and are distasteful in their society; others being unsavoury to them, as they are to others: another thing they hinted, which was very observable, that he had met with many, and those he could nominate who had no feeling, and least in their hands, where that sense commonly is most tender; for they handle not their affairs first, and make trial before they proceed; but being hurried with a certain eagerness, their hands neither ponder their actions, nor their reason compares them with former examples. But he whom Critilo thus occasionally met, was one different to all others; for besides those five senses which were most acute and vigorous in him, he had another sense, which was more advantageous than all the rest; for it is that which gives life to men, and awakens them to discourse, and searches out the most hidden secrecy, contrives, invents remedies, gives us tongues, with confidence to speak, feet to run, and wings to fly, and a prophetic spirit to divine future accidents; and this is necessity, it is a thing very admirable and useful, for though the object wants, yet the defect is supplied by the ingenuity it begets: it is witty, inventive, cautious, active, acute, and is a sense which for its excellency has pre-eminence over all the others.

Critilo had no sooner this knowledge of him, "but how well," said he, "may you and I join in company together; I am glad I have met with you, and though misfortunes do usually attend me, yet now I account myself happy," and so related to him the whole story of the misfortune which had befallen him in the court.

"I believe you," said Egenio, for so was both his name, and nature, "and though my journey is to the grand fair of the world, published on the confines of youth, and manly age, the great gate of life; yet to serve you, let us go to the court, where I will employ all my six senses in search of him, and whether man or beast I make no doubt, but to discover him."

So having entered in, they sought him with all attention; first on the theatres, and amongst the comedians, in the commonest streets, in the openest markets, where they met great mules tailed one to the other, every one followed treading on the heels of him that went before; their baskets were so laden with gold and silver, that they groaned under their burden, their sumter-clothes were fringed with gold, and silk, and some of these wore plumes of feathers on their heads, being oftentimes the trappings of beasts, and their pectorals of gold made a jingling as they moved.

"He may be some of these," said Critilo.

"No," replied Egenio, "for these are, I mean, have been great men, on whose backs the heavy burdens of the commonwealth have been laden; and though you now see them gallantly adorned, yet take but off their rich saddles, and you shall discover their backs so galled and festered, that there is scarce a place free from the boils of vice."

"See if he be amongst any of these country people, who drag and draw the cart with creaking wheels."

"Nor none of these neither, for these cast their eyes downward, having no thoughts of honour, and therefore contentedly suffer."

"See yonder is a parrot which calls us, perhaps it may be he."

"No, no, don't give ear to his call, for this is but a flatterer, which never meant what he speaks. There is a kind of a politician of this sort, that has one thing in his beak, and another in his heart; a prater which only repeats the words of others, that imitates men, but is not such, and goes clad like a parrot all in green, expects to receive the reward of jests, and accordingly receives it in earnest."

"Nor does this formal cat seem to be he which hides his claws and shows his beard."

"There are many," said Egenio, "of this sort who lie at the catch, and strike not only at open, but at secret and guarded evils; but to judge rightly, we may call these men of the pen."

"And that old dog which stands barking yonder, what is he?"

"He is a bad neighbour, one who never spoke well of any, he is emulous, of a bad intention, melancholy, and that passes for one of the seventy."

"I know he cannot be that baboon which makes mimical faces, and screws himself in so various postures in yonder balcony."

"O he is a grand hypocrite! who would seem, and only imitate good manners, and piety of the religious, and yet is not so; he may be some grave accountant, or some licenciado, some clerk, or writer of burlesque; and being a man always in jest, never deals in earnest, but is made up all of flashes, and little substance. Nor can he be amongst the lions and tigers of the retiro, for those are a people made up of processes, writs, and executions. Nor yet is he amongst the swans in this pond: for those are scriveners and lawyers, men of the quill."

"Yonder I see an unclean beast prodigally wallowing in the mire of his own beastly appetite, which he calls and believes to be flowers."

"If it be any it must be he," replied Egenio, "for these are the unclean and lascivious, who are so choked in the filth of their own vile delights, that whosoever sees them, does abhor and abominate them, and these think the mire to be Heaven, and smell not the ill favour which proceeds from the putrefaction of the world, which they esteem to be a perfume, and a fragrant odour, far excelling the sweetness of paradise."

"Let me see if this be he."

"No, no, it is not he, but a wretch whose riches and pampered body, shall at his death make a joyful day for his heirs, and feast for the worms."

"Is it possible, complained Critilo, we cannot find him amongst all these brutes we have seen, nor amongst these many droves we have encountered?"

"Neither drawing the coach of the harlot, nor carrying the chair of one greater and heavier than he; nor is it he who sits in his litter in false Latin, and out of it scarce in good Spanish, or that pack- house of corrupted customs. Is it possible these Circes should disfigure and disguise a man in this manner? Thus may sons beguile their fathers, and make them mad with jealousy that they are not their own, who are not content only to strip them of the garments of their bodies, but of those also of their mind, degrading them of the very formality and essence of man."

"But tell me, Egenio, when we find him thus changed into a beast, how can we reduce him again, and restore him to his former condition and shape of man?"

"When we have found him," replied he, "the business will not be difficult, for some have perfectly recovered and become themselves, though others have always retained some tincture and savour of their former condition. Apuleius was worse than any, yet with the role of silence, an admirable medicine against folly was recovered of his infirmity: for material pleasures being well ruminated, and our own corruptions considered, it is a sovereign means to take off the mask which makes them appear amiable. The companions of Ulysses were metamorphosed into beasts, and with tasting the bitter root of the tree of virtue, recovered the sweet fruit of humanity. We will give him some leaves plucked from the tree of Minerva, which are planted and highly esteemed in the garden of the courtly and learned duke of Orleans; and if not, we will give him some leaves of the moral sage you know of, and I am sure it will prove an infallible remedy to bring him to himself, and to restore his lost reason."

They having thus given a hundred turns with more pains than success, "at last," said Egenio, "I have considered of a better device; let us go to the same house where he was last, and perhaps, raking there amongst the filth and ruins of it, we may find this lost jewel."

So thither they went, entered in, and sought him with much diligence.

"This is but lost time," said Egenio, "for already I have narrowly searched that place. But hold," said Egenio, "let me apply my sixth sense, which is the only remedy in this condition."

And now he observed that from one great heap of lascivious filth proceeded a smoke very thick. "Here," said he, "is fire," and removing some moral rubbish and uncleanness, there appeared the door of a horrid cave, which when they had opened with some difficulty, they saw by a confused twilight of infernal flames, many disanimate bodies stretched out in the coffins of their sensualities. There were some young gallants as shallow and short-witted, as they were long haired; some also learned men, but fools, rich old usurers, whose eyes, though open, yet saw nothing; for some blinded them with a linen napkin cast about their eyes; some had no other life than what they gave signs by their sighs and groans. in fine, all were frantic, asleep, and naked, no not a rag left them to make a winding-sheet, wherein to bury their inanimate bodies. In the midst of these lay Andrenio so changed and disfigured, that his father Critilo scarce knew him. But than he cast himself upon him and wept, and called aloud to his deaf ears; his hands were as cold as clay, no pulse beating, nor any symptoms of breath or life. Egenio observed that that dim light, which was not the light of a torch, but of a hand proceeding out of a wall, which though pale and cold, was yet adorned with bracelets of pearl, purchased with the sighs and tears of many; the fingers, which were ringed with diamonds, bought with falsity, burned like tapers, though they gave not so bright a lustre, as that fire which scorched and consumed their bowels.

"What dead man's hand is this," said Critilo, "one that was hanged?"

"No," replied Eugenio, "of the hangman's rather, which destroys, strangles, and stifles breath."

They had no sooner removed this a little away, but suddenly they began to revive; for whilst this did burn, their sleep was so profound, that there was no possibility to awake them. They endeavoured to extinguish it with water, but could not, for this is the fire of Naphtha, blown by the blasts of amorous sighs, and is more enflamed by the water of tears; but the way is to cast dust and earth upon it; for fire, though as violent as the infernal, is smothered by it. This being done they all awaked, and every one began immediately to excuse the fault which had brought him into that lethargy: the graver sort much ashamed alleged that the disease was epidemical, and that these flames of uncleanness were not only nourished in dry fuel, but in the sappy moisture of greener sprouts; the judicious exclaimed against their own folly, and that Paris in affront to Pallas, was young and ignorant; the discreet called it a double madness. Andrenio amongst the Benjamites, or younger sons of Venus, had a dart pierced through his heart; and now seeing and acknowledging, Critilo went towards him.

"What do you think now?" said he. "How well has this wicked woman treated you? in leaving you without estate, health, honour, conscience, hereafter by experience so dearly bought, you will give both credit to my words, and add caution to yourself."

With that they all unanimously began to exclaim against her; some called her the Scylla of Ivory, others the Carybdis of Emeralds, a painted pestilence, poison in nectar.

"Where there are reeds, said one, there is water, where is smoke, there is fire, where evil women are devils."

"There is no greater evil than a false woman," said an experienced Don, "except it be two, for than it is double."

"There is enough comprehended in this," said Critilo, "that they are witty in nothing but in evil."

To which Andrenio replied, that he must ingeniously confess, that notwithstanding all this evil they had cast upon him, he could neither abhor nor forget them; "for I assure you, of all those excellencies the world boasts of, as gold, silver, stones, palaces, gardens, flowers, birds, stars, moon, and Sun itself, there is none of that beauty to me as the woman; nor can Heaven itself afford me more happy bliss and felicity than one of the female sex, that is amiable in her countenance, and kind in her embraces to me."

"These are lofty expressions," said Egenio, "but let us go from hence, our time here is misspent, and those invectives I have to utter against a false woman, are such, that our time is too short to vent them: so we will double down the leaf for our discourse in the way."

In this manner they all went forth, and proceeded to the light disguised to others, but better known to themselves, to visit the temple of their own amazement, there to render thanks to undeceiving light, hanging upon her walls the spoils of their shipwreck, and the chains of their captivity.

The Thirteenth Crisis

"It is a report of ancient times, that when God created man, he imprisoned the licentious nature of evils in a profound abyss, which some say was in the Fortunate islands, and from thance they take their name and appellation; for there he restrained the exorbitancy of crimes and troubles, vice, & punishment, war, famine, pestilence, infamy, sadness, and the very pangs and torments of death itself. These he linked and chained one within another, and not trusting to these vile canalia, made a gate of solid diamond, which he shut with a padlock of steel, the key thereof he delivered to man's free-will, to make his enemy the more sure, giving him to understand that unless he opened the door, they could never escape out to all eternity. Contrariwise he gave freedom to all other good things in this world, namely to felicities, virtue, content, peace, honour, health, riches, and life itself, permitting them to walk and range the world as they pleased; so man lived happily till the woman, moved out of her own curious fancy, was impatient to discover what was contained in that fatal cavern; so that one day taking man in an amorous humour by her caresses and embraces, she hugged from him his heart, and with that the key; which she no sooner obtained, but without farther consideration, she rashly set her hand to open the prison, where evils were enclosed. The key was no sooner put into the hole of the lock, but the universe trembled, and the bolt thrust back, out came a flood of evils, which crowding in multitudes, flew like a whirl-wind through the whole circumference of the world. pride the captain of the band took the front, and met with Spain the first province of Europe, and finding it a place agreeable to its humour, resolved to take up his habitation there, where he now lives and reigns, set in the same throne of his kindred, self- estimation, contempt of others, desire of sovereignty, and to be commanded by none. Much is he pleased to be styled Don Diego, and to boast his lineage and blood from the Goths, to make great ostentation to praise himself, to speak high and hoarse, and that with gravity, disdain, action, and with all kind of presumption, which is not an affectation only of the nobility, but an humour common to every plebeian. Covetousness overtaking pride, and finding France in the hands of none, possessed itself of it, from Gascoigne to Picardy. Its beggerly family spread misery in every part, a base ignobleness of mind, and a servile disposition fit to be made the slaves of other nations, who apply themselves to vile and mean offices, selling their selves to bondage for interest; their toil always laborious, their bodies naked, their feet unshod, unless with sabots, all workmanship being cheap by the multitude of such slaves. in fine, a disposition to commit the most base and vile attempts for money, that it may well be said that fortune, compassionate of their low spirits, made some recompense for the common baseness in the rare endowments of their nobility, who so much differ in excellence from the vulgar people, that they are become two extremes, without a middle. Deceit passed into Italy, taking deep root in the Italians breasts. In Naples for their words, in Genoa for their dealing; for in that whole country is the army and kindred of falsity numerous and strong; deceit, artifices, inventions, plots, treasons, all which they style the effects of honest policy, the order and good management of a profound brain. Anger took another course, and passed into Africa, and her adjacent isles, being pleased with the fierce and rugged conversation of the Alarves, and African monsters. gluttony with her sister drunkenness (exempting that precious Margarite of Valois) has devoured both upper and lower Germany; for there they spend days and nights in luxurious diet, their estates and consciences are drowned in their bowls; and though some are drunk but once, yet it is a continual intoxication their whole life; these vices in war devour provinces, lay fields waste, and for this reason Charles the Fifth composed the belly of his army of Germans. Inconstancy flew into England, simplicity into Poland, infidelity to Greece, barbarity into Turkey, craft into Muscovy, morosity into Sweden, injustice into Tartary, deliciousness into Persia, cowardice into China, rashness to Japan, and Sloth coming late, found all places taken up before, and no room left, that so she was forced to pass into America, and take up her habitation amongst the Indians. Luxury, that famous and renowned piece of gentility, as great, as powerful, esteeming the bounds of one province too narrow a confinement, at last extended itself through all the world, filling it from one end unto the other: and so incorporating itself with other vices, has taken so deep a root in every nation, that it is hard to be resolved which part is most polluted with this growing infection. Woman being the first subject which evils encountered, made her their first prey, and from head to foot swelled her with the venom of malice."

    This was the discourse Egenio used to his two companions, after he had conducted them out of the court, by the gate of light, which was of the Sun, to bring them to the grand fair of the world, published in the great empire which divides the pleasant meadows of youth, from the rough and rugged mountains of manly age, where multitudes of people flock to buy and sell, some such as the most discreet came only to see and observe the conditions of the vulgar; they entered through the broad path of convenience, the universal garden of pleasure, and contentment; some praising what others abhorred; as soon as they set footing on one of these entrances, for many there were, came two prating sophisters, which they called philosophers, one of one sect, and the other of another; for all men are divided into several opinions, and every head begets a fancy like his own brain. Socrates invited them (for so the first was called) to one part of the fair, where those commodities were sold, which most conduced to accomplish a man, and to enrich him with the treasury of imperishable virtue; but Simonides (for so the other was named) told them, that all the merchandizes of the world were reducible into two classes, honour, and profit; honour was always full of vapour and smoke, and empty of substance, or solidity; but the other was an inexhaustible mine of gold, the coffer of riches, and a compendium of all worldly advantages. This I profess to you, but the choice I leave to your own arbitrement. These different offers greatly perplexed their friends which way they should incline, their opinions being as disagreeable as their humours; and as they were thus divided, came a man to decide the difference; in his hand he brought a piece of gold, with which he rubbed theirs, pretending to know them thereby.

"What does this man mean," said Andrenio.

"I am," replied he, "the cunning critic in judging men's affections, the touch-stone of their humours." "How," said Andrenio; "the touch-stone?"

"This it is," said he, showing him the gold.

"That is a strange touch-stone," said Andrenio, "for it is the gold that is tried, rather than the stone."

"It is true," said he, "but the touch-stone of men is gold, and those to whose hands it cleaves, are not true, but false men: so that a judge to whose clammy palm the gold sticks, we presently condemn him for a tried man, and dismiss him from his bench of judicature. That prelate that hoards his fifty thousand dollars rent, is not so much to be esteemed golden mouthed, for his pious and florid sermons, as his chest is for the treasure it amasses. That officer that struts in his gold lace, and is clinquant, and vapours in his plumes of feathers, shows that he has deplumed his soldiers, and does not succour them like the valiant Borgonon d. Claudius Manricius. That cavalier who rubrics his executions with the blood he has drawn by the instrument of extortion from the poor, is indeed no gentleman. When the wife goes gallant, and the husband poor, it breeds suspicion. In fine, all these whose hands are not clean, nor well wiped from the clammy birdlime of interest, cannot be men of honest integrity."

"And so you," pointing to Andrenio, "to whose palms gold will stick, and leave its impression, pass over to this side."

"But he," pointing to Critilo, "who has not that clammy palm, nor has the print of coin on his fingers ends, let him turn up by this way of integrity."

"But that he also," replied Critilo, meaning Andrenio, "may do the same, it is necessary I should follow him."

And thus going forward, they began their discourse by the rich shops on the right hand, where they read an inscription, "here is sold the best and worst," and going in, they found that they were tongues, the best were those that held silence, which they bit between their teeth, and fixed to the roof of their palate; and a little farther stood a man making signs that they should be silent, so far he was from crying his merchandise.

"What is it this man sells," said Andrenio; and with that the seller clapped his fingers to his mouth. "How shall we know in this manner what it is you sell?"

"Without doubt," said Egenio, "he sells silence."

"It is a merchandize rare and important," said Critilo, I thought the whole store had been spent in former times, or that it was a drug now, and in no demand."

"This commodity is brought from Venice, especially secrecy, which is a fruit that these parts do not produce."

"Who is it than that spends it?"

"This," replied Andrenio, is a commodity for melancholy hermits, anchorites, and monks, who only know the use of it, and suck from it their best advantage."

"For my part, said Critilo, I believe the most that use this, are generally, not the good, but the bad. For the dishonest conceal their sin, the adulterers dissemble their uncleanness, the assassinate covers his cruelty, the thief enters with the silent steps of his woollen socks. In fine, sin as ashamed of itself, arrives not to that impudence, as to blow a trumpet before it, but treads softly, speaks not high, and goes veiled in all its enterprises."

"But the world is changed now," replied Egenio, "and this age is arrived to that pitch of impudence, that those who should be silent speak most, and the debauched person boasts in the number of his iniquities. You shall see another, whose nobility is disgraced by his unseemly carriage, and whose lascivious pastimes give him but small content, unless they appear impudent and shameless in the face of the world. The fencer who plays prizes, is proud of the many scars in his face. The amorous boy is pleased to have his locks and features commended. The dissolute wife neglects her household affairs, only to dress her face. The thief is not ashamed of the gallows, and the ambitious pleads for a title to inscribe over the list of his base ancestors. In this manner we see the worst and most wicked, are those who in the world make the greatest noise and bustle."

"Who than, sirs, are those who buy?"

"He that acts and does not speak; he who performs him employment, and says nothing, is like Hippocrates, who never incurred the censure of any."

"Let us know the price," said Critilo, "for I would buy some quantity, for perhaps this commodity is not to be afforded in another place."

"The price," replied they of silence, "is silence also."

"How can this be? For if that which is sold, is silence, how can the price be satisfied with the like return?"

"Very well, for the benefit of one's silence is repaid with that of another's; for one replies not, because the other speaks not, and all say do you be quiet, and we shall be silent."

Than they passed hence to an apothecary's shop, where there was an inscription written, *here is sold the quintessence of health.*

"A thing, said Critilo, of no small excellence," so that he was importunate to know, what it was, which they told him was the spittle of one's enemy.

"This," said he,"I should rather call the quintessence of poison, being more mortal and venomous, than the foam of the basilisk: for I should rather a toad should spit on me, a scorpion sting me, a viper bite me, than to be bespattered with the froth of an enraged enemy."

"The spittle of a faithful and true friend is balsamic, and the only remedy to cure our infirmities."

"You do not yet well understand me," said Egenio, "for the flattery of a friend is a more dangerous charm; that passion by which he encourages our faults, that affection by which he dissembles our infirmities, and persuades us that our estate is better than it is, hastens his friend who is sick with the abundant humours of his sins into the grave of his destruction. Believe me a true censure will better advantage him, though distilled from a bitter potion which an enemy administers, for that scours out the spots of his honour and reputation, and cleanses the stains of fame; for as it takes off the acrimony of the envious from us, so it keeps us constant and close to the line and point of virtue and reason."

After this some others called them to another shop in great haste, for the merchandize was almost all sold and exhausted, and that was truth, and this was the only time to buy it. Of which asking the price, they told them, it was now given freely, but hereafter the smallest quantity would be inestimable, and not to be sold, though we would buy it with our dearest sight. Another cried out heartily to come and buy, for the longer they stayed, the more they lost, a commodity which could never be purchased hereafter, and no price could redeem it, and that was time. Another cried his ware, which he sold for nothing, and the value great; and that was admonition, a thing which fools buy at their own cost, and the wise at another's.

"Where is experience sold?" demanded Critilo, "a thing of an inestimable value;" and for that they directed him a great way off, to the shop of years.

"And where is that of friendship?" demanded Andrenio?

"This is not bought," said they, "though many sell it: but bought friends are not indeed such, nor are they worth anything."

In letters of gold in another place, was wrote, *Here are sold all things, and that for nothing.*

"Here I will go in," said Critilo: but there they found the merchant so poor, that he was totally naked and stripped of all, forsaken, and nothing in his shop; so they asked how his dealing was correspondent to his motto?

"Very well," replied the merchant.

"But how is it you sell all things without price?"

"Yes, by despising of them, setting no value nor estimation on them; for he who can over-rule himself, and do thus, is master of the world, embraces all in his arms, and he who contrariwise esteems and adores them, is rather the slave and servant, than master of them."

Hard by was wrote, *He who gives to another, bestows on himself, and those who receive are obliged by the gift.* This they supposed to be courtesy, and civil respect which honours all the world.

"Here is sold," cried another, "that which is every man's own, and not another's."

"This is not much," said Andrenio.

"Yes," said the seller, "but it is, for many sell that diligence they perform not, and the favour and interest which they have with others, and many times those actions and labours they never sweated or laboured for."

Thus passing from one shop to another, they met with one, where merchants with much trouble and perplexity drove away their customers, and discouraged all that came to trade with them.

"Do you sell, or not?" said Andrenio "I never saw so absurd an action, that the merchant should deny access to their chapmen, and hinder their own profit and sales. What is it you mean by this? "

With which they uncivilly treated them, and desired them to be gone and trade farther off.

"Do you sell," said he, "or not? What is it fraud, or poison?"

"Neither one, nor other, but rather the most esteemed jewels of the world; for it is estimation itself, which a reservedness only can preserve: familiarity destroys it, and intimate society disenables it."

"This is agreeable," said Critilo, "to that saying, *that honour inhabits at a distance, and that there is no prophet in his own country; and that were the stars themselves fixed near us, they would in few days loose their lustre and esteem*; so ancient years are valued by the present, as the sages of our times will be the admiration of succeeding ages."

"Yonder," said Egenio, is a rich jeweller, let us go thither, where perhaps we may buy some precious stones at a cheap rate, in which are not on-lustre, but virtue also."

Being entered in, they found the discreet duke of Villa Hermosa in person there, desiring the lapidary to show him some of the finest sort, and of greatest estimation. He answered that he would, for he had some of great value and price: and as all expected some rare oriental stone, some diamond, or emrod, whose sparkling brightness cheers up those who behold it; he drew out a piece of black jet, as dull and melancholy as himself.

"This," said he, "excellent sir, is a stone the most worth your estimation and value; in this has Nature instilled the quintessence of virtue; into this has the Sun, the stars, the elements, conspired to drop their most precious spirits and influence."

At these high expressions, they were all amazed, and remained silent, giving way to the discreet duke to spend his judgment; who replied, "What is it you mean by this? is not this a piece of jet? What than can this lapidary pretend by it? What need is there of all these extravagant praises of it? does he take us for Indians?"

"This," said the jeweller, "is more precious than gold, more profitable than rubies, more bright than the carbuncle: pearls are not to be compared with it. In fine, it is the stone of stones."

The duke not being longer able to let him run on in these extravagancies; "is this more," said he, "than a piece of jet?"

"No," replied he.

"Why than do you give these exorbitant commendations of it, for of what virtue or beauty is this stone? Or what novelty or strange effects have been found lately in it? it is not pleasing to the sight, as these of a shining and transparent lustre; nor is it physical or medicinal, as the emrod, nor comfortable as the diamond, nor purifies as the sapphire, nor an antidote against venoms, as the bezar, nor can facilitate birth like the eagle's stone, nor is a remedy to ease distempers; for what more than can it serve, than as toys for children?"

"Your excellency," said the lapidary, "must pardon me, for it is only useful for men, and those of the wisest sort, for it is the philosopher's stone, which teaches, and instructs us in the precepts of morality, and in one word, that which most imports, it gives us rules which way to guide the course of our lives."

"In what manner?"

"By condemning and scorning the world, by yielding to it in nothing, that neither cares should weaken our stomach, nor troubles make us start from our sleep; nor as fond fools affect the world too much, but to walk as free and disinslaved, as the king of it, made us; this is to live, this is a business in whose right management the world is most ignorant."

"Give it me hither," said the duke, "for I will chain it in my house, and enclose it in the most secret drawers of my cabinet."

"Here is fold," cried one, "a sovereign remedy against all diseases;" to which there crowded such a multitude of customers, that the shop could not receive their feet, but their heads being empty, and without substance, were more easily contained in a narrow compass. Andrenio impatiently desired them, to give him suddenly of that merchandize; and they told him: " yes, for we know you have need of it, and therefore have patience;" but he presently after again importuned them to dispatch him.

"Sir," said the merchant, "have I not already given it to you?"

"How given it me?"

"Yes," replied another, "I am an eye-witness of it."

Andrenio growing angry hereat, denied it with fury.

"It is true," replied the seller, though he has no reason neither in what he says, "for though they have given it to him, yet he has not received it; wherefore be patient and expect it: the seller having thus wearied the expectation of his customers, desired them to retire, and give way for others, having that which they came for."

"What means this?" replied Andrenio. Do you affront us, see with what patience we attend, give us our desires, and we shall soon depart."

"You may go," said the merchant, "for I have already given it you, and that twice."

"To me? You have only bid me have patience."

"How precious a commodity," laughing aloud, said the merchant, "is this? it is so admirable a remedy against all disasters, that all generally, from the king to the peasant, that are not masters of it, are unarmed soldiers against the worlds revolutions."

"Here is," said another, "to be sold what all the riches of the world have not value enough for to buy. Who than can trade for it?"

"Those who will not loose it," was replied. And that is liberty: a thing which we ought most to esteem; for not to have our dependence on another's will, especially to be disengaged from obedience to an ignorant ruler, or of him, whom we would be ashamed to own, not only for our master, but for a servant; for there is no pain nor trouble greater than to have men impose weights on our heads, and to make them serve instead of backs for burden.

Amidst this came in a chapman into the shop, who told the merchant he would sell him his ears; at which motion they all laughed; but Egenio especially, who informed them, that it was the principal thing, and first that we should buy; a thing as useful as any, for as we have bought tongues to keep silence, so let us buy Ears that we may not hear, which will be of excellent use being set on the shoulders of a strong poror miller.

In all this fair, it was a rare sight to find one, who sold his own commodities; things also not esteemed, for what they are, but for what they appeared, and men not seeing, nor hearing with their own eyes, and ears, but with those borrowed from others; whose very taste was regulated by another's palate; and their whole knowledge and judgment beholding to their own credulity and others information. But a thing very much observed was, that the famous men of the world, as Alexander, the two Caesars, Julius, and Augustus, and others of that rank, and order of time, together with the moderns, as the invincible captain don Juan of Austria did much frequent a shop on which there was no inscription; their curiosity of knowing the mystery thereof, and the unwillingness of the people to inform them what was to be sold, made them more desirous and inquisitive; besides the merchants were those, who were the most discreet and judicious.

"There must be some deep mystery in this," said Critilo; and going to one of them, asked him privately, what was their sold? Who replied, that there was nothing sold, but given at a high rate.

"What is that?"

"It is that inestimable liquor, which makes men immortal, deifies their memories, and makes them only known, and chronicled in the world, whilst millions besides are buried in perpetual oblivion; as if they were not only dead, but never had lived?"

All confessed it was a precious thing, saying, "what an excellent fancy had Francis the First, Mathew Corvinus, and others."

"Tell us if there may be any left for us?"

"Yes," said they, "there may be, upon condition you repay as much, I mean of your own sweat; for so much as a man sweats with his industry and travel, so much does he obtain of fame and immortality."

The virtue of Critilo seemed deserving of it, to whom they gave a glass of that immortal liquor; who looking on it with much curiosity, believing to see the influence of the stars smile upon it, or some quintessence of the Sun's rays, or some distilled spirits of Heaven, he found it to be nothing but a little ink mingled with oil; and therefore in contempt he would have thrown it away, had not Egenio hindered him.

"For know," said he, "that the oil of the student's lamp, and the ink of historians, mixed with the sweat and industry of famous worthies, and sometimes with the blood of their wounds, compose an immortality of fame. In this manner the ink of Caesar deified Achilles, and that of Virgil, Augustus; Caesar was immortalized by his own, that of Horace renowned his mecoenas, that of Jovius his invincible captain, the ink of Peter Matheus, Henry the Fourth of France; but the reason why all arrive not to this pitch of excellence, is because they want success in their enterprises, or at least the fortune of a good historian to transfer them to posterity. Tales Milesius sold works without words, saying his deeds were men, and words only handmaids to them, or servants of the female sex. Horace says that the first step to wisdom is to be free from folly. Pitacus, another of the wits of Greece, moderated exorbitant prices, and reducing all things to the just balance of *ne quid nimis*."

There were many reading an inscription, which was, *Here is sold the best at a bad price*; but few came into the shop.

"Do not wonder," said Egenio, that this should be a merchandize, so little esteemed of in the world." "Some wise men," said the merchant, "trade here by returning good for bad, and thus employ their talents with no small advantage and happy returns."

"This is a place," said another, "neglected by all, every one being suspicious, that he who is his greatest friend to day, will to morrow be his enemy; and indeed few country-men of Valentia enter here no more than they do into the shop of secrecy."

At the end of all, there was a common office, to which all people applied themselves to know the value and estimation of every commodity, but the way and means how to prise and rate them, was odd and strange, it being to beat them in pieces, to spoil, burn, and in fine, to destroy that which we most love, and value, as our health, estate, honour; in short, what is either dear or precious to us.

"Is this," said Andrenio, "the way to raise estimation?"

"Yes," replied they; "for till our folly has made us sensible of the want of goods, either of Nature or fortune, our judgments can never set the due price, and value upon them."

At the request of Andrenio they passed to the other part of the fair of human life, notwithstanding the unwillingness of Critilo to be drawn with them, for oftentimes to please fools, wise men err: on this side there were many shops of different conditions each from the other. The first inscription was, *Here is sold him who buys*.

"This is the first step to folly," said Critilo.

"And pray God it proves not mischievous to us," replied Egenio.

Notwithstanding which saying, Andrenio had precipitated himself in, had not they pulled him back, warning him of the danger, and that his entrance there was the gate to captivity. To confirm which they saw some afar off, and those none of their smallest friends, captivated in chains, and sold slaves to unworthy masters. On another shop it was written, *Here is sold that which is given*. Which some guessed to be rewards. Others the remuneration and presents of these times.

"Without doubt," said Andrenio, "it must be that which is given, and bestowed too late, which is as much as not to give, and deserves a thankless return."

"No," said Critilo, "it may be gifts, or alms, bought with demands; for requests cost a certain reluctancy of Nature, fearing to receive the discourtesy of a denial."

But Egenio said, "they were the gifts of this vile world."

"How bad a merchandise is this," cried one at the gate;" but however they were impatient to enter in, and when they returned again, they complained of most accursed ware; for if you possess it not, you are tormented with a desire to enjoy it; when you have it, your care to keep it, is troublesome; and when you loose it, you consummate all your misery with vexation. They observed another shop full of nothing but empty glasses, and chests, and yet full of people. To this hurly-burly and crowd came Andrenio, and asked, seeing nothing, what was sold there?

They answered, "wind and air, and something else, both of less substance and advantage."

"And is there any that will buy it?"

"Yes," said they, "and some are so covetous of it, that they esteem their whole estates too small a price wherewith to purchase it. That chest yonder is filled with flatteries, and sold at the highest rate; in that glass are words the price invaluable; in that box is a conserve of favours, generally asked for and demanded; That vast trunk is swelled with falsity, a commodity of more demand than truths, especially if craft and cunning can for three days conceal the fallacy. As the Italian say, 'in tempo di guerra bugia, cometerra.'"

"Is it possible," considered Critilo, "that any man should buy air, and pay himself with it too?"

"Do you wonder at this," said they, "what is there in the world but air, take that from man, and you shall soon see what than remains. And yet here is sold something less than air, which notwithstanding is very satisfactory, and men are paid sufficiently with it."

For there they saw a young smock-faced lad, actually dealing out many and rich jewels, caresses, and gallantries, which always go together, to an ugly jade, of whom he was enamoured; and being asked what he thought pleasing or amiable in her, he answered, "a certain mien and little air she had."

"And is it but a little air," said Critilo, "and yet is it capable to enkindle so much fire?"

There was another fellow, that was delivering out many ducats, to some, that should kill his adversary; and said one to him, "sir, what hurt has he done you?"

"Done me," said he, "he has not done much; but there was a kind of word which he spoke."

"- what was it, affrontive?"

"No," said he, "but yet methought, he spoke it in a certain manner, and air, that offended me much." "Alas," said Critilo, "is it not so much as air, which is likely to cost you and him so dear?"

Here was one great prince to be seen that consumed all his estate and revenue in parasites, and buffoons; and he said, he did it because he was pleased with their gestures, their fashion, and behaviour; and in that manner at a dear rate are sold the punctilios' of honour, the vanities of the mode, the air of songs, and a debonair behaviour.

But that which was beyond all admiration, was a certain woman so fierce, that she run through the market like an infernal fury, scratching and tearing all that came to her shop, crying out, "who buys sorrows, head-aches, potions to break sleep, bad dinners, and worse suppers;" and yet whole armies entered in, and the worst was, that when they came to number them, few remained alive, and such as did, came forth all besmeared with blood, and with more stabs and wounds than Marquis Borro; and notwithstanding such as saw these passages, and newly came, did not forbear to enter in. Critilo was startled to behold so much cruelty.

"See," said Egenio, "how many evils entice and ensnare poor mankind, gold moves his avarice, delight affects his luxury, honours raise his ambition, meats please his gluttony, ease cherishes his sloth, only anger affords naught but blows, wounds, and death, and yet many fools and madmen purchase it at the dearest rate."

There stood another making an outcry, "Here are sold bonds and fetters of matrimony." Some came to cheapen them, and asked whether they were bands of iron, or women?

"That is all one," said he, "for they both hold fast alike, and for their price, you may have them for nothing, or something less."

"How can that be?" said one, "what less than nothing? it must certainly be a bad sort of merchandize."

"What, women?" and those cried too.

Considered another: "for my part I will have none of them, neither seen, nor unseen, known nor unknown."

Howsoever there came one, and he demanded a handsome wife, which they sold him at the price of an aching-head; and the match-monger assured him, that the first day would be his own happiness, but that for other days he must be content to share them with other men. Another came, who was well warned hereby, and he would have an ugly wife.

"And for this," said the seller, "you shall pay with a perpetual trouble."

They invited a young man passing by to take a wife; but he answered, that it was too early yet for him; and asking the same of an ancient man, and he said it was too late. But when another, who thought he had more discretion than the rest, asked for a wise woman; they brought him out a most ill-favoured creature, all bones and tongue. But said one wiser than he, "let me, good sir, have one that is agreeable to me in all things; for I am assured that a woman is the other half of a man; for that at first they were both really one, till God separated them for not obeying his divine command; and this is the cause why man seeking his other half, is transported with a vehement propensity towards the female sex."

"You have some reason," answered they, "but it is very difficult for every one to find his other half, for all things are confused and shuffled together; so that the half which belongs to the choleric man, we give to the phlegmatic, that of the melancholy to the cheerful, that of the handsome to the hard-favoured, and sometimes that of a young man of twenty, to an old decrepit dotard of seventy; which is the occasion that most married men live in a repenting state."

"But Mr. Matchmonger by your leave," said Critilo, "you have no excuse in this, for the inequality is sufficiently apparent between fifteen years and seventy."

"What would you have me do," replied he, "they are blind, and will have it so, and the reason hereof is, sir, because that they, being girls, desire speedily to be women, and the men being old and doting, turn children, and as ill luck will have it, when they have not young men by their sides, they are displeased to have such lie by them, who are troubled with coughs, phthisis, and rheums. But as to this woman now, there is no remedy, take her as you desired."

But the chapman reviewing her again, found that she came short in two or three particulars, both as to her age, her quality, and her riches, and willing than to disclaim his bargain, declared she was not agreeable to his desire.

"Take her however," said he, "for in time you may accommodate her to your mind, for otherwise she may become much worse; but have a care you afford her not all that is necessary, for in giving her that, she will quickly come to arrogate that, which is superfluous."

One being invited to see a wife, was much praised for his answer, that he would not choose a wife by his eyes, but by his ears, and in reward thereof obtained one, who had a good fame for her dowry.

At length they were invited to the house of good cheer, where there was a banquet prepared.

"This must be the quarter of gluttony," said Andrenio.

"It may be so," replied Critilo, "but those that enter seem the eaters, and those that go forth appear to be the meat that is devoured."

And here were rare sights, for there was a great lord set up in state, encircled with gentlemen, intermixed with dwarfs, buffoons, and flatterers, like the ark of ---- he eats well, but the account was large, for they avouched that he had eaten one hundred thousand ducats a year rent, which account was passed without any question or scruple.

Critilo considering hereof, said, "how can this be? for he has not eaten the hundred part of what they pretend."

"It is true," replied Egenio, "but what he has not devoured, these have. Than according hereunto," said he," let them not say, that such a duke has a hundred thousand crowns a year, but only a thousand, and that the rest only consists in troubles and vexations of mind."

There was a sort of people like chameleons, that sucked in air, and pretended that they grew fat with it, but at length all vanished into air. Some ate all, and some drank all, some sucked in their spittle, and others chewed upon an onion; and at length those that ate were eaten themselves, and that to the very bone. in all these shops was sold nothing of substance, or true benefit; howsoever on the right hand, were wares of the most precious quality, and truths of the purest touch, which were sold to men's own selves; such as these, *the wise man is with himself; and God is all-sufficient.*

In this manner they came out from the fare, discoursing as they went. Egenio being other than what he was before, because now rich, intended to return to his lodging, for in this life, we have no house, or abiding mansion. But Critilo and Andrenio resolved to pass the gates of virile age in Aragon, of which the famous king gave this testimony, that he was born to make as many knights of St. Jago, as should be conquerors of several kingdoms, and comparing the several countries of Spain to the different ages of man, attributed the robustious and manly age to that of Aragon.

The Conclusion

If men change their inclinations every seven years; how much more must their judgments alter in every period of their four ages. He that understands little, or nothing, lives but by halves; the faculties of our souls are feeble in our infancy; and the common or inferior, as well as the more noble powers lie buried in an insensible infancy, exercising only an animal life, and increasing with a vegetation like flowers, or plants. But the time comes when the soul proceeding out of its mantles, enters into the jovial stage of youth, which being sensual and luxurious, is most naturally expressed by such epithets. He that understands little, indulges his genius, and pursues those inclinations, to which youth and Nature prompt him, neglecting the use of the sublimer faculties. Howsoever at length, though late, he arrives at the rational life which appertains to man; his judgment being awakened, he reasons, and discourses, desires to be esteemed, thirsts after great actions, embraces virtue, cultivates friendships, pursues knowledge, treasures up wisdom, and attends to every noble and worthy action. He that compared the life of man to the swift current of a stream, did apply an apt similitude rightly fitted to the transient condition of humane nature, which glides away like a passing water. For infancy is a lively brook springing from amidst little sands, the muck of our bodies being produced from the dust of nothing. It twinkles as bright as a little spark, it smiles, but does not laugh, it runs after the little bubbles of wind, tumbles amongst the pots, and binds itself with the green stays with which the nurse keeps it from falling. But youth follies forth like an impetuous torrent, runs, leaps, precipitates its waters like cataracts, bubbles on the loose pebbles, turns into a thousand eddies, troubles the clearness of its streams, and casts all into froth, and fume. But the fury of this brook tumbling into the age of manhood, glides than with a more quiet stream, and is as smooth, and still, as it is deep: it than diffuses itself without noise towards some good end or design; it overflows the meadows to make them fertile and rich; it encompasses cities, to carry their vessels of provisions, and fortify them against their enemies; and in short enriches whole provinces with all things necessary and useful. But alas! at length this placid river comes to discharge itself into the froward sea of old age, emptying every drop of itself into the profound abyss of infirmities, and diseases: here it is wherein rich men loose the vigour of their strength, their pleasures, and the remembrance of their very names: here it is wherein the shattered vessel drives to leeward, leaking in a hundred places; and being beaten on all sides with gusts, and storms, is at length cast away, being shipwrecked in the gulf of the grave, and swallowed up in the sands of perpetual oblivion.

Critilo and Andrenio, our two pilgrims of life, were now arrived in Aragon, which travellers call, *the good Spain*, where being entered, they found themselves engaged in the greatest stage and course of humane life. They had now insensibly passed the cheerful and pleasant fields of youth; and the plain and wanton paths of delight, and were ascending upwards on the steep mount of manly age, which was full of sharp rocks, covered over with briers and thorns, and in every respect a most difficult, and troublesome passage. Andrenio, like such who would arise unto virtue, strained hard to mount aloft, he laboured and sweat, and was out of breath; whilst Critilo encouraged him with prudent remembrances, and comforting him in a way where no flowers grew, with the prospect of trees above laden and overcharged with fruit which were more plentiful, and in greater abundance, than the leaves of those books which they carried in their hands. At length they were got so high, that they seemed to be raised above all that this world contains, and to rule and govern inferior things.

"What is your opinion," said Critilo, "of this new region? do not you think that we do now breathe in a more pure air?"

"Yes indeed," replied Andrenio, "methinks we now carry another sort of air with us. We are entered into a good station, where we may repose, and recover our strength."

"Let us now reflect," said Critilo, "on the journey which we have made. Do not you observe those green and trampled paths, which we have left behind us, how mean, how vile do all those matters seem, which we have already passed? How childish and vain appears every thing in respect of that great province into which we are now entered? How empty and void do past matters appear? How little do they show from our sublime place of residence? it were a madness to return to them again by the same steps which have wearied us already without satisfaction or contentment. And here we will leave our pilgrims in the confines of Aragon, having attained to the virile, and robustious age of manhood."

FINIS.

Made in the USA
Monee, IL
27 December 2023